MAKING THORPE PARK

CHRIS ATKINSON

CONTENTS

INTRODUCTION

Located between the unassuming towns of Staines and Chertsey in Surrey, Thorpe Park is one of the UK's most popular theme parks, attracting around two million visitors every year. After over 40 years of welcoming guests, it is now well-known around the UK, thanks to regularly hitting the headlines, sometimes in controversial circumstances. In recent times it has become widely known for hosting over 30 thrill-centric rides and experiences, along with classic rides. It was a very different place to begin with, for a long time forcing revolution as the UK's answer to the Disney theme parks in the USA.

When I was a kid growing up, going to Thorpe Park was the greatest treat anybody could offer me. Thorpe Park was seen by my parents as the wholesome family day out, and despite us living much closer to Chessington World of Adventures, we would always make the effort to go to Thorpe Park, it was our tradition. As I grew up and started to seek more intense experiences, so did the park, and family trips turned into group visits with friends. I would eventually work for Chessington World of Adventures, and despite using my adult freedom to explore other theme parks around the world, my affection for Thorpe Park continues.

Because of this I've always followed the development of the park with fascination and intrigue. Fuelled by my warm childhood memories, I've always adored the creativity and planning that goes into producing a truly wonderful experience. Keen to find out more about how such unique and abstract ideas come to fruition, I've enjoyed reading books and watching interviews that detail the work that goes into giving people such joy and escapism. However, despite some excellent books already existing on parks such as *Tales from the Towers* about Alton Towers, I've spent a long time expecting somebody to release the definitive one about Thorpe Park. Tired of waiting I've decided to give it a go myself, which frankly is a lot more hassle.

Foolishly thinking that I already had a decent knowledge of the park's history, the research and exploring of archives has given me another level of admiration for the part Thorpe Park has played in the history of the UK theme park. Although many have tried to boast the title, Thorpe Park has without doubt a strong claim to be the first true theme park in the UK. Regardless of ownership, there has always been ambitions to continually move forward and be at the forefront of the industry. This has led to rides and attractions from all corners of the earth making their way to leafy Surrey, packed together on a regularly evolving manmade island. It's something quite special, but regardless doesn't seem to receive as much admiration as its peers.

I hope you enjoy re-visiting and exploring the creation of some classic attractions Thorpe Park has offered over the years, alongside some spectacular failures. Personally I find both equally as fascinating.

PART ONE

AN ADVENTURE IN LEISURE

"The first thing to understand about Thorpe Park is that you have never been anywhere like it before. Because there isn't anywhere like it.

Thorpe Park is unique, an adventure in leisure, a 400 acre wonderland where everyone will find something of interest and delight"

Thorpe Park – The Book of the Park (1981)

CONCEPT - 1979

Tim Hartwright was having a day off from his job in the mid-1960s, when he took his young family to Longleat House in Wiltshire[1]. The grounds of the stately home were in the process of becoming a safari park, with animals such as sealions sitting inside the glorious traditional grounds a huge hit with guests. The development of the attraction was rather unusual for the UK at the time, being led by Jimmy Chipperfield of the legendary *Chipperfield's Circus*. Hartwright left that day inspired and struck by an idea of how it could benefit his employer, the Hall & Ham River Company. They were a builders' merchants and large supplier of aggregates in the south east of England. Hartwright proposed that some of the land laid waste by the company's excavations could use the Longleat model and be adapted into a new type of water safari, but when he enthusiastically suggested the ambitious plan his colleagues laughed him out of the room[2].

> "Everyone thought I was a raving lunatic and the proposal went no further"

Whilst Hartwright's plan was foiled for now it didn't go away completely, and in 1968 the Hall and Ham River Company were purchased by Ready Mixed Concrete (RMC). RMC had been established by a young Danish engineer called Kjeld Ammentorp in 1930, who located their headquarters in Bedfont, a suburb of Feltham in the London Borough of Hounslow, West London. They made a loss of £399 in the first year[3]. To make ends meet they excavated materials from appropriate pieces of land they could purchase and sold them on to developers. Concrete was not considered crucial for large construction projects at the time, but as the industry developed it became increasingly popular, aided by a post Second World War building boom. By 1958 RMC were expanding rapidly producing 500,000 yards of concrete each year, compared to just a tenth of that amount at the start of the decade[4]. A listing on the London Stock Exchange followed in the 1960s, and by the time that the Hall & Ham River Company deal was proposed business was strong, with RMC also supplying large construction projects such as the nearby motorways.

However, the gravel pits created by their work had a finite lifespan, and when it was no longer feasible to use the land to extract gravel and sand, a new use had to be found. In addition to their own sites, RMC now had a new flurry of additional locations from the Hall and Ham acquisition. So in 1969 their open minded finance director Alan Endsor asked for ideas about how best to do this, and Hartwright (who was now an RMC employee) re-pitched his idea. This time the proposal was met with a lot more positivity, with RMC keen to diversify away from specialising exclusively in concrete[5].

Keen to replicate the success of Longleat Safari Park, a call was made to Chipperfield's Circus to see if they were interested in partnering on a new leisure facility. They were indeed open to the idea and RMC arranged a fact finding tour to the US for Hartwright, Endsor and CEO John Camden who were joined by representatives of *Chipperfield's Circus*. This was to visit various theme parks to gather as much useful information as they could. During their trip they visited Disneyland and Six Flags theme parks, and left convinced that the UK was lagging behind others when it came to such leisure facilities[6]. Upon the group's return there were serious disagreements about how the proposed new development would be run, and unable to agree on an acceptable way forward, Chipperfield's left the project. Endsor was however convinced this was still the right move for the company and set about pushing forward plans for what he would deem the UK's most spectacular leisure complex.

To manage the significant new project a new subsidiary of RMC was created called Leisure Sport Ltd. Endsor would eventually relinquish his finance director role entirely to become managing director of the new creation, but to begin with Hartwright was given the position. They knew quickly that the most significant decision was to decide where the new leisure facility would be located, with a number of pits that they owned as possibilities. Recalling this stage of the project Hartwright wrote[7]:

"It is said in the leisure industry that there are three essentials for any successful leisure park, they are, LOCATION, LOCATION, LOCATION"

To guide their decision, they created six criteria which they felt were the most important to the project being a success[8]. These included being near a large population of people, proximity of major roads, public transport, and also a good network of local roads to the site. Additionally, they wanted the immediate surrounds to enhance the development itself, and most specifically they desired "an established tourist area where the planning authority and local inhabitants would recognise the benefits of the development". The final criteria would ultimately prove to be harder than they imagined.

After considering all the options, a site owned by RMC was chosen in Surrey, in a location close to Staines and Chertsey called Thorpe. It was close to the M3 motorway and near to the proposed M25 which was due to be constructed over the following decade. Whilst not close to an existing tourist location as such, the argument was that London itself was one, and that public transport could be easily introduced. Best of all for Hartwright was the surrounding area[9], which he felt was perfect for the tone of the attraction he was looking for:

"Thorpe Park was chosen because its location was outstanding. Despite its proximity to London the site's surroundings are heavily treed, including fine wooded slopes of St. Anne's Hill which provide a perfect backdrop to the park"

At the time the only considerable concern of all the criteria they had established was the local roads leading to the Thorpe site. Something they would eventually invest heavily in to rectify. However, the criteria they had underestimated was the reaction the local area, and the planners, would have to their ambitious plans. Thorpe was a largely quiet and traditional part of Surrey, and the locals were going to need some convincing.

Back in the 16th Century the area of Thorpe had been divided between two rival families, who resided in the only large properties in the village, titled Hall Place and The Manor[10]. For many years a peaceful but bitter rivalry existed between them, until members of both households joined the Great War, resulting in 18 out of a population of just 500 in Thorpe tragically being lost in battle. Shortly afterwards the owners of Hall Place (later to become Thorpe Place) decided to leave. So in 1930 the estate was split, with the house being purchased by an order of Anglican nuns, the Convent of St Mary the Virgin. In 1955 it was bought by The American School in Switzerland (TASIS), who would go on to also purchase The Manor (now known as Thorpe Manor) in 1977, bringing the two rival properties under the same ownership.

The land that was split from the estate in the 1930's was eventually purchased from the Lord of the Manor by RMC, and excavation of the land that would eventually become Thorpe Park began in 1941, with the average thickness of the deposits around four metres[11]. However, as the site was on the flood plain, the areas became wet and left behind flooded areas that later became the distinctive lakes. As the pits at Thorpe reached the end of their useful life, the area was selected at the beginning of 1970 as the ideal spot to position Leisure Sport's ambitious new project.

A strong vision was created for the future of the Thorpe site, which included huge landscaping works, proposing to move millions of tons of soil to re-define the land and create a series of permanent lakes. This would create a large pleasant area for visitors to explore and relax, which would be complimented by a number of activities and exhibitions. The overall concept had evolved slightly from Hartwright's original water safari into what was being labelled *The History of the British People as a Maritime Nation*. Describing the proposition, he said[12]:

"It is British through and through and not a carbon copy of an American theme park. The aim has been to blend together Britain's fascinating past with the latest in entertainment to fire and stimulate the imagination and to provide a day of pure fun for all ages"

An opening date in 1974 was established with RMC fully behind the project still and determined to offer an "upmarket" experience but for an entry fee of just four shillings. Hartwright wanted it to be affordable for all[13], telling the *Evening Post*:

"This park is going to be for the public in general. If we make it expensive or exclusive it's going to die on its feet. This is a completely new concept and we think people from all areas will come here"

There was a substantial elephant in the room of the whole project, and that was the not insignificant issue of RMC being concrete specialists with no prior background of creating or running a leisure attraction. This would to an extent come back to bite them when it came to approaching the planning authorities in 1970 to ask for permission to develop the new visitor attraction. Whilst the planning department were open to their ideas, this was on the proviso that people who lived in the local area would not object to the new use of the land. Leisure Sport set up a number of meetings with local groups to discuss the project with them, which were met with strong opinion[14]. Some demanded that the site simply be filled in and the land returned to agriculture. Others opposed to the attractions proposed to include cafes, aquariums, tropical houses, and ski machines, suggesting these would be better suited to Regent's Park or Chessington Zoo than sandwiched between Egham and Chertsey. Others were more positive though, taking the view that the facility would improve the leisure and employment opportunities in the local area.

At the time the idea of a theme park in the UK was not well known. Disneyland/Disneyworld in the United States had filtered into the public's consciousness, but locally it was a new unfamiliar concept. Alton Towers was an estate with beautiful gardens, but no rides until the early 1980s. Chessington was a classic zoo, and what is now Legoland

Windsor was then a safari park. Disney would not enter the European market until the 1990s. Residents of Thorpe and the surrounding areas had no point of reference for what was being proposed, and the fear of what this new concept might do hampered any quick progress. Officials were quick to point out that if the plans for what was being tentatively called Thorpe Water Park were denied, then the likely outcome would be many more years of constant heavy goods vehicles taking deliveries from the site, and that in all likelihood the land would eventually be used for a massive residential development instead.

It took two years, but outline planning permission was granted for the project in 1972 allowing basic preparation work to begin[15], but Leisure Sport would have to apply separately for the buildings and attractions they wished to construct. To appease concerns surrounding local traffic they agreed to install directional signage to the park that would ensure cars avoided residential areas (in the days before *Google Maps* or a satellite-navigation) and invest a hearty £200,000 (over £2.5 million in 2020) in a roundabout outside the main entrance[16]. A frustrating period followed for Leisure Sport as they struggled to get permission for the attractions they wanted on the site. Proposals rejected included an ice rink, amphitheatre, and children's rides. Plans for a log flume were also submitted and denied, but would be revisited at a later date. Looking back at this period a decade later, Hartwright would admit they were possibly too ambitious to begin with:

"Wishful thinking is dangerous and costly and yet time and again would-be developers have been carried away by their own enthusiasm only to find frustration and rejection by the local planning authority. Designing a leisure facility is so stimulating and exciting that it is all too easy to fall into this trap"

Determined that they would still get the park open a year later than originally planned, a deal was struck to sponsor and host the *Water Ski World Championship* in 1975[17]. It was seen as a good fit to showcase the new venue and bring attention from the wider world. By 1973 though they had already spent £150,000 on landscaping[18], with a further £100,000 planned, but with no guarantee the venue would open on time. Additionally, the concrete business was starting to falter, with a sudden deteriorating market for ready mix. The financial struggles of the parent company caused questions to be asked internally about continuing with the project, with suggestions that it simply wouldn't be viable anymore. John Camden was resilient though and pushed for the plans to continue despite them taking far longer than initially projected.

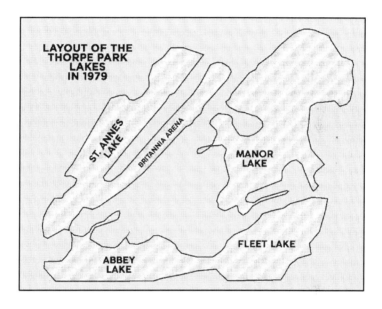

By the time the *Water Ski World Championships* arrived in 1975, much landscaping had been completed, including introducing 24,000 trees and shrubs to make the manmade lakes and islands appear more natural. This would also help encourage wildlife to the area and soften the lake edges. The southern area of water used for the tournament was named Britannia Arena/St Ann's Lake. It is no longer part of the facility, but continues to be used for aqua activities, becoming Thorpe Lakes Watersports Resort. In the 1980s it would regularly feature on Saturday afternoons on *BBC One* sports show *Grandstand*.

The other areas created as part of the initial landscaping were designated

Abbey Lake (to the south east, between the car park and the island), Manor Lake (the main body of water to the west), and Fleet Lake (as you are crossing the bridge to the island, this is on your right). A public footpath called Monk's Walk exists to this day between the water sports facility and the modern theme park, allowing you limited views of the park even during the closed season.

Unfortunately, when athletes from around the globe landed in Surrey the leisure park had yet to begin construction, and there were only minimal facilities compared to what was originally envisioned. Worried about Thorpe's draw without the planned attractions, a boat and angling show was added along with demonstrations by the SAS and a small funfair[19]. Despite the setbacks the event was a success. Competitors and crowds assembled from far and wide to witness Venezuela's Carlos Suárez and USA's Liz Allan-Shetter take home the top prizes[20], and help raise the profile of the location. One of those in attendance was minister of sport Dennis Howell[21] who praised how the event had been hosted[22]:

"These championships have been staged here at Thorpe in a manner which reflects the greatest credit on this country. I have talked to many competitors and they are unanimous that Leisure Sport has created the world's number one water ski arena"

Howell's attendance was an opportunity to educate him on the wider plans for the Thorpe project, and when he heard of all the hold-ups, he wanted to help, feeling it was an early chance to fulfil government policy after an election win the previous year. He asked for the planning committee to join him at the final day of the tournament, where he expressed the importance of the project. This was a considerable boost for Leisure Sport, and although there were still a number of planning hoops to jump through, it meant construction on the leisure park could finally begin in earnest the following year.

Finally, after years of planning frustrations the troubled project was becoming a reality, and Leisure Sport could start planning for the opening. The final name decided upon was Thorpe Park, losing any reference to water in the title. An estimated £3 million was being spent on the new facility, with the cornerstone being one of Europe's largest single span structures, initially called the *Royal Pavilion*. The now familiar dome was constructed out of, of course, concrete, reaching 37 feet high[23]. The interior is a lot larger than you might imagine, hosting offices and facilities on lower levels, as well as the spacious public area you are most likely to know above. Originally it contained a number of food, drink and souvenir shops around the edge, with a stage and loose seating in the middle. Depending on your mood you could choose from the *Crown and Anchor* pub, *Oasis Restaurant*, or *Oliver Twist*[24]. Sweet treats could be purchased from Sundae Best. There was also an early arcade, featuring what was described as a "hillbilly shooting gallery".

The Dome, as seen in 2020. Credit: Alex Rowe

The outdoor section was huge, much larger than the modern theme park, with guests allowed to walk and explore almost the entire way around Manor Lake. A number of exhibits were created on the grounds which were supposed to offer both entertainment and education for visitors. One of the highlights was *Model World*, a collection of over 40 recreations of famous landmarks from around the world, in a consistent scale of 1 to 36[25]. Together they took up four acres of land in the centre of the park, and were presented in a delightful terraced garden. The models were created by David Ward-Fear and even included a four-foot-wide version of the new Thorpe Park dome. The other choices were somewhat eclectic, ranging from iconic world landmarks to infamous vehicles such as the

R101 airship. Because all models were to the same scale, it meant that some were far larger than you might expect, for example the *Eiffel Tower* was towering almost 30-foot-tall and visible from a long distance. It was on a different level to your local model village.

MODEL WORLD IN 1979

Bodiam Castle	Pyramid of Cheops
Cardington Airship Sheds	Pyramid of the Sun
Cardington Mooring Mast	Red Arrows
CN Tower	S.S. Great Britain
Colossus of Rhodes	Saturn V Rocket
Eiffel Tower	Sears Tower
Graf Zeppelin	Shwe Dagon Pagoda
Hercules Flying Boat "Spruce Goose"	Space Shuttle
Le Krak des Chevaliers	St Basil's Cathedral
M.V. Queen Elizabeth	Statue of Liberty
Matsumoto Castle	Taj Mahal
Mausoleum at Halicarnassus	Temple of Artemis
Motherland Statue	The R101
Nelson's Column	The Sphinx
Neuschwanstein Castle	Tower of London
Pont du Gard	Tower of Pisa
Post Office Tower	

The other big attraction for the launch was the *Invaders of Britain* exhibition, which was designed by Terry Catliff[26]. This extensive and large-scale recreation was built on land between Fleet Lake and Manor Lake, which nowadays is not publicly accessible. It explored the various forces that had tried to take control of Britain over many centuries, and allowed guests to explore recreations of their homes, transport and culture. Unlike *Model World*, these varied in scale, but many were impressively large. You could for example go inside a Celtic farmhouse, explore a Roman timber watchtower, or walk through a stunning recreation of a Saxon Hall. All were done to high standard using the original materials where suitable. There was also some local history thrown in, with a recreation of King John signing the Magna Carta at Runnymede in 1215[27]. The historical figures in this section were complimented by a pet dog, which was actually a real taxidermy canine.

Possibly the highlight of *Invaders of Britain* though was a specially constructed galley called *Britannica*. This type of ship was a historical icon, propelled by oars, and used by many cultures over hundreds of years. Leisure Sport had commissioned a recreation of a *Liburnian* which was a Roman destroyer. Britannica was constructed in a Devon shipyard, before being sailed along the coast and making its way up the Thames to its new home on the lake[28]. It was a gorgeous piece of work that remained static and could be accessed by a small wooden bridge.

The Atkinson parents enjoying Invaders of Britain.

Another large original exhibition was the *Royal Naval Air Service World War One Airfield*[29]. This was a selection of planes that chartered the intense development of air battle between 1914 and 1918. During this period necessity really was the mother of invention, leading to planes at the end of the war flying 50 percent faster, 50 percent higher and carrying three times the firepower as they did at the start. For a certain generation this display was fascinating, but younger members of the family would struggle, as there was little engaging or interactive about it. Of a similar nature was the *Schneider Trophy Exhibit*[30], which showcased seaplanes and flying boats that had competed for the award between 1913 and 1931, which at the time had drawn crowds of up to 1.5 million spectators. *The Fleet Air Arm* also had an exhibit close to the Dome.

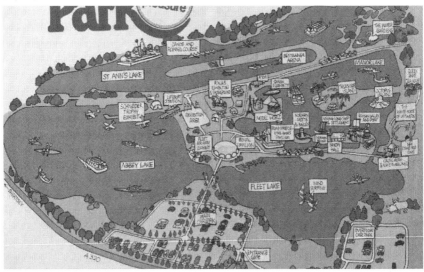

The land closest to Thorpe Village was transformed into *The Water Gardens*, a peaceful area, far away from the hustle and bustle near the main entrance. The space was designed to attract exotic species of wildlife, not commonly found near Staines. Brochures[31] proudly boasted that the parkland Leisure Sport had created was "worthy of Capability Brown", commonly regarded as England's greatest gardener. Another piece of land that protruded into Manor Lake was dubbed *Treasure Island*, free to explore on foot to begin with, although in later years this would be developed into a full attraction.

In order for visitors to explore the immense new facility, they'd need to commit to walking long distances, so to support those who didn't fancy doing the whole thing on foot, a number of land trains were purchased. There was no charge for using these, and visitors could hop on and off to see the various areas as they wished. Additionally, you could take to the water on one of the two catamaran waterbuses on a voyage around the various lakes. Christened *Lady Amhurst* and *Lady Caroline*[32] these distinctive yellow vehicles would run regular services throughout the season, and boasted climate control, anti-glare glass and toilets on-board.

After years of planning, battling and construction, Thorpe Park was officially opened to the public on the 24th May 1979[33]. The special guest to perform ribbon cutting duties was Lord Louis Mountbatten, who was a suitable choice given his nautical history. Lord Mountbatten was maybe best known at the time for being uncle of Prince Philip, Duke of Edinburgh, but he also served an eventful fifty-year military career, and was the final Viceroy of India. To honour his appearance the new dome was re-named the *Mountbatten Pavilion*. After a truly fascinating and extraordinary life, Lord Mountbatten was assassinated later in 1979.

With the park open, and the new exhibits ready, the first of many seasons to come got underway, with the entry fee set at £1 for adults, 50p for children, and 75p for senior citizens[34]. This would soon rise to £1.50 later in the year, with the facility open every single day apart from Christmas. Adverts in the local press promoted the new attraction, calling it "a new experience in entertainment"[35] and "Britain's first theme park"[36]. Advertising also proudly promoted the first special event to grace the park, the less than enticing *International Concrete Canoe Regatta*, although more events were promised later in the year. Each of the spots finished with the slogan:

"It's new, it's different, it's unique, it's the latest adventure in pleasure"

To complement the edutainment was the opportunity to participate in a number of activities on the lakes themselves. Available to hire were both rowing boats and pedalos, depending whether you would rather propel yourself by arms or legs. In a move that further suggests health and safety might have been a little laxer, if you were over 18 and held a driving license you could also hire a 1300 cc Ford engine jetboat to speed around Abbey Lake for ten minutes. Also added shortly after were *Bumper Boats* near *Model World*, which were on a basic level a version of dodgems on water. Continuing the nautical theme next to the *Bumper Boats* were remote control boats, that were themed as scaled down luxury cruisers. Depending on when you went, and the great British weather, you could also witness a number of other special events such as a selection of the World War One planes taking off, sea planes landing, regional water ski championships and battle re-enactments. A showground proudly sat in the middle of the main land to host such excitement[37].

From the beginning Hartwright and the management team were keen to ensure they employed team members who would represent Thorpe Park well and leave a positive lasting impression for guests. Hartwright would admit they were still learning how to best run the new facility in the early days, but was keen to instil the values he had seen on his tour of the US, writing[38]:

"Cleanliness and staff behaviour at the utmost importance and have considerable bearing on the conduct of the visitor. People are far less inclined to leave litter if the place is spotless"

To make further use of the facilities, and generate additional revenue, prominence was given to hiring out the *Mountbatten Pavilion* for private events. A Saturday night disco for over 21s was also introduced to appeal to the young adult audience.

The gamble taken by RMC and Leisure Sport had been significant, but with the park now open, the long-term dream of Camden, Endsor and Hartwright was now a reality. The experiences were generally being received positively, and the herculean effort to get everything ready, combined with positive word of mouth, led to 313,000 people visiting in the debut season[39] (around 250,000 of which had paid[40]). The park was awarded a *Come to Britain* trophy for best new attraction in the UK by the British Tourist Authority. The vast amount of money invested in creating the park was going to take a long time to recoup, but the success of the opening gave Leisure Sport the confidence they needed to be even more ambitious in the years to come.

As for the original attractions? *Invaders of Britain* remained for just over a decade, being known as *Our Heritage* for a period, and also *History of Man*. As interest in the concept waned, the 1990 season was its final bow, before that part of the park was blocked off to the public and most of the exhibits removed. A ride maintenance warehouse now sits on part of the land. Many of the planes and boats from the *World War One Airfield* and other exhibitions were used in different shows, or went to other collections by the mid-eighties. *Model World* stood the longest of the original attractions, although as the park developed around it the number of exhibits slowly shrunk, before the final models were removed in 2004. Some of these models were outdated but it is unfortunate that some of them could not be repositioned around the park.

The *Dome/Mountbatten Pavilion* still stands to this day, and whilst the contents have changed regularly throughout four decades, it still serves the same purpose. It features a number of restaurants, bars and central hub for the park staff. Updates have included installation of a large digital screen showing information about the park, refurbishment of the facilities and an expansion of the arcade. The Mountbatten name was eventually dropped, becoming known as *The Port*, *Port Atlantis* and simply *The Dome* during different periods.

1980

A successful opening year meant the park could return in 1980 with few changes, although Thorpe Park would still be operating at an annual loss until 1985. The steep learning curve Leisure Sport had experienced the previous season helped them make better informed decisions about investments and park operations. It became obvious that certain dates such as bank holidays would be the biggest test of their resources, with huge spikes in attendance as Britons flocked for a day out. The ambition was to eventually reach one million visitors per year, and the holidays could help contribute up to 30,000 guests per day to that.

The theoretical capacity had been worked out using what seemed like fag packet maths, but turned out to be quite a solid indicator. Hartwright knew that most people would come by car. They had created two large car parks on over 50 acres of land, which could hold on average 180 cars per acre[41]. If each of those 9,500 cars brought roughly three people, that would add up to around 30,000. The parking lot had been split being a main area directly outside the car entrance, and a large overflow some distance away that reached behind Fleet Lake. A small second entrance was introduced at the far end to be used on the busiest days. Because the facility was so spread out, it meant the number of guests it could cope with was much higher than the present-day park.

A jetty was added by Fleet Lake close to the Dome so visitors could easily board the waterbuses, offering trips in two different directions. If you went one way, it was a round trip showing off the *Invaders of Britain* and *Model World* from the water. The other option was to head to the *Water Gardens*, via Abbey and St. Ann's Lake. Here you would be dropped off, and could choose to return by foot, land train or the next waterbus[42].

Journeys on the waterbuses were usually very pleasant and peaceful. You could choose to sit indoors, or venture outside and watch from the front or back. The waterbuses were driven by staff who earned a reputation for being friendly and would occasionally let children take the wheel for a few moments much to their delight. It seemed to take great skill to moor them effectively, and guests would watch with anticipation as the driver would try and line up their approach perfectly. This could become significantly more difficult if hampered by a blustery day with choppy waters.

A waterbus service continued serving the park for over two decades. The routes would often change as the park evolved, depending on developments elsewhere, but for many years they served an important dual purpose of entertaining guests, and transporting them to another corner of the park. Eventually another two boats were added, called Diana and Alex. The waterbuses also offered another commercial opportunity, with the chance to hire them out for parties and corporate events.

There was also a focus on providing more extreme water experiences, and visitors could now pay to try out windsurfing, water skiing and board surfing[43]. This was making the lakes a hive of activity in the summer, and had the added benefit of offering a spectator experience for visitors. These early days were a chance to throw different ideas into the mix, ideally those that didn't require planning permission, and see what worked. The park was becoming a smorgasbord of entertainment, with ever changing activities taking place from live bands, to show jumping and outdoor plays.

An early sign of things to come were apparent when only a year after opening the entry price was nearly doubled to £1.80, and visitors would have to pay extra for experiences outside of the exhibitions. Despite the hike in entry fee visitors seemed to remain positive about the experience, even the *London Archaeologist* magazine gave the park a warm review[44]:

"Generally, the archaeological reconstructions are very good given the constraints and the operators are to be congratulated on providing such a sense of atmosphere without bringing in the Disney Land ballyhoo"

Also available was a spacious crazy golf course which was located on land in the centre of the current theme park[45]. It was quite basic stuff by modern standards, but at the time the obstacles and challenges were far more of a novelty. It was enormously popular and signalled that those visiting were looking for more interactive and fun experiences, not just museum like exhibitions. A bouncy castle and small children's fairground rides were also added, with management finding the temptation of adding less educational, more fairground like attractions hard to resist.

No longer being able to fall back on the once hugely profitable concrete business, RMC were now desperately trying to diversify into different areas, not just theme parks[46]. In a sporadic investment spree, they took stakes in other areas such as insurance, Rentokil and even ended up with two vineyards (one each in Surrey and Hampshire). Although they did turn down the offer to purchase a moderate sized company in 1979 for £18-20 million, that would turn into DIY behemoths B&Q. They would eventually enter the home improvement market with less success.

Attendance rose around 50% in 1980 to 450,000 visitors[47]. Knowing that reaching that one million target was unlikely without some extra pulling power, Leisure Sport were ready to follow up on the eight figure sum already invested with further spending on new attractions.

1981

Cracks were already starting to appear in the original claims that the facility would be focused on the *History of the British People as a Maritime Nation*, as just two years after opening the emphasis was switching to new forms of family entertainment. Addressing the criticism of the concept changing Hartwright was clear[48]:

> "This was inevitable as the original concept is now twelve years old and at that time could not be based on any previous operational experience or known public acceptance"

By 1981 a small go-kart track was enticing children to race, where it was claimed that "You sit so close to the ground that even ten miles an hour feels like fifty"[49]. The petrol-powered vehicles were located in the centre of the park just before the *World War One Airfield*.

Roller skating had seen a sharp rise in prominence and popularity during the seventies, and as part of a wave of additions Thorpe Park had constructed their own large 200x60 foot rink just outside the *Mountbatten Pavilion*. Those not wishing to participate could watch others and relax in the grass spectator areas surrounding the rink. Those who owned skates could bring them, but keen to add a more modern angle not necessarily available at home, you could also try out "the world's newest skating sensation" *Triskate*[50]. Unlike traditional skates which have two rows, each with two wheels on each foot, *Triskate* was one of the very first examples of inline skates. This meant that you had three wheels in a row, creating an experience more akin to ice skating. It was claimed that this formation would allow you to move twice as fast, and perform impressive jumps and turns.

Visitors who wanted to try out *Triskating* could do so for the hire price of 60p, and special conversion kits for skates from home were also available. To reduce injuries from the inevitable crashes helmets and safety pads were offered too. A suspiciously unnamed "New *Triskating* Champion" was quoted in advertising stating[51]:

"There's so much to do at Thorpe Park I'm surprised I found time to become Champion"

Triskating never quite took off in itself, however inline skating did eventually become big in the 1990s. This was led by the brand Rollerblades which was largely the same skate but usually with four wheels. Three wheeled variants of inline skates do exist, although the craze has seen a steady decline in the twenty first century. The rink at Thorpe Park was popular and the following year had a permanent roof built to protect skaters from the elements, with removable covers at the side for the winter months. The arena stayed in action for the rest of the decade, before being removed to make way for new developments opening in 1991.

Another big new attraction was to debut in 1981 too, which offered further insight into the future direction of the park. Located in a much smaller dome located close to Abbey Lake, *Cinema 180* was a UK first[52]. Described by the park as "A new visual experience from the USA", it consisted of a curved screen with a film projected at 180 degrees around it, offering a far greater level of immersion usually capable from watching a movie. Twelve-minute performances would take place regularly throughout the day, consisting of a film that had been shot exclusively for the format[53]. Different sections varied from driving a car at high speeds, to performing aerial stunts in a fighter jet. The most memorable section for most seemed to have been captured on a rollercoaster, giving visitors an opportunity to get a feeling of what it was like to ride such an exotic attraction. The UK already had some rollercoasters at the time, but they were not as prominent, and certainly not in Surrey.

The *Cinema 180* technology was created by a company called Omni Films in Canada. They shot the footage required using fisheye lenses that created the effect required to wrap the finished film onto the curved screen. It was projected in a similar manner, and at a higher frame rate than usual cinemas adding an additional layer of realism. Although

Omni Films created their version in 1979, the idea for this type of attraction was by no means new. Disney had been using a 360-version called *Circle-Vision* in their parks for decades. Other examples had also toured fairs in America and been available at the Six Flags parks. With International travel far less prominent than today, and little competition in the UK, Thorpe Park had an exclusive on their hands that was completely new to the vast majority of the British public.

When combined, the finished Omni Films product was surprisingly effective, with up to 300 audience members at a time regularly swaying and screaming along as the action unfolded. Because viewers stood watching, rather than sitting, it would also confuse some guests who would struggle to retain their balance with many falling over[54]. It was a further sign that thrill rides and special effects were becoming desirable, with *Cinema 180* overshadowing much of the edutainment. The popularity of the concept meant it endured a longer stay than you might imagine, being in operation for 14 seasons until the end of 1994. This was no doubt helped by the fact the film could be changed occasionally, giving a fresh experience for returning visitors. The technology itself would lose popularity around the same time, with trends heading towards more immersive and 3D versions of traditional cinema screenings, something Thorpe Park would dabble with themselves eventually.

The additions of *triskating* and *Cinema 180* were offering a tantalising taste of a possible future, rather than the originally announced plan to focus on the past. In many ways it shared hints of EPCOT, the brand-new park being constructed by Disney in Florida at the time. The EPCOT name standing for "Experimental Prototype Community of Tomorrow", and due to open in 1982 alongside the existing Magic Kingdom park in Orlando. Whilst Thorpe Park was obviously being developed on a much more modest budget, the focus on nature, showcasing heritage, and highlighting the latest technology was loosely shared by both.

To take advantage of the busy summer period the decision was made to extend opening on Friday, Saturday and Sunday evenings until 11pm from the end of May[55]. Those arriving after 7.30pm could receive a reduced admission price of just £1 (compared to the full price of £2.50). Local advertising was heavily pushing the extended hours and using another new tagline which was:

"One visit is never enough"

Possibly the most eye-catching advert run by the park this year was in the form of a fake newspaper report positioned in the local press[56]. The headline was:

"FAMILY OF FOUR LOSE THEMSELVES IN PARK"

The report went on to detail all the places they could be missing inside Thorpe Park's 400 acres, before reassuring readers they were expected back at their car by 6pm. The advertising, strong word of mouth, and the new attractions raised attendance to 600,000[57].

1981 also saw the *World Water Ski Championships* return, but this time with the facilities complete[58]. Crowds gathered from Tuesday 1st September to watch the competition, reaching a climax the following Sunday in front of 20,000 people. This time Karin Roberge and Sammy Duvall, both from the USA, were the overall winners[59]. The return of the event combined with the new additions were clear attempts to establish the facility in the minds of the public, and offer different experiences to entice them back. Leisure Sport were still facing planning issues though, with plans for two new additions for the following year worth £3 million rejected. Hartwright was adamant[60] that to survive they would need to continue to refresh the offering:

"New attractions must be added and existing facilities updated at frequent intervals to stimulate repeat visits. This need for constant change and updating of facilities is difficult to convey to planners"

1982

After a succession of new additions close to the entrance, the latest new feature of the park would utilise space over a kilometre from the turnstiles. This had the benefit of encouraging crowds to spread out further around the facility. Taking advantage of existing farm buildings close to Thorpe Village, on the west boundary of the park, Thorpe Farm was created out of the remains of the previously named Manorhouse Farm[61].

Thorpe Park had unsuccessfully applied to use this land as part of the facility previously, but as was becoming common, the request was denied. Leisure Sport appealed on the grounds that the holding had been reduced significantly from 1,000 acres to just 100, which would make its use as traditional farmland uneconomical[62]. They argued that the only way that the depleted assets would receive the capital expenditure they required, was by making it part of Thorpe Park. This would ensure the restoration work could take place on the farm buildings. After considering the appeal, permission was given, and *Thorpe Farm* was born.

The concept of the restored area was to introduce a working recreation of a 1930s British farm where visitors could see real animals, and learn about the process of caring for them. As many of the buildings from the estate were Grade II listed, great effort went into restoring these to a safe and working condition, whilst keeping the original structures protected. To run the farm and look after its many creatures, they turned to a man who had been working with animals all his life, Ian Minshull[63]:

"I answered an advert in *Farmers Weekly*. Their basic spec was to do a farm from the past with a bit of everything, so that's what I did. It was a blank sheet of paper, with a lot of loose papers everywhere, and falling down sheds"

A range of animals were being brought to the park including pigs, cows, horses, sheep and goats. Some animals would not remain all year, and could be moved during the closed season. Minshull worked tirelessly to create a genuine and welcoming environment, doing endless hours of care for the animals, and living in a building on the farm itself. His hands on approach led to him receiving the nickname of the "Thorpe Park Compo", his smell often arriving at management meetings before he did. He felt no shame in this, he was doing his role, and was proud of the progress he was making. In addition to the animals, a number of classic pieces of tractors and farming machinery were displayed.

"I bought loads of machinery from sales, and people got to know I was in the market for it. We had a milking display, and many more. People loved to see things moving. I had a load of engines circulating water and people loved to see that"

Although further modern rides were being planned elsewhere, the farm epitomised the original mission of the facility, giving educational value to visitors. Displays were created with information on each of the pieces and animals on show. Friendly and enthusiastic seasonal staff, regularly including veterinary students getting experience, would chat to families visiting. When *Thorpe Farm* opened it was an instant success:

"The people just loved it. Most of the visitors came out of London, and have very little knowledge of farm life. We had a beautiful short horned cow called Rosie, and people couldn't tell if it was a horse or a cow. We had seasonal youngsters come and work every year, and I don't think we had ever had a spot of trouble"

Although some of the time guest ignorance to how farms worked went against them:

"I had a ewe with fly strike (a common condition) and I had to have a member of staff there all day long, just to explain what it was"

Ian Minshull fondly remembers working with the original management, who gave him a lot of support during their time:

"Terry Catliff looked after the day to day of the park, and Tim

Hartwright the strategy. Terry would come down to the park regularly. Once we had 20 lambs killed overnight by dogs. I was distraught, and Terry was picking them up himself to take them away. That was the sort of person Terry was, he understood the animals"

Minshull was a consummate professional who cared personally for each of the animals, but was also keen to offer guests an experience not available at other leisure facilities. Visitors regularly flocked to see sheep giving birth:

"Everybody loved the lambing. I used to lamb all the way through from March to September. Used to have about 300 ewes across the season.

Always lambs being born, it was very wearying, I would stay up all night lambing. They were within a foot of you, the women loved it, the men would often walk away in disgust"

It wasn't just sheep though, the emergence of adorable piglets would melt hearts:

"We had an American girl visit for the day, and she witnessed ten little piglets being born, and she left saying it was the best day of her life"

With Thorpe Farm sitting a distance away from the other team facilities, the staff felt part of a slightly different community, as Minshull fondly remembers:

"We did our own thing, we were a little bit naughty. We had our own parties and own football team. We had bungle the lamb as our mascot in the team colours. We had a great crew"

To help develop the far end of Thorpe Park further, Minshull's son Jonathan created the plans for the *Nature Trail* through the *Water Garden*. The *Craft Centre* was also introduced which was a big hit with visitors:

"In the craft centre we had potters, somebody making bronze figures, corn dollies, painting, all sorts of crafts. People would stand and watch for hours as they loved to see things being made"

The introduction of *Thorpe Farm* also gave further credence to school trips, that were becoming a big market, and had the added benefit of boosting business during the quieter weekdays. In fact, the farm's introduction in 1982 helped boost school attendance to 150,000 people alone, up from 107,000 the previous year[64]. It was also garnering the attention of other ambitious leisure facilities:

"We were one of the first to have a big farm that was open to the public, Alton Towers came down to see how we did it and went back and opened theirs."

One of the highlights as a visitor was feeding time for the animals, and these were well promoted, with lucky kids often getting an opportunity to help. It was old fashioned, wholesome, family friendly entertainment. To compliment the farm a duck pond sat in the middle, and a small playpark was added. There was also a sit-down restaurant called *Potbellies* complete with cheeky pig logo. The food served was pretty decent, but sometimes the pungent smell wafting in from the nearby animals could be a little off putting. A *Thorpe Farm* gift shop and ice cream parlour gave families another opportunity to part with their hard-earned money.

Minshull found the farm environment especially wonderful for those with special needs. He put a heavy emphasis on ensuring children who might feel left out elsewhere, had the chance to do something quite different to their normal lives. His experiences during the early years of *Thorpe Farm* provoked him to set up a dedicated special needs farm near Heathrow. The original site of this was between the two airport runways, but when Terminal 5 started construction, it was moved to another nearby location in West Drayton, where it still operates to this day.

Noting the majority of the demand for visits was during the core summer season, all year-round opening had been replaced by a seasonal operating calendar. This meant the park re-opened for business on Thursday 1st April 1982[65]. To help guests who didn't fancy the long walk or land train ride visit *Thorpe Farm*, the routes of the waterbuses were changed. This change allowed visitors to board via a second jetty next to *Model World* and sail directly there. The new advertising slogan was seemingly keen to justify the £2.50 entry price[66], stating on all promotions:

"More to see. More to do. More that's free"

At this stage Thorpe Park had also introduced some basic character mascots, Mr Rabbit and Mr Frog, who would wander around the park. Although by modern standards their appearance was terrifying, with outfits looking like basic onesies. Regardless they did the trick, and children would often pose for pictures with the odd shaped animals. Eventually Mr Frog would hop off, leaving the cuddlier Mr Rabbit to be developed into a more traditional mascot figure during the 1980s.

Thorpe Farm continued to welcome visitors for many years to come, and although little changed about the experience, the shifting of focus to the core area in front of the *Dome* meant it became more isolated. Many of the animals were kept on a 40-acre field off-site, but when this land was excavated for gravel, the farm had to downsize. Other attractions around Manor Lake would eventually disappear, leaving the farm as the sole destination away from the core theme park area. This was because no loud rides could be built close to the village. After 18 years dedicated to managing *Thorpe Farm*, Ian Minshull was made redundant in 2000[67].

Maybe the toughest test of its existence followed shortly after in 2001, when a huge foot-and-mouth outbreak spread across the UK. During this time visitors were asked to walk through disinfectant when they arrived to reduce the chances of the disease reaching the animals. Although the farm continued to operate through this, it would eventually close its (barn) doors a few years later.

Things were looking good for the fledgling park, and Leisure Sport would be confident enough to plough further resources into their flagship project. After the introduction of *Thorpe Farm* their intentions no longer seemed to prioritise historical exhibitions. Thorpe Park had eyes on becoming a ride driven theme park.

1983

New experiences had been promoted the previous year, where the park map handed to each guest as they entered[68] had areas marked out in red which promised "major new rides for 1983". When choosing these Tim Hartwright said that consideration had been given to how they would impact the atmosphere[69]:

> "Each ride or attraction must be capable of handling large numbers of people to avoid long queues – A sure way to build customer dissatisfaction….They must combine to provide a new experience for people, thrills and challenge and yet not upset the balance of the park, be too noisy or too dominant in the landscape"

Not content with a variety of water-based experiences on the many lakes surrounding them, the next venture was to be a boat ride on the main "island" itself. Permission was given to introduce an attraction commonly known in amusement parks as an *Old Mill*, which is a leisurely ride on a boat as it floats down a predetermined course. The concept and technology had been around for a long time, with the first example at the very end of the nineteenth century. By 1905 Blackpool Pleasure Beach had added their own version *River Caves* which still operates, with variants also opening in Southport and Margate. Similar rides had proven massively successful for Disney, most notably the *It's A Small World* attraction. Unlike many existing versions which took place inside a large building, Thorpe Park's would largely stay outdoors. For the finale there would be an indoor section, which would ultimately give the attraction its name, *Magic Mill*.

This would be the first of several collaborations with Mack Rides, who had opened their own theme park called Europa Park in Germany in the mid-seventies, partially to showcase their various ride systems to prospective buyers. The family owned business had been running for over 200 years, and amongst the many products they had to offer was an *Old Mill* style ride. Unlike many versions in operation the model supplied to Thorpe Park had no guide rail taking it through a wide river,

instead it followed a trough filled with flowing water, meaning there
was no illusion of following anything other than the designated route.

Construction started in 1982, with a location chosen by the *World War
One Airfield*[70]. A number of covered boats were delivered that could sit
riders in three rows, which would be boarded from a static station
platform. Landscaping and gardening teams went about complimenting
the ride's route by creating grassy inclines around each of the many
bends, which had ornate flower beds planted regularly around but not
much else to see. The boats would barely move at a walking pace, and
with the relaxing surroundings created by the team, it really was
something you could take your grandparents on. The slow speed also
meant you had around 4-5 minutes to enjoy the setting, which also had a
few small buildings, bushes and multiple gnomes added so there was
something to look at.

For the final section guests would pass a spinning water mill, before
pushing through the doors of the building and flinging them open. In

quite the juxtaposition to the sparse outdoor section that preceded it, the inside of the mill was jam packed with exotic sights and sounds. Suddenly it appeared as if you were travelling through some kind of jungle, with creatures such as herons and frogs battling for your attention alongside wildlife and ancient artefacts. You could probably quite fairly describe the first four minutes of the ride as pleasant but completely forgettable. The final section was a real treat, and most would need to ride several times to take everything in. Shortly after opening the tropical sound effects were added to inside the mill[71], with the song *We All Stand Together* by *Paul McCartney and the Frog Chorus* played on a constant loop. The novelty song had been recorded for a short *Rupert the Bear* film and charted at number three in the UK. The song became a somewhat iconic part of the ride, with the frogs appearing to sing along with the tune.

Entering the Magic Mill

This in many ways was the very first proper amusement park ride ever installed at Thorpe Park. There were plenty of other activities, but the now familiar prospect of boarding a vehicle, doing a predetermined circuit on a transport system, and then getting off, was a step up. This also meant they had a ride that handled a decent number of visitors per hour, with guests almost constantly being loaded onto the boats, helping to achieve Hartwright's wish that long queues would not form.

The other new attraction this year was on the already established *Treasure Island*. This was a piece of land that protruded onto Manor Lake from the south side, around a 250 metre walk away from the likes of *Model World* and the *Magic Mill*. Thorpe Park collaborated with a company called Space & Place[72] to develop what they hoped would be another winner with families. The new experience would use both theatre and transport to help tell a tale loosely inspired by Robert Louis Stevenson's classic novel a century on from its original release in 1883.

To help bring *Treasure Island* to life, a small, looped railway track was installed using two-foot gauge steam trains each pulling four passenger carriages. Steam trains are probably not the first thing that comes into your head when you think of pirates, but this was going to be a very British makeover. Riders boarded one of two trains and were taken on a short journey to an area hidden from general view where the train would stop. Here actors portraying pirates would perform a short show and interact with the train passengers on a basic sandy set with wooden cabins, one of these called the *Admiral Benbow Inn*[73]. There was an enormous amount of overacting and terrible jokes, which always went down well with the predominantly family audience. After the main show element, the train would depart, and head through an impressively large replica pirate ship that had been installed. The ship was broken into two so the train could pass through, and occasionally have cast members hidden inside who might throw water or pick on certain guests.

What everybody seems to remember about *Treasure Island* was the "black spot". In the original novel the black spot was a circular piece of paper/card given to those who were deemed guilty of wrongdoing. On the Thorpe Park version one of the children would be given the spot, and it became a recurring joke throughout the act. Despite its gloomy origins, kids would be desperate to be chosen as the one to receive the spot and play a part in the show. For a time if you received the black spot, you would find it contained a voucher on the back to claim a free reward such as an ice cream.

A pirate in action on Treasure Island

The trains had to be driven manually, and this took quite a bit of skill as the driver would also need to perform to passengers at the same time[74]. When technology advanced this was replaced with a pre-recorded voiceover which allowed drivers to concentrate on the train, but maybe lost a bit of the character. Staff who performed on the ride seemed to enjoy it, especially as its location away from the main park gave them a little bit of freedom away from management. Later in its life some of the pirates seemed to be enjoying themselves a little too much when cannabis plants were found growing behind the *Admiral Benbow Inn*![75]

Both of the new rides went down well with the public, further establishing Thorpe Park as an annual family day out for many in Surrey and the South East. *The Magic Mill* was to remain in its original form until the end of 1994. *Treasure Island* spent eleven seasons entertaining visitors, before being retired at the end of 1993. The trains were still in working order, and it's understood that at least one train and its carriages went to the *Lynbarn Railway* which opened in 1995 at the Milky Way Adventure Park in North Devon[76]. Another was kept and used as an engineer vehicle on another Thorpe Park railway line.

1984

Development was continuing at a lightning pace, and now just five years after flinging the doors open to the public as a local leisure facility, there was no hiding the fact that the park had become something rather more extensive, going well beyond the original remit granted after public consultation. This left them in a delicate situation in regarding building bigger and better rides. A step too far and local residents who were already starting to kick up a fuss about the heavily increased traffic and noise could make it very hard for Leisure Sport to achieve their ambitions. It's a common consideration for attractions in the UK, and although the casual visitor might believe parks are only limited by their designers' imaginations, the case is that visual impact and noise disruption are one of the key barriers that stop many attractions progressing from a pipe dream.

When Leisure Sport wanted to add their very first rollercoaster and dark ride, they anticipated it was not going to be easy. However, Hartwright had been concocting a cunning plan to circumvent the rules for a while. In 1982[77] he declared:

"One possible solution is to site them (rides), within buildings clad with facades, possibly examples of different periods of British architecture, to retain the character of the park and to add the element of surprise to the attractions they contain. Utilising the inside of buildings in this way, and by making full use of modern technology in electronics, lighting and simulation, it is possible to create magic. Disney has done this to magnificent effect with such rides as *Pirates of the Caribbean* and *It's a Small World*. The company must follow his lead even if the cost is high"

This is exactly what they ended up doing for both rides, with an indoor rollercoaster having walls made from thick concrete to stop screams of delight escaping. As suggested, an attempt to portray some kind of educational value relating to British history was made, with building exteriors themed to represent various facades from periods of time. A new area called *Central Park* was created to accommodate the additions, sat very much where the name suggests.

For both transport systems Thorpe Park would return to Mack Rides who were able to showcase working versions at Europa Park. For the dark ride they were inspired by the ghost train *Geisterschloss*, that had opened in 1982. Whilst winning many fans for their ride systems at the time, they certainly weren't winning any awards for original theming, and many of Europa Parks attractions were basically close as legally possible copies of Disney's popular rides from the USA. In the case of *Geisterschloss*, the similarities with the iconic *Haunted Mansion* were obvious, possibly most notably due to the ride's vehicles. These were a type of Omnimover, which is an Endless Transit System, where all the cars are connected to each other in a loop and there is seemingly no end to the constant vehicles coming through the station. The first time these were ever used by any theme park was an attraction called *Adventure Thru Inner Space* at Disneyland in 1967. One of the core advantages of this ride system is that it allows a huge number of riders per hour, higher than nearly every other ride type available. Making no attempts to hide their inspiration, the ride cars are even shaped the same as creepy "doom buggies" that fit two people who are held in by a single lap bar. These move at a constant slow speed, and have the freedom to turn, directing the rider's vision to different areas throughout the attraction.

The vehicles for a dark ride, certainly at this time, are really only the enabler for any attraction. Whether it succeeds or not completely depends on the journey you take the riders on. To help create the environment guests would travel through, Thorpe Park turned to designer Keith Sparks, who had experience working on a number of dark rides. These included collaborations at Europa Park, a boat ride at Alton Towers called *Around the World in 80 Days*, and the *Haunted Hotel* at Blackpool Pleasure Beach. Sparks was known for being a big character, with a wicked sense of humour, which would often come through in his work[78]. He was an expert in puppetry and one of the few people in Europe at the time who knew how to successfully execute a story-based attraction. The decision was taken not to stray too far from the existing formula. The ride would be a ghost train like *Geisterschloss*, using 79 connected cars, but with some added British flavour.

To entertain riders for the near five-minute ride, dozens of scenes and models were created. Some of these were ideas "borrowed" from similar attractions, but many were completely original. Sparks and his team who were based in Colchester, were constantly learning as they worked on each ride, and that meant Thorpe Park's ghost train would have the benefit of many years' trial and error. The experience contained a considerable number of things to see, leaving you with little time to savour one scene, before the next grabbed your attention. The general tone was a little scary, however overall it was deliberately more humorous than terrifying, meaning it was still very much a family ride.

Amongst the many items installed were ghosts, monsters, skeletons and mummies[79]. Some of these items remained static, whilst others were animatronic and moved as each vehicle passed. A replica high street was constructed, featuring an undertakers and Sweeney Todd's Barber Shop, with riders given a chilling glimpse inside each. An animatronic undertaker continually nailed a coffin closed with a moving hand showing the victim was not yet dead. Whilst Todd got to work giving a shave to an unsuspecting customer, with the resulting pies being sold in the next shop along. Further along a visit to Henry VIII's banquet takes a shocking turn when the ghosts of his ex-wives come to visit seemingly out of nowhere. This scene was achieved using the old magician's trick *Pepper's Ghost*, which future Thorpe Park designers would turn to again over three decades later. Elsewhere a Frankenstein like mad scientist is busy in his laboratory, experimenting on bringing his monster creation to life. One of the largest scenes in the whole experience was towards the end and resembled a famous scene from Disneyland's original *Haunted Mansion*. In a large ballroom extravagantly dressed figures dance around in circles, but as you continue round the scene it's revealed that these are actually the undead.

An incredible amount of time and effort went into creating the ride which was christened *Phantom Fantasia*, and many believe it to be the best themed attraction in the UK at the time. Sparks Creative used a huge variety of skills, mechanics, and illusion tricks to bring the whole thing to life. The full details of which could potentially fill an entire book by itself. The completed sets were complimented by a soundtrack of unnerving creepy noises, at one point featuring a tolling bell which features in one of the scenes. It was a quality addition, which had the added benefit of eating through queues at a rapid pace. With over 20,000 people visiting each day during a scorching Easter period[80], this was most necessary. Visitors who weren't paying attention though might not have realised what they were getting themselves into, as the entire ride was hidden inside one of the new facades, with the entrance through a quant looking Tudor building.

The new rollercoaster that would sit inside the other building in *Central Park* was a more basic, but nevertheless equally as exciting affair. Mack Rides had a rollercoaster system called *Blauer Enzian*[81], presumably named after the railway line with the same title that runs between Frankfurt and Klagenfurt. Most rollercoasters use gravity to propel them after being pulled up a lift hill, however this version was powered all the way round meaning no lift was required. This system is not suitable for high speed, adrenaline fuelled coasters, as the motors wouldn't cope. It has the benefit of being able to propel riders round at a steady speed without the need to build it particularly high. As the ride would need to sit inside a building around three storeys tall, this suited Thorpe Park's needs just fine. The track layout chosen was of a common but effective design, that in basic terms followed a figure eight with straight track either side, one of these forming the station.

Powered rollercoasters also have the ability to do multiple laps of the circuit, and on the default layout it can take until the second lap to get proper momentum and advance at a more rapid speed.

Now truly buying into the impact adding immersive theming to an attraction could have, the opportunity was taken to heighten the ride experience and provide more character by giving it a space theme. According to the general manager at the time Henry Heath, the name and theme had a surprising origin[82], as he told *The Stage*:

"My nine-year-old son came up with *Space Station Zero*. We said to the Sparks people, 'Here's the name, here's your building, give us a space ride'"

Once again there was more than an inkling of a famous Disney ride here, with strong vibes of the successful *Space Mountain* indoor rollercoaster. The inside of the building was given an intergalactic makeover to match the *Space Station Zero* name. This included replica control panels and white plastic walls that were very 1980s science fiction. The train provided was styled as a (not particularly aerodynamic) spaceship, blue in colour, with orange trim[83]. Completely unnecessary over the shoulder restraints would hold riders in place but gave the impression something intense was to follow. As much of the ride itself was hidden in the darkness, it could portray the perception of greater speed and height, with guests unable to accurately judge the drops and velocity. In fact, the ride was only just over six metres high, and didn't even reach 20 miles per hour, but the setting really amplified the feeling of speed.

Another rollercoaster opening the same year at Alton Towers would use many of the same tricks. The also space themed *Black Hole* was a much larger gravity powered rollercoaster, which sat inside a massive tent that blocked out any light. It was their fourth rollercoaster added since 1980, when the *Corkscrew* ride forever changed the direction the park was heading. News spread of Alton's attraction and seemingly everybody wanted to try it out, causing overcrowding and regular queues of over five hours[84]. Since then Alton Towers had been adding further coasters to cope with demand. Thorpe Park were openly advertising *Space Station Zero* as a family ride, but it was a rollercoaster, and that was a massive deal in 1984. For those living in the south east a journey to Alton Towers was a short break, and short of some coastal locations and travelling fairs, there really wasn't many options if you wanted to try out a modern rollercoaster.

Some finishing touches were added to *Space Station Zero* that really helped add to the experience. The indoor part of the queue line ceiling had a window into space added, and mirrors as you walked towards the station. When strapped into the ride and ready to go, a countdown on screens would signal the ride was about to start, which really built the anticipation for first time riders as they would have no idea what was to follow. Around the track there were neon lights and at one point apparently a disco ball. To their credit Thorpe Park had once again gone the extra mile to create an enjoyable full experience, rather than taking the easy option to just buy a basic ride and plonk it somewhere. The extra costs even today of properly theming a ride can be hard to justify to senior management, as it's money that it is not absolutely necessary to produce a new draw to the park, but the lasting impact it has on visitors undoubtedly rationalises it in the long run.

Despite the effort that had gone into turning a concrete shell into a space station for the interior, the exterior had the same weird contrast as *Phantom Fantasia*. You'd queue for *Space Station Zero* and enter through a the façade of a Georgian House. As this was a period long before electronic queue time boards or phone apps, visitors would therefore have no idea what the likely wait would be. Apparently one measure parks including Thorpe Park used to use to deal with this was to ensure a large section of the queue line was visible outside, therefore giving guests the chance to make a visual judgement and encouraging them to try elsewhere if it was unsuitably long. This also had the benefit for the park of spreading the crowds around, at a time where live communicating was much more difficult.

With the significant new attractions in place, the entry fee was again raised, now reaching £3.50[85] (accounting for inflation that's about £10 in 2020). It didn't seem to be deterring anybody though and crowds continued to flock through the gates in massive numbers. Although not everybody was delighted with all the fun the park had to offer, as in July four members of the Hunt Saboteurs Association were arrested at the park[86]. They were protesting against trout fishing, which was offered as one of the many lake activities. In fact, at one point you could take any fish you caught in the lake to be cooked for you at a small hut. On this occasion the protests were unsuccessful, and fishing continued to be offered for years to come.

Both the big new attractions in *Central Park* would prove to be successes, but each would go through transformations over time. *Phantom Fantasia* remained in its original form until 1993, however *Space Station Zero* would only stay in place until 1989. That wasn't the end of the story though and both would play significant parts in the making of Thorpe Park later.

There are only a few other examples of similar rides to *Phantom Fantasia* in the UK, certainly in terms of ride hardware. One of the most prominent installations was at Madame Tussauds London, where visitors are invited to board vehicles styled as black taxi cabs on the *Spirit of London* ride. This still operates to this day, where its never-ending chain of cars can cope with tens of thousands of tourists every single day. When Alton Towers decided to install their own ghost train in 1992, they also teamed up with Sparks and Mack Rides, however the ride system was changed to allow individual cars to travel through the scenes[87]. It was felt this offered a better experience as riders were not alerted to upcoming scares by reactions of guests in front.

Geisterschloss continues to operate at Europa Park, although it has undergone some serious makeovers over the years. This may be in part due to the park's desire to change its reputation of allegedly copying Disney, which became more urgent when the Parisian Disney opened in the 90s. For those who miss Thorpe's version(s) it is a nostalgic experience to take a spin nowadays, and Europa Park is one of the world's finest examples of a theme park, so worth a visit if you haven't already taken the opportunity.

Powered coasters are still commonplace across the world, regularly being used as a type of stepping stone ride to offer children their first taste of a rollercoaster. The height restrictions are usually lower (around 1.1 metres) than many larger coasters. Numerous manufacturers offer versions of this, but the Mack version that was used for *Space Station Zero* has been installed around 29 times[88]. Creatives have developed how the technology is used, with possibly the most colourful use so far at Universal's Islands of Adventure in Florida. Here they have turned the same basic technology into a transport touring ride called *The High in the Sky Seuss Trolley Train Ride* which can cope with multiple cars on the track.

1985

1985 welcomed *EastEnders*, *Back to the Future* and *Live Aid* into the public consciousness. At Thorpe Park though it was to be the year visitors were introduced to a banjo playing dog, who was the star of *Cap'n Andy's Revue*.

The latest new addition to the line-up had one of the more unusual journeys to north Surrey. The story of this attraction begins in America, where in 1977 a pizza restaurant called Chuck E. Cheese had been opened by Atari founder Nolan Bushnell in California[89]. He envisioned a new type of family restaurant that offered decent but reasonably priced food, and plenty to keep children occupied such as the cuddly mascot Chuck E Cheese himself. Importantly for Bushnell this included arcades, which at the time were located mainly in adult locations, that could promote Atari's video games to a younger audience. As a massive fan of Disney's theme parks, it was also decided to install their own version of the *Bear Country Jamboree* from the Magic Kingdom in Orlando into the restaurant.

The Chuck E. Cheese show ensured it legally had enough differences from any existing attraction, and used audio-animatronic animals to perform for guests on a loop, every eight minutes or so. Along with Mr Cheese, a wisecracking Jersey rat, one of the main animatronics was Jasper T. Jowls, who is described by *Western Foodservice* as a "banjo-strummin' hound". The show was a lot of banter between the two leads, along with interactions from several other characters. President Gene Landrum described his new pizza restaurant as:

"Disneyland carried to American families in their neighbourhoods"

The concept was an immediate success, and expansion plans were put in place to try and roll Chuck E. Cheese restaurants out across America as quickly as possible. After investing $1.5 million into creating the first couple of animatronic shows[90], they were confident future versions could now be produced at a fraction of the price.

With the new style restaurant packing families in, it didn't take long for others to try and replicate the formula. One of the first to try this was called *Captain Andy's River Towne* which promised "Fantastic food 'n' fun for everyone"[91]. Playing the mascot role at this joint was not a rat, but a character that looked suspiciously like Jasper T.Jowls named Captain Andy. This banjo strumming dog even wore the same style hat. The River Towne restaurant would also be serving up pizza, hosting children's parties and boast the latest arcade games. When it came to an animatronic show, they had ambitions to completely outdo their rivals, and went about developing a longer show, featuring more characters and even more advanced animatronics. The creators of the show were a set of former Disney employees who had formed their own independent company, including Dave Schweninger and Tom Reidenbach. Original engineer drawings were made by one of the all-time great Disney Imagineer's Bob Gurr, who amongst a glittering career had also worked on the original *Haunted Mansion* that had inspired *Phantom Fantasia*.

The finished show was set in a turn of the century river town, presumably in southern America. The star of the show was of course Captain Andy himself, who was also a fireman when not performing on the banjo. He was joined by half a dozen other characters, including a saloon's busty barmaid hippopotamus, some hounds, frogs and cats. They would perform along with the soundtrack being played, whilst moving on, in and around the impressive stage set. Songs performed by the various characters included *On the Sunny Side of the Street*, *Proud Mary* and *Take Me Out to the Ball Game*. A beautiful animated fire engine was also used in the show, along with the set that included the firehouse and saloon.

Despite working hard to create a series of restaurants and an impressive show, the business failed to replicate the revenue and growth of Chuck E. Cheese. By the mid-eighties the restaurants began to close. With the animatronic show still in good working order it was decided to offer these for sale. Thorpe Park were not necessarily looking to install such an attraction at the time, but when the opportunity came to purchase

Captain Andy's show at a price of under £100,000[92] it seemed like a great deal. To host the incoming show from the US a new dome, similar in size and design to the one hosting *Cinema 180* was constructed. Benches were laid out in rows inside, and the animatronics and sets reassembled upon arrival. A large colourful sign was added to the entrance revealing the new name as *Cap'n Andy's Revue*.

You might reasonably think that operating the animatronic show would be just a case of flicking a switch and watching it work. However, this was before digital technology had been introduced. All the sounds and movements were based on large reels of tape. Unlike a modern audio file this would require some skill to ensure the timing was correct and needed maintenance when the physical tape was wearing out. The addition was never supposed to be a big hitter like *Space Station Zero* or *Phantom Fantasia*, but it was another investment in offering a full family day out, showcasing technology you were unlikely to find elsewhere.

Captain Andy and his crew would stick around at the park for a decent stint, performing their last revue in 1998. After finishing at Thorpe Park, the animatronics made their way to New Pleasurewood Hills in 2001, where it only lasted a year before being moved on again. The most unusual of journey's currently ends at Watermouth Castle in Devon[93]. Here the animatronics have been lovingly cared for and re-programmed to perform a selection of more familiar hit songs such as *Sweet Caroline* and *Big Spender*.

Despite some rough financial times in the 1980s Chuck E. Cheese restaurants have continued to operate in the USA, and are now in over 500 locations, plus now expanding into other territories[94]. It has become a part of American pop culture, and for a long time stuck with animatronic shows to entertain guests. In more recent years the decision has been taken to move on from the animatronics[95], and although some remain for now, their days appear numbered.

Around this time Thorpe Park also welcomed the addition of the *Bronco Bikes*. Located on the hill by the Exhibition arena, these were bicycles with offset axels and other components switched, making them incredibly difficult to ride. Children would be challenged to ride them round a designated course, leading to much frustration and hilarity as they struggled to go the right way. They remained until the end of the decade, when they were removed shortly after a child got their foot wedged firmly between the frame and pedal of one of the bikes[96].

The momentum the new attractions were bringing had helped attendance for the year reach the ambitious target that was set, rising to 1.1 million visitors. It was also receiving acclaim, picking up the Premier Award by the *Business and Industry Panel for the Environment*. The same year it received the Green Line Award for Travel Achievement[97]. Forming and creating Thorpe Park from scratch had been a battle but resulted in triumph critically and finally financially too, making an annual profit for the first time. The *Litchfield Mercury* summed up the achievement in November 1985 stating:

"Thorpe Park is unique in world terms in that no other site of a similar nature has ever been developed as a public amenity on a similar scale and met with such public acclaim. The creation of Thorpe Park has taken place without any aid, financial or otherwise, from outside sources – its very existence is entirely due to the foresight, effort, investment and commitment of the RMC Group and will continue to provide a balanced mixture of excitement, adventure, learning and fun for everyone"

It was around this time Thorpe Park sadly lost one of the people who had been imperative to its creation and early development. Tim Hartwright passed away before he reached his 60th birthday[98]. Impressively he had completed the mission he had set out on, unsuspectedly inspired by that trip to Longleat two decades earlier, but sadly would not get to enjoy seeing many of his other ideas come to life. He was a gentleman ahead of his time, a true visionary of the UK leisure industry, who just so happened to work for a concrete company.

For Leisure Sport the honeymoon period had ended, and on the horizon was a new batch of challengers.

PART TWO

RIVALS EMERGE

1986

In March 1986 the news was confirmed that Chessington Zoo, which is situated under 10 miles away from Thorpe Park, would be transforming itself into a fully-fledged theme park. The zoo had been operating since 1931, eventually adding a fun fair and circus, but was now struggling. The Tussauds Group were the owners, and at the time had some experience operating visitor attractions such as Wookey Hole and Madame Tussauds, but little in the way of theme park knowledge. Upon receiving advice from ride consultant John Wardley, Chessington would now undergo a massive £10 million[99] overhaul to be turned into a modern themed attraction to accompany the existing zoo, opening in the summer of 1987. Reporting on the news, the *Kingston Informer* revealed some early details of the plans to the public[100]:

"By 1987 visitors will be able to travel through the screen of a computer, visit a western town and career over the Rocky Mountains, sail round the exotic lands of the Far East, become part of a circus fantasy world and enjoy the atmosphere of a perfect old English village"

The new version of the park was being dubbed Chessington World of Adventures, with the plan to significantly increase their annual visitors from the 550,000 a year they were already welcoming. They had struck a deal with frequent Thorpe Park collaborators Mack Rides to provide the hardware needed for the new attractions, which included a log flume, monorail and dark ride. They were also going to install a near identical version of Thorpe Park's powered coaster *Space Station Zero*, but themed to a mine train.

If the news that a massive rival theme park was to open in the south was a blow to Thorpe Park, then the fact it was so curiously close must have been plain infuriating. Wardley says that like Leisure Sport's original planning, the proximity to the new M25 was one of the deciding factors when choosing to go ahead with the overhaul[101]. He felt that Chessington would be a better representation of what a theme park could be, and that he found Thorpe Park's ideas at the time "esoteric". To add insult to injury another rival was in the pipework too. John Broome, then owner of Alton Towers who had overseen their hugely lucrative transformation into a rollercoaster thrill park, had won permission to turn the iconic Battersea Power Plant into a giant leisure complex[102]. His vision for a multi-level attraction filled with entertainment and rides was planned to open before the end of the decade at a cost of over £100 million. When pressed about the Battersea development during an interview with *The Stage*, General Manager Henry Heath was somewhat sceptical[103]:

"I feel very strongly about Battersea, but only because I'm a resident and live far too close to the site. I think Broome's figures on traffic density are absolute cobblers but the Battersea Leisure concept is fantastic"

In fact, theme park fever had hit the UK big time. Another, titled American Adventure, was due to open near Derby and Nottingham at the same time as the new look Chessington. Drayton Manor in Tamworth had long been a relaxed amusement park, but now had plans to install bigger rides and become a full-scale theme park too. It was a similar story at Camelot in Chorley and Frontierland in Morecambe, everyone now saw the potential.

Seemingly willing to back themselves against the upcoming fierce competition, Thorpe Park agreed to their biggest investment yet to open at the same time as the relaunched World of Adventures. Whilst that project got underway, it was time to do what all great British people do in a time of crisis, sit back, and have a cup of tea.

Another Mack Rides creation would be making its way over from Germany to be the new addition for the 1986 season. A teacup might be a familiar concept if you are a theme park fan, but in truth it's quite a bizarre notion. Once again opening at Europa Park first in 1985, Mack had created a spinning flat ride which saw four guests sit inside one of 15 giant teacups, sat upon a saucer and located around a large tea/coffee pot. The entire circular floor rotates, and inside that trios of teacups sit on another circular spinning floor, meaning you are being flung both around the central pot and in a smaller ring. If that wasn't enough spinning for your group, you have the ability to turn a large wheel in the centre of your vehicle/teacup to make your individual car spin. The speed and direction are controlled by the riders, depending how much momentum you can get. The result is a fun ride, suitable for all the family, but deceivingly nausea inducing.

After a successful debut at home, the Mack teacups were to make their way to two British theme parks in quick succession. The first of these would be Thorpe Park, where they would proudly sit near *Model World* in a new section of the park being developed over two years. The appearance and experience were near identical to the German original. A permanent canopy was constructed over the top to shelter riders and those queuing from the elements. Feeling that simplicity would be the best option name wise, it was christened *Tea Cup Ride*. It was a solid attraction, and the ability to control the intensity to an extent meant it appealed to a wide audience. The length of ride is also controlled by the operator, meaning that you could get a longer spin on a quiet day, and shorter rotations to get through the queues at peak times. Entry to try out all the rides Thorpe Park had to offer, including the new teacup attraction, was set at £5 for 1986[104].

After over 30 years the teacups continue to be a staple of Thorpe Park, still sitting in the same position as they always have. Although it's understandably not as popular as it once was, it's a credit to the manufacturing of the attraction that it remains incredibly reliable and shows little sign of disappearing. Thorpe's version has undergone some minor changes during its lifetime, mostly cosmetic. The first change was a small amendment to the name in 2000, with *Teacup Twisters* deemed to be far more twenty first century. Then in 2004 the vehicles and surroundings were given a more weathered look, complete with artificial cracks. The distinctive handles were also removed, and the ride was given the updated name of *Storm in a Teacup* to match the surrounding theme of an area devastated by a tidal wave. In more recent times the attraction has formed an appropriate partnership with Tetley Tea, who have some branding present, but it's surprisingly not too intrusive and hasn't affected the name.

The Teacups in 2020. Credit: Alex Rowe

The year after their debut in Surrey, Alton Towers would install the same ride, again deciding on the familiar look and feel. Since redeveloping the area in 2008, the ride resides in a pirate themed section. Updated vehicles represent barrels, and the name changed to *Marauder's Mayhem*. Impressively it seems that as of 2020 all the numerous versions of this classic Mack flat ride are still in operation, including one themed to the *X Men* in Florida at Universal's Islands of Adventure. The original happily still sits in the Dutch area of Europa Park.

To end the season the park opened until 10:30PM on Guy Fawkes Night, promising "one of the largest organised fireworks displays in the UK"[105]. Over seven years the annual event had been gaining popularity, with 20,000 people reportedly in attendance to see a finale that involved over 1,000 colourful fireworks, organised by the experts at Phoenix Fireworks Displays. Unfortunately, the display was marred by groups of youths "fighting, swearing and carrying out acts of vandalism", who had travelled from far and wide. Feeling the atmosphere reflected badly on Thorpe Park's reputation the display was cancelled for future years[106].

1987

With Chessington World of Adventures opening just around the corner, Thorpe Park were willing to spend £2.2 million[107] (equivalent to £6.5 million in 2020) to try and blow them away. To do so they had identified a concept they felt was ready to trump their new noisy neighbours.

In 1980 the world's first river rapids ride had opened at AstroWorld in Houston. The concept was created by the park in conjunction with Swiss ride manufacturer Intamin and supposed to realistically recreate the feel of white-water rafting. The premise was to travel down a hostile, raging river in a circular boat which would ride the waters, taking passengers on an exciting and unpredictable adventure. Unlike many boat rides there would be no track as such, with the guests instead being directed by the designed environment and general flow of water, allowing for a wildcard element to the experience. Whilst each journey is broadly the same, boats could spin, and travel at different speeds depending on a number of factors, including weather, number of passengers, and how you entered certain elements. The rapids sections are created in a surprisingly simple manner, by placing circular tubes under the surface of the water. The result of the clashes with the water, was more often than not, riders being drenched. The system also allowed for small drops, and interactions with other boats and rocks by using a large tubular bumper all the way round.

After seven years of planning and $3,000,000 in investment[108], AstroWorld called their new ride *Thunder River*. Despite some serious teething problems with the operation of the ride, it had been a huge hit with the public. Parks all over the United States immediately ordered their own versions, and by 1985 there were at least 14 in operation. Inevitably the popular ride type would make its way to the UK, and Alton Towers commissioned Intamin to create a version as part of their 'rapid' expansion. The *Grand Canyon Rapids* debuted in 1986, and its high capacity helped crunch through the crowds at a time when they were the most popular theme park in the country.

Seeing a rapids ride as the perfect complement to the still predominantly water styled park, Thorpe Park set about working with Intamin to work out how one could be added before the opening of the new World of Adventure. A site was identified between *Treasure Island* and *Central Park*, and planning permission submitted to the council[109]. This was, however, the most flagrant example yet of the park going against its original concept, and local residents were starting to lose their patience. This was not helped by the park's seemingly casual attitude towards previous planning applications, where they had recently only asked for permission retrospectively, when the construction had already been completed. The independent councillor representing Thorpe residents, Jack Smith, was not impressed stating in April 1986[110]:

"The law of the land is ignored by these people... They are the cowboys of industry"

At the same time seemingly, reasonable concerns were raised about the noise the rapids would make from riders screaming and music being played. The fear being they would be a constant disturbance in Thorpe Village. Thorpe Park director Terry Catliff strongly hit back saying that "We are not high-handed", "There will be no music on the rapid water ride" and that "It's no-where near the village"[111]. In fact, Jack Smith was becoming a constant irritant for the park, despite admitting to never having set foot inside. It seems not all residents were against further development, with local A.G. Richardson writing a strongly worded letter to the *Herald & News* local newspaper. In it he sets out a case in support of the park, and says that is preferable to the alternate options, also pointing out that the park pays a six-figure sum in rates to the local council every year[112]. His letter included:

"Yes, Thorpe Park is different to what we may have originally envisioned. Yes, it gives pleasure to hundreds of thousands during summer months. Yes, we should keep our eye on their planning applications"

The letter ends imploring Jack Smith to bury the hatchet with Thorpe

Park to ensure a better co-existence moving forward. The final permissions were sought requesting to extract 2,250,000 gallons of water a day from Manor Lake for use in the ride, although any that didn't end up soaking guests would be returned[113]. Confident any planning quarrels would be sorted, advertising of the new attraction started earlier than ever, with visitors the year before promised "Wild Water Ride - New for '87" on park maps[114].

Construction started in 1986, with a 470 metre long fake river being created from scratch[115]. As the boats would need to be returned to their original starting height after each circuit, a large wooden conveyor belt was constructed, which would be the slightly underwhelming final aspect of the ride. The station where guests would board and disembark the boats was an updated version of the early rapid's rides, unlike those which stopped on a conveyor belt, this would involve a large continually rotating platform. Boats would be pushed tightly against the side, giving a certain amount of time to swap riders over as the boat travelled round roughly 180 degrees. This system adds a certain amount of urgency to visitors as they don't want to miss their chance to board, and keeps the ride moving at a steady pace. A large wooden bridge was constructed to allow people to and from the rotating station area, which would also form the queue. Its position would allow those waiting to watch the boats in the final stretch, which was an entertaining way to pass the time.

Alongside construction of the ride system and pathways, work was underway to create a jungle style setting to travel through. Landscape manager David Hill was overseeing the work, which would require subsoil to be delivered by 50 22-ton lorries every day for several months[116]. Alongside the new forested areas there would be a cave-like tunnel created for boats to travel through. Inside would lie a furious waterfall along one of the walls. 23 bright yellow boats were delivered, each able to hold six riders for their near five-minute journey. This would theoretically allow 1,500 people an hour to experience the new ride. In the middle of each boat was a circular safety bar, allowing riders to grip on during the more turbulent moments. Although other parks were marketing their rapids rides as family attractions, Thorpe Park were looking to play up the thrill element, and it was certainly more exhilarating than many of the other entertaining but relaxed rides installed previously.

With presumably no nine-year olds around to offer creative support on a new name this time, the decision was taken to keep it the same as the original rapids ride. Thorpe Park would have its own *Thunder River*. The ride would form part of a new area in the park designated *European Square*. This corner would also boast a lovely replica *La Fortuna* fountain, and Italian restaurant of the same name. Also included were a Bavarian Fest Halle and French café[117].

On Wednesday 15th April, a few months ahead of the official opening of the re-imagined Chessington Zoo, *Thunder River* was ready to be unveiled to the public. The official launch was attended by the Prime Minister's husband, Denis Thatcher. His attendance also seemed to attract a stream of local government officials, who were suddenly keen to try out the ride themselves. Thatcher was full of praise for the park, and added his claim that it was indeed Britain's first theme park[118]. For his debut ride he was given what was described by the press as a "faintly ridiculous" yellow plastic cape to wear, but seemed to enjoy the experience immensely. He was still drenched despite the poncho, but completed two circuits of the ride in good spirits. Speaking about Thorpe Park, and referencing his own business history, Thatcher declared[119]:

"Those of us in the extractive industry have a responsibility, indeed a duty, to return the land to the environment and Thorpe Park is one of the finest examples of environmental repair in Europe. This ride is a magnificent achievement and is an example of the British construction industry at its finest"

Counsellors from Runnymede and Chertsey also took turns to ride *Thunder River* with the park's latest managing director Gerald Tyler, although Runnymede mayor Maud Austin declined the offer of a ride being quoted as saying "I don't like getting wet".

Predictably the press was quick to ask questions about what Thatcher's high-profile wife, the Iron Lady herself, would think of the new attraction. Denis Thatcher commented:

"It was great fun, but I'm not quite sure whether it's her sort of thing"

The ride contains many spins and corners, and she was after all, not for turning. While enjoying a beer in *European Square* he joked of his inadequate choice of clothes for the event, saying[120]:

"I never actually thought to wear any special clothes. It was not frightening but it was certainly wet-making. It was absolutely magnificent"

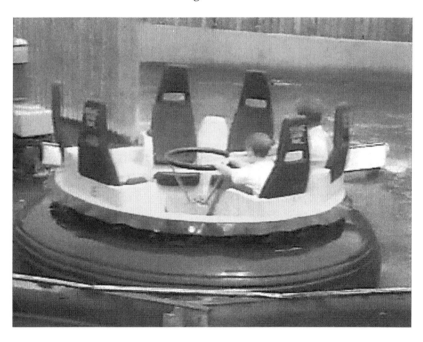

With the pleasantries and dignitaries out of the way, the public were now to get their chance on Thorpe Park's largest ride yet. Queues formed along the newly constructed wooden bridge as visitors waited their turn to try out this concept that must have been alien to the large majority of them. Judging by the regular laughter and screams of joy, the rapids were proving to be the most enjoyable ride yet for many. However,

Thunder River was experiencing some of the same issues that had dogged the original, especially in sections where the course was wider, allowing boats to become stuck. On the second day of operation boats were getting stuck in the tunnel, and Intamin were called back in to make some modifications[121]. Whatever changes were made, however, were not enough to stop a major incident later that year.

On Tuesday 28th July Pauline White from Reading visited the park with a group including her family[122]. Towards the end of the day the group of six climbed into a *Thunder River* boat, keen to try out the high-profile new addition. When the boat reached the tunnel section it became jammed, unable to continue with the flow of water. As other boats reached the tunnel they slammed into the stranded vehicle, which eventually capsized, flinging all six passengers into the raging waters. Panic stricken, they were dragged downstream as other riders screamed for help. Four members of the public dived in themselves in an attempt to save them, and heroically managed to pull them to safety. Unfortunately, by the time they reached Pauline's seven-year-old son Liam, he was covered in blood. Liam had been dragged against rocks further down the course, and his ear completely ripped off. Staff stopped the ride, and were instructed to drain all the water, as a search got underway to try and find the severed ear. Liam was rushed to hospital, with his hearing thankfully not impacted by the accident.

Following the dramatic scenes of that evening, *Thunder River* was shut pending an investigation into the accident. Alton Towers were put under pressure to close their rapids too, but resisted, with spokeswoman Liz Taylor claiming that their ride was safer than the Thorpe Park version[123]:

"Our ride has underwater guide rails and logs specially positioned to keep the rafts moving – there is no possibility of them stopping or getting stuck"

The White family were understandably seething and called publicly for *Thunder River* to be completely removed. Headlines such as "Mum tells of fun park horror" and "Shut ride, says mum of severed ear boy" were seen in multiple media outlets[124], complete with Pauline White quoted as saying:

"I feel very angry now and as far as I am concerned they should shut the ride down and get rid of it"

The timing of the accident could hardly have been worse for Thorpe Park, taking place at the start of the key summer holiday period, and shortly after the official launch of their new rival. Chessington World of Adventures had been opened by Prince Edward on Monday 6th July[125], and would now have a further advantage as the two theme parks vied for the public's footfall.

Liam White underwent a number of skin grafts and further plastic surgery in hospital. The media followed his story closely, reporting on his release from hospital almost two weeks later[126], and his eventual return to school in September[127]. He was commended for his bravery, and even decided that he would go without an artificial ear. *Thunder River* was closed for around a month whilst an assessment was made of its safety, finally re-opening shortly before the end of the summer holidays after both Intamin and the Health & Safety Executive had given it the all clear. A Thorpe Park spokesman was quoted in the *Evening Post* saying[128]:

"Modification has been completed. The prohibition notice issued by the Health & Safety Executive has been complied with and therefore it's been permitted to reopen the ride"

The incident came at a time when rides were under intense scrutiny in the UK. A number of accidents in a short period of time had led to many calling for greater health and safety checks to be put in place. Incidents included somebody falling to their death on a Blackpool Pleasure Beach rollercoaster, a five-year-old being killed by a rotor ride in Aberdeen, and fourteen people being rushed to hospital when a chairlift collapsed in Skegness[129]. Most of the wrath was aimed at travelling fairs, but the boat capsizing on *Thunder River* had firmly brought Thorpe Park into the debate. Speaking to the *Evening Post* James Tye, who was director general of the British Safety Council, wasn't holding back in his criticism of those responsible:

"Showmen are lazy. They don't care about safety checks. All they're concerned with is making the most money for the smallest outlay. Our advice to parents is not to take children to fairs this summer. There are plenty of other, safer places to go"

No major changes were made to *Thunder River*, although measures were put in place to ensure boats could not capsize in the future. Ever since things have operated pretty smoothly, and after a dramatic opening season it shook off any negativity to become a firm family favourite at the park for many years. Many millions of people have now ridden, enjoyably and safely. Many would agree that it's one of the all-time classic Thorpe Park rides. Graham Clatworthy would be one of the ride's operators in the 1990s and remembers it well[130]:

"Thunder River was always my favourite, definitely. For me it was the park's best ride. Other rides were all computerised, and all you had to do was to respond to buttons and noises, whereas at Thunder River you really had to properly operate the ride and there was a bit of skill involved"

Understandably it would attract especially large queues on hotter days, and some of the announcements in the queue even reached cult status, with many regulars able to recite the frequent "There's no doubt about it, you will get wet" plus "and hey, have a super day" wording as it happened. The announcements were pre-recorded by park staff, and different voices played on a loop.

Despite installing a more thrilling new attraction, management were keen to stress that Thorpe Park still had a family focus. In an interview with *The Stage* Heath was clear stating[131]:

"We are increasing the amount of family entertainment at Thorpe Park although the last thing we want is to get the rowdy fairground element coming in to spoil a family's day out"

When pressed on the increasing competition he was buoyant about the future of all theme parks, and in a prophetic mood claiming:

"As mechanisation extends, there will be less jobs and earlier retirement. Realistically, unemployment must rise and the working week is likely to be reduced. Catering for the amusement of those at leisure will be a constantly expanding industry"

1987 was also the year that the park would host the *World Water Ski Championships* for the third and final time. Once again, the USA were the dominant force, Sammy Duvall retaining the overall male prize, with fellow American Deena Brush claiming overall female[132].

Thorpe Park's *Thunder River* remained in its original, most cherished form, until 2002. Rapids rides continue to be a theme park staple around the world, with in excess of 150 versions now having been constructed in all corners of the planet. Although technology has advanced to an extent, they largely work in the same manner as the original. In more recent times they have hit the headlines in tragic circumstances. The similarly named *Thunder River Rapids Ride* at Dreamworld in Australia suffered a malfunction in October 2016, resulting in four people being killed[133]. The incident happened when two boats clashed on the conveyor belt leading to passengers falling out. The horrific incident led to the ride being demolished. The following year an eleven-year-old schoolchild died at Drayton Manor in Tamworth, when she fell into the water on the *Splash Canyon* rapids during a school trip[134]. Thorpe Park's rapids were closed as a precaution the day after the incident whilst waiting for any learnings, but re-opened soon after[135].

Despite a stuttering opening, Thorpe Park had another key attraction to entice families, but the battle with Chessington World of Adventures was only just beginning. The next few years would only see the conflict intensify.

1988

After touring Europe to find inspiration, Thorpe Park concluded that offering a series of rides was not enough to provide magic for guests, they needed to put on a show. In fact, from 1988 onwards they were planning to put on a stack of them to keep visitors entertained and amazed throughout their day.

The centrepiece of this renewed effort was a brand new 630 seat theatre in the heart of the rides and attractions, called *Park Palladium*, constructed at a cost of over a million pounds[136]. In addition, shows would continue elsewhere such as in the Dome, and a further £100,000 was budgeted for "impromptu entertainment"[137]. The latter would be entertainers such as jugglers, stilt walkers and clowns who would roam the park freely so guests would barely have a moment to get bored. Marketing manager Derek Oliver was buoyant about the plans:

> "The idea is to have entertainment going on all around the place so that even when people are standing in a queue they are being entertained. The aim is to make Thorpe Park a spontaneous place of amusement where visitors never quite know what to expect next"

The expensive new theatre was to host up to eight shows a day during peak times, lasting around 20-30 minutes each. Peter Jennings was asked to create the original performances which included shows called *Hooray for Hollywood* and *Up the Charts*[138]. Typically, these involved young entertainers singing and dancing to familiar hits, depending on the genre of the show. The park was trying to give itself something of a seaside resort feel, and even dabbled with calling their staff "Yellowcoats". A not-so-subtle nod to the iconic Butlin's Redcoats, with *Yellowcoats* also featured in the TV series *Hi-di- Hi*! Howard Keel, who starred as Clayton Farlow in one of the biggest shows of the eighties, Dallas, was asked to officially open the new theatre in June 1988. Keel had a musical and recording background himself, making him an apt choice for ribbon cutting duties.

Whilst the theatre was now the largest capacity venue in the park, much effort was still focused on shows elsewhere, especially inside the Dome where 30-minute performances where offered up to five times a day under the banner of *Variety in the Dome 88*[139]. Unlike the theatre seating, the Dome had tables so guests could enjoy food and drink from the surrounding vendors whilst the shows unfolded in front of them. The hectic schedule required the seven core performers to appear for 146 days in a row. These shows were actually devised and produced by two actors, Graham Hunter and Nigel Taylor, who had previously met and worked together on the *Treasure Island* ride as pirates. After catching the eye shivering their timbers, they were entrusted to create and star in variety shows that would appeal to the whole family.

A typical day would see them start at noon with *The Cockney Show* which featured East London classics including a sing-a-long rendition of *I've Got a Lovely Bunch of Coconuts*. Following this would be *The Sunshine Show*, with feel good songs such as *Everything's Coming Up Roses* from the musical *Gypsy*, and an eye-catching final dance to *One* from *Chorus Line*. In a review of the various performances in *The Stage*[140], Eric Braun singled out 19-year-old Carolyn Luck for praise saying her Chorus Line finale performance was "very agile" and "an arresting climax". Later in the day the *Rock 'N' Roll Show* offered renditions of Elvis and Billy Fury classics, and the day finished with the *Cabaret Show* where guests had the chance to see The Charleston and songs from *Hello, Dolly* before heading home. Despite admitting the offering in the Dome wasn't particularly sophisticated, Braun praised Hunter and Taylor's work calling *Variety in the Dome 88* "A remarkable display of sheer, slick, non-stop entertainment: this is music expertly angled for family audiences". Hunter and Taylor's efforts were replaced in 1989 by the ice lolly inspired *Calippo Disco Show* to chillier reviews.

The extra entertainment around the park was a popular with guests, and certainly helped retain the feeling of wholesome family fun that Thorpe Park had earned a reputation for. It also helped justify another increase in entry fee, which now stood at £6.50, although much of this was still being re-invested into the overall experience including a completely re-worked admissions area[141]. The hope was that the new variety shows would help boost annual visitors by a further 100,000 to reach the 1.2 million mark. Oliver's latest sales slogan said Thorpe Park was *"For the time of your life"*, and claimed they had no ambitions of taking on the likes of Alton Towers and Blackpool Pleasure Beach in the thrill stakes[142]:

"The main development of the park has been geared towards attracting families, which account for about 90% of our visitors, unlike some other places which aim to provide the larger stomach-churning rides. We are a much gentler park"

Park Palladium opened its doors again in 1989, this time overseen fully by new entertainments manager Stephen Gold, who had an extensive background in live theatre and music performances. An initial show he inherited was titled *Live at the Palladium*, presumably in a nod to the classic TV series that went by similar names on ITV from 1955 onwards. The smorgasbord of entertainment included live performances of popular disco songs, magician Andy Leich performing tricks and comedy, and ventriloquism by Jack Edgar. Nick Lloyd led the song and dance routines, which were choreographed by George May. Also featuring at the time was Adrian Kaye, who went on to have an esteemed thirty-year career as a clown and street performer. He joined Thorpe Park having just finished at *Guildford School of Acting*, initially portraying Charlie Chaplin[143]. Roaming around the park to entertain the crowds were clowns Aero, Lupi and Kiku, plus the double act *Slap & Tickle*.

The theatre continued to offer variety shows for another decade, alongside more ad-hoc performances. At points cartoons were shown inside to keep younger children entertained, and during the 1989 season the theatre even welcomed 17 Can Can dancers from West Germany to perform for one day alongside a local Egham band[144]. Unlike the rides, the shows needed to be updated more regularly as visitors tended to enjoy the more topical aspects. Therefore, Gold introduced a new variety show that he had written himself, directed by his long-time partner Penny Hogan[145]. *Space Fantasy* was developed from one of his previous touring shows, and featured some classic 80s hits with a fantastical futuristic theme. A largely new generation of performers belted out the likes of Kylie Minogue, David Bowie and the Carpenter's *Calling Occupants of Interplanetary Craft*[146]. The popular *Star* Wars music brought smiles to the audience, along with a robot character that required an actor to wear silver paint. With the show lasting around 35 minutes, and being performed up to six times a day, it required a dedicated and disciplined attitude from the cast, something Gold felt would hold them in good stead for their future careers. Looking back on the time Gold was rightly proud of his achievements, calling the performances "a real first for the UK theme park industry"[147].

The next iteration of the Palladium shows for 1993 was the action-based *Legend of the Ring*, which Stephen Gold again devised and produced, with Hogan on chorography and staging duties. It riffed heavily on Spielberg films such as *Indiana Jones* and *Jurassic Park*, and promised a "live" dinosaur. This time a number of original songs were used, along with the distinctive chart hit *Don't Give Up* by Peter Gabriel and Kate Bush[148]. Max Hutton and Michelle Musty starred in the show[149], which took advantage of some new screens and projectors to display a dastardly villain's face. It was another family-friendly hit.

Gold was a big admirer of the *Park Palladium* theatre, calling it "quite remarkable for a theme park". He admitted it had some limitations though, with the stage having little depth to it, and no curtains, meaning they had to get creative at times. When it came to *Park Palladium's* final and biggest budget variety show, it meant making some changes. *Merlin's Magic Castle* opened in 1995[150], and combined special effects and music with the classic tale of King Arthur, Merlin and Co. The inside of the theatre underwent a medieval makeover complete with turrets and balconies where some of the actors performed. The stage was also extended and featured a sword in the stone moment close to the audience[151]. After several successful years the final curtain went down on

Merlin's Magic Castle in 1998, ready for the theatre to be refurbished for a new attraction.

Gold was complimentary about the freedom he was given when creating the shows, claiming to never have received creative interference from his fellow management[152]. Hogan and Gold would later form their own independent company called *Parkshow Production Associates*, based locally in Shepperton. The new company specialised in creating theme park shows for a variety of attractions and training specialist staff[153].

Shows and entertainment were to also remain a core part of Thorpe Park's offering outside the theatre throughout the 90s. The attendance in 1988 didn't reach the target of 1.2 million visitors, but remained just over a million[154]. A new addition the tenth anniversary would ensure they had no problem increasing that number next time.

1989

Just a decade after opening, Thorpe Park had already transformed from its quaint leisure origins to an ambitious full-on theme park, spending over £20 million to continually update the experience. Since the launch of *Thunder River* in 1987, references had been made to a big new investment for the 10th anniversary[155], and all was ready to be revealed in 1989.

An area in the south east corner was identified to develop into a whole new themed land. The space was previously home to the *Schneider Trophy Exhibition*, as well as some other smaller attractions in the mid-eighties such as a *Commando Test*. The expansion was an opportunity to draw crowds away from the busy *Central Park/European Square* area. Early on a partnership was struck with the Canadian Tourist Board to theme the new development to the North American country[156], which helped unlock a budget of £4.5 million[157] to invest in the land and several new attractions.

Identified as the centrepiece of the new area would be a log flume ride. Proposals around introducing one of these had been about since the 1970s, but had initially been rejected. John Wardley suggests there was a gentleman's agreement between Chessington and Thorpe Park, that would see them introduce different water rides so they didn't cannibalise each other[158]. Because of this in 1987 Chessington had a log flume, and Thorpe Park installed a rapids. However, if that was the case, then Leisure Sport were about to go back on their word.

Log flumes are based on how lumber used to be transported in chutes quickly down mountainous terrain to reach sawmills in the 19th Century. The modern attraction version sees riders seated in hollowed out logs, usually single file between each other's legs, and travel down a flume in much the same way the Magic Mill worked, but usually at a faster pace. The finale of a log flume is almost always a large drop, where riders hurtle downwards with the boat slowed at the bottom by impact with the water, leading to a soaking for passengers. This type of water ride was already very popular both in the UK and around the world, becoming a staple of the American amusement park since the 1960s.

Chessington World of Adventures local log flume was one of the key rides in their 1987 re-imagining[159]. *Dragon River* had an oriental theme, after initial Egyptian designs were rejected. Its introduction had been a huge hit, with pictures of the 45+ foot drop being used everywhere to promote the fledgling theme park. Alton Towers had introduced a flume in 1981 (as part of their swift expansion into rides after the success of the Corkscrew), with theirs claiming to be the world's longest, although its tallest drop was a pretty standard size. Around a dozen others were in operation elsewhere across the UK of varying standards and design, and Thorpe Park realised they would need a point of difference to stay ahead of the opposition.

This would be another collaboration with Mack who weren't as experienced as the likes of Arrow in building this style of ride, but had already provided the successful flumes at Alton Towers and Chessington. The answer, which would eclipse the opposition, would be height; with the manufacturer finding a way to go bigger than before. The finale of the ride would be a 55-foot double drop, the tallest in the UK, beating rivals Chessington by a short distance. The drop would initially dive down, before straightening out momentarily, and then continuing back down. Mack were happy that this could be achieved safely. Plans were drawn up for the rest of the ride to compliment this, complete with a second smaller drop early in the ride, which would take place inside a cave-like tunnel section. In between the two drops the log boats would wind through around a 500-metre journey, reaching the furthest corners of the park.

To compliment the log flume, which was going to easily be the most thrilling ride Thorpe Park had ever built, would be a more tranquil classic train ride. This served a dual purpose as it offered yet another family attraction, and would also be transport to and from *Thorpe Farm*, allowing the land trains that had been in action since opening to be retired. There would be a station at either end of the park, one at the farm and another a little over a kilometre away in the new Canadian section. The train would pass right by some of the animals, with drivers having to occasionally have to wait for them to move from the track, but *Thorpe Farm* manager Ian Minshull was a fan[160]:

> "The train was great, it bought loads of people. The animals, it didn't bother them, no problem at all. It was great"

Whilst most of the trainline was simply a straight line following the previous footpath past *Treasure Island*, there was a lovely touch added where the trains returning from the farm would follow the new log flume round the ride, returning to the station shortly after witnessing the final dramatic drop. The loop also helped turn the trains, so they were facing the right way for the return journey.

With plans firmed up in good time for the anniversary, Thorpe Park requested permission for the new area in December 1987 from Runnymede Council[161]. The plans revealed the project's name as *Canada Creek* and confirmed further specifics of their ambitions. The new railway would be 600mm gauge and host two trains, each with five carriages, capable of carrying roughly 150 passengers. The flume ride would operate 22 logs at a time, with a theoretical capacity of 1600 riders per hour, sections of the ride heading through rugged scenery with tumbling waterfalls. Like *Thunder River*, it would use water from the surrounding lakes to operate, with an expected 15.5 million gallons a day required from Abbey Lake[162]. The flume would circle part of the lake, which would offer a fitting backdrop. A total of five buildings would need to be amended or constructed to make *Canada Creek* possible. Another advantage of using this particular underdeveloped corner of the park was that it was the furthest point from the village, meaning any noise was unlikely to trouble them, and meant a smooth passage to the plans being accepted.

Whilst the new theatre was being opened in the centre of the park, construction on *Canada Creek* got underway in mid-1988. To give the surroundings a more authentic Canadian feel 500 red maple trees and 4000 quick growing conifers were planted[163]. To create the mountainous terrain around the lakes and ride areas one million tons of rubble was brought in including excavations at the Houses of Parliament, Barbican, Old Bailey, Alexandra Palace, Heathrow Airport, and most bizarrely Queens Park Ranger's old artificial football pitch[164]. To carry the logs up inclines ahead of the drops, and control their movement through the station, conveyor belts were installed. The lift sections would include anti rollback mechanisms which make a distinctive clanking noise as boats travel upwards. Fibreglass was used to add theming around the tunnel and the lookalike log boats. With crowds expected to flock to the big new ride, a lengthy queue was created in an uninspiring cattle pen style continuous backwards and forwards layout. To keep those queuing entertained televisions were added showing a seven-minute-long video created by the Government of Ontario and Air Canada[165].

Construction took nine months, and with a large launch event planned for Wednesday 22nd March, installation went right down to the wire. Just the week before the two new *Canada Creek Railway* trains were delivered, complete with their bespoke bright blue and yellow colouring and tenders. The American style locomotives were built by the experts at Severn Lamb Ltd who were based in Stratford upon Avon and transported down to Surrey[166]. They looked absolutely fantastic, a real quality design with bespoke touches, and matching carriages. *Loggers Leap* was chosen as the name of the new thrill ride, but with it still not ready when advertising footage was required, video of a similar ride at Europa Park was used instead. With the prospect of having to cancel their biggest ever launch event, project teams worked through the night to ensure the rides were ready, and bar a few planned totem poles, they succeeded.

The new area was possibly the best yet, with effort made to surround visitors with an authentic Canadian feel, including the materials used and surrounding refreshment stalls. Canadian flags were added throughout, and specially designed level crossings installed to allow the railway to pass through. A further addition to the area was *Fort Ontario*, an adventure playground with slides, tunnels and cargo nets for children to explore. It was surprisingly large, and would allow youngsters to lose themselves, whilst siblings were off braving *Loggers Leap*. Its logged wall perimeter really helping to fit it into the surroundings. The development was most likely the first to have been truly influenced by the new areas at Chessington World of Adventures, having been designed at the time the new attractions were revealed. It seemed like a response, showing that Thorpe Park were ready to match the level of detail and theming that had gone into the likes of *Mystic East* and *Calamity Canyon*.

With such effort going into creating *Canada Creek*, it was a huge shame that when the 22nd March came, the weather was absolutely dreadful. Heavy rain and strong wind weren't able to stop things though, and 1,400 invited guests assembled to witness a ceremony. This included around a thousand school children from the local area, plus VIPs from the Canadian Government and Ontario Tourist Board, who joined their Surrey counterparts and various members of the press[167]. Television personalities Timmy Mallet and Michaela Strachan were enlisted to get proceedings underway. Both were presenters for TV-am, although Mallett was also known for his own show *Wacaday*, which involved him hitting people with a giant pink and yellow hammer (the 80s!). In her review of the day the *Evening Post's* Rosalind Renshaw was particularly smitten with Strachan's appearance[168]:

"The beautiful Michaela Strachan whom every male in Britain over the age of four is madly in love with, and no wonder. She is the only grown woman I have ever seen who manages to look sexy in socks"

Mallett and sexy sock fan Strachan arrived in *Canada Creek* jumping through a giant hoop, accompanied by music and loud fireworks. They were then given the opportunity to be the first official riders on *Loggers Leap*, and duly obliged as cameras captured their delight crashing down the large drop. The newly constructed drop looked especially intimidating at the time, as none of the landscaping had time to grow, leaving the ride's surroundings a little bare. In later years large tress and foliage would help the ride blend in more, but for now the fresh surroundings stood out. When asked what he thought of the new experience, Mallet was pretty succinct in his thoughts:

"Wet but wonderful"

Loggers Leap closed very shortly after as the maintenance team ironed out some final issues, and dignitaries went off to try out the railway and the rest of the park, with the overall reaction extremely positive. With some pride and a little relief, it became clear that Thorpe Park's biggest investment to date was going to be another winner, and crucial to keeping up with the new wave of theme parks hitting the UK. The reaction for the press at the launch was strong too. Some may forget how different expectations were at the time, with no rollercoasters towering over the landscape. *Loggers Leap* was the tallest ride about, and a seriously daunting prospect to many families. Renshaw's *Evening Post* review made it clear just how much of an effect it had on some bystanders, and refused to let her son try it out:

"I had no intention of letting him go, and if I'd been Michaela Strachan's mum, I wouldn't have let her go either…..I am glad I am not a well-known television personality, as no amount of money including free mortgage repayments for life would have induced me to go on *Loggers Leap*"

Thankfully others were more willing to try it out, with both *Loggers Leap* and the *Canada Creek Railway* instant hits with the public. The final ride experience for *Loggers Leap* would see passengers squeeze inside a slowly moving log travelling through the station, which most likely was already filled with a little water from the previous trip. Everyone was required to sit in a straight line, and although several sections were split by a cushioned barrier, there was a good chance you'd find yourself awkwardly wrapping your legs either side of a family member/friend/complete stranger to cram five of you in. The station was decorated as a saw mill, complete with various cutting instruments on the wall, and the conveyor belt would eventually jerk you out into the main ride. Here you would meander through troughs at a leisurely pace, as the boat constantly bumped the sides to find the correct way around the corner without guide rails. After a minute or so of winding you enter the indoor cave section, which was impressively dark, successfully concealing the first climb and drop. Although the climbing was apparent, there was no way of telling how high you were going, or when the drop would happen, adding an excellent level of suspense. This made the most of a rather small drop, often leaving riders screaming twice in quick succession, once as they dropped into the dark, and again shortly after as a surprise splashing of water hit them at the bottom.

The famous Loggers Leap double-drop. Credit: Thorpe Park Nostalgia

After leaving the tunnel, there was more winding troughs far from public view, as the headline drop approached. Here riders were reminded by several signs to remain seated, as there was nothing holding them in, apart from the warm thighs of the passenger behind you. The 55-foot climb, featuring several conveyors and the distinctive clanking, took around 30 seconds and offered increasingly impressive views of the surrounding area. Eventually the boat would reach the top, and the key tipping point where the boat would leave the safety of the climb, and plunge down the double drop. Riders would often feel a quick pop of air-time in the middle bump, before continuing downwards and being drastically slowed down by the water, which would spray over everyone. If you were particularly unlucky and at the front, you would occasionally get a wave of smelly lake water come over the front and into your lap. From here it was a few more turns back to the station, where you had an excellent view of the next few boats behind you crash down the drop, and see the amusing reactions of others. It was a fantastic ride, with just the right amount of intensity to entertain those families with older children who were possibly a little under catered for.

After the successful launch, a couple of incidents later in the 1989 season led to small changes having to be made. The first of these in early July saw five-year-old Sharik Mirza fall from the *Canada Creek Railway* whilst the train was moving with the local newspaper claiming he was "dragged screaming along the track after getting his leg caught"[169]. The young boy suffered a fractured shinbone and fibula, and required plastic surgery. The *Canada Creek Railway* was closed for a couple of weeks whilst an investigation was held, and new guard operated doors fitted to replace safety chains. It re-opened later that month with the Railway Inspectorate of the Department of Transport happy with the changes stating "new measures were more than adequate from a safety point of view".

Over at *Loggers Leap* there was a minor incident in September[170]. It was reported that a log vehicle failed to slow down after the large drop, hitting the next turn at high speed, and injuring four riders. One of these suffered a fractured wrist, with the others thankfully more minor. The ride was closed for two days for Mack to identify the issue, which was a faulty sensor. The water level had dropped below that required to slow the boats, and the ride should have automatically stopped. Mack claimed it was a one off they had not experienced before, and *Loggers Leap* returned to action.

The attraction was a bit hit with the staff too, with Tony Hall occasionally sneaking off to have a go himself[171]:

"Once you got on the ride and were away, it was lovely and quiet. And it was breezy, away from the rest of the park. It was used in all the adverts, so it had panache. It was a really good ride too. You got a great big splash, it was fun, it was really nicely themed and fitted really nicely in the area"

Steve Day also has fond memories of riding with his friends[172]:

"As soon as the boat left the station and out of the view of the crew, you'd start cheekily splashing your mates with water. The spray at the end seemed to drench you, and you'd often come off pretty soaked"

The investment gave the park the desired boost in attendance, and although a new capacity of 22,000 people a day was in place, they managed to hit 1.3 million visitors which was a 22% increase on 1988[173]. This was especially impressive as it was set against a tough economic climate of rising interest rates.

One of the key members of the team from the early days, Terry Catliff, tragically suffered a heart attack in his office and passed away[174]. His eventual replacement as general manager was Colin Dawson, a veteran of many years at parent company RMC. He had a passion for ensuring high standards and putting families first, and came from a surprising background, having been an original member of rock band *The Who* alongside Pete Townshend and Roger Daltrey, before going on to work in concrete. The latest career switch would turn out to be a long and successful one for him, eventually earning an OBE. Entertainment manager Gold worked with Dawson over many years at Thorpe Park, and held him in high regard[175]:

"Colin Dawson was a great supporter, and really latched onto ideas. He was great to work with, a very good general manager. He always listened to what you had to say"

Thorpe Park was now being advertised with the latest slogan 'A fortnight's fun in one'[176], although some were critical of the latest pricing structure which saw the cost set at £6.00, and free for those under three foot six[177]. Responding to the incidents and criticisms at the time Dawson was resilient:

"Over a million visitors will come to Thorpe Park this year and we take
every possible precaution in all areas of the park....It is a value for
money day"

One area Dawson was less happy about was the drop in school trip
numbers. Thorpe Park continued to rely on these to boost attendance on
weekdays in term time, but with a 24% drop in educational visits he was
planning to mail 23,000 schools with details for the following season[178]:

"The new curriculum has meant more demands on the teachers'
timetable with increased commitment to in-school activities resulting in
less time available for organising school trips. We might have had an
outstanding year had the school business held up this season"

Not included in the attendance numbers were up to 24,000 people who
purchased tickets to a fictional Acid House Party that sellers claimed was
happening on Saturday 5th August. The con men raked in around
£360,000 from the fake tickets, claiming those purchasing would get
access to all the rides in the park, followed by a massive party[179]. With
direct communication to the ticket holders impossible, police planned a
massive operation to turn away revellers on the day. Predictably
Dawson was furious telling the *Reading Post*:

"This appears to be a massive case of fraud where somebody is
capitalising on the obvious popularity of our facilities"

To cope with the increased crowds throughout 1989 the park trebled the
amount of queue line entertainers and claimed that theoretically no ride
should have more than a 30-minute queue, although this would often
not be the case[180]. This included entertainers *Luke 'n' Floyd* who dressed
up as hillbillies and played four 45-minute music sets every day in the
Loggers Leap queue[181]. One particularly popular day was Sunday 14th May
when the *Capital FM KitKat Roadshow* rolled into Thorpe Park[182],
complete with celebrity presenters Pat Sharp and Mick Brown. They

broadcast live in front of the surrounding guests, and distributed free KitKats.

Elsewhere on the park a new temporary dome was installed for three months, as the premiere location for the *Hazards at Home* exhibition[183]. The purpose was to educate families on common dangers in the house, presumably stuff like "don't use your toaster in the bath or lick the hob". It was a big government initiative costing £360,000 and paid for by the Department of Trade and Industry, with the plan that the *Hazard Dome* would then travel round the country to educate others. For the launch celebrity Floella Benjamin and Consumer Affairs Minister Eric Forth attended, and were keen to show off the many videos and exhibits in the structure - many of which featured their new mascot *Doc Hazard*. The event backfired slightly when contrary to the *Canada Creek* launch earlier in the year the weather was scorching, and when some marketing materials were ditched by the air conditioning it overheated, leaving guests too hot to stay inside.

Leisure Sport had one further surprise up their sleeve for the 1989 season, in the shape of six new animal mascots called the *Thorpe Park Rangers*[184]. One of these was a re-modelling of the previous mascot Mr Rabbit, who now looked far more personalised in a smart uniform of hat, yellow trousers and blue blazer. Joining him in matching uniforms were Chief Ranger, Mr Giraffe, Mr Elephant and Mr Monkey. What was quite impressive about the original outfits was how they varied significantly in size and design making them easily distinguishable. The Giraffe neck was huge, with the character towering over the rest, whilst Mr Elephant was short, plump and had a facial expression like he was perpetually constipated[185]. The leader was Chief Ranger whose tall, broad bear costume depicted an imposing alpha male figure. The final mascot was Baby Bear, who was apparently the child of Chief Ranger and deemed too young to wear a replica uniform. Extra ranger characters such as a lion and kangaroo joined the line-up in cartoon form, but didn't seem to ever exist as physical mascots. The *Thorpe Park Rangers* would initially roam the park and adorn marketing materials, but their popularity would see them play a larger part in years to come.

With the introduction of *Canada Creek*, the *Thorpe Park Rangers*, and record attendance, this was a significant year in the history of Thorpe Park. Whilst not a complete victory against the new band of theme park rivals, it at least showed they were well set to compete, and continue to grow.

Loggers Leap went on to become one of the most adored attractions in the history of the park. It developed into an emblem of Thorpe Park, proudly staying one of the most cherished rides for over two decades, the success of which future additions would struggle to replicate. Little changed to the experience over time, and it would commonly feature whenever filming took place in the park, becoming well known amongst the general public. After 27 years in operation the iconic ride was closed at the end of the 2015 season, with the initial communication from the park that it would re-open in future after undergoing some extensive maintenance. Sadly, after several years of being closed but not removed, Thorpe Park confirmed the ride's fate in a February 2019 statement[186] reading:

> "It's with a heavy heart that we announce the time has come to say goodbye to a much-loved ride here at Thorpe Park Resort and what was the UK's tallest log flume, Logger's Leap"

The reaction to the closure on social media was strong, with the park seemingly surprised by the volume of overwhelming love from nostalgic visitors throughout the years. However those fans were to be left disappointed, with no final rides, or opportunity to say goodbye. So why was the decision taken to permanently close the still popular attraction? It seems it was very much death by a thousand cuts, with no one issue being the problem, but a series of smaller concerns mounting up until a re-opening became unfeasible.

Unsurprisingly most of these revolved around health and safety, in one way or another. The state of the ride had deteriorated greatly over time, and repairs were required. This included the ride hardware and station, but also the tunnel which had much of the roof removed several years before the closure when it was found to be structurally unsound. Chessington's similarly aged log flume underwent hearty renovations by a company called Garmendale Engineering[187] at a not insignificant cost, and it would have been possible for *Loggers Leap* to have similar action taken, but it's rumoured the budget had to be used to upgrade other rides in 2017 instead. Regulations were also changing regarding ride safety, and that meant you couldn't just throw a huge amount of filthy lake water over people anymore. The lack of restraints holding riders in were also a constant concern. Any ride in the twenty first century that relies on passengers behaving, or operator vigilance to detect misconduct, rather than automatic safety measures is going to come under scrutiny. Safety is absolutely paramount, and the thought of somebody standing up at the wrong time on *Loggers Leap* must have given the park's lawyers nightmares.

An abandoned Loggers Leap in 2020. Credit: Alex Rowe

The legal team already had their hands full, when in April 2014 a teen claimed she received life changing injuries from riding *Loggers Leap*[188]. 14-year-old Leah Napolitano reportedly received £20,000 from Thorpe Park's insurers after she became stuck in the front of one of the log boats, pushed forward by her family crammed in behind her. Speaking to the *Manchester Evening News* several years later Napolitano said[189]:

> "My legs were completely trapped. I couldn't move them for the whole way round. I got to the end and couldn't get out"

Although originally able to carry on with her day, the injuries worsened and meant Napolitano was unable to return to school or take part in any sport. The pay-out opened the door to the potential of other claims unless changes were made to the boats.

It's highly likely that Thorpe Park intended to open a refurbished *Loggers Leap* again after the 2015 season, but with a growing list of issues, they eventually made the call to pull the plug. Alton Towers interestingly made the same decision at the end of 2015 too, closing their flume ride to make way for future developments, likely influenced by similar concerns. Whilst not quite as popular as they once were, log flumes do still appear frequently at theme parks across the world, and continue to be installed albeit many with increased safety measures. As of late 2020 *Loggers Leap* still stands abandoned, but not yet removed, giving hope that there's still the very slightest chance of a unlikely revival.

Alongside *Loggers Leap*, the rest of *Canada Creek* survived into the next century, and one of the small rotating Mack train rides from the children's area was eventually added in the centre of the area in the 90s and named the *Rocky Express*. The main *Canada Creek Railway* eventually stopped its regular service in 2011. After the removal of the original rides, and with the partnership with the government long finished, the area was eventually renamed into its current incarnation, simply called *Old Town*.

1990

As a new decade dawned, the battle of the UK's theme parks was about to escalate further. Alton Tower's owner John Broome's plans for a leisure facility inside Battersea Power Plant had turned into a financial mess. Years of throwing money at the listed building had failed to properly fix major issues with its suitability, and it was becoming apparent that the project would likely never come to fruition[190]. Tussauds were buoyed by the initial performance of Chessington World of Adventures and had been searching for a new location in the middle of the country to open a second UK theme park. After considering several locations including Warwick Castle, they became aware of Broome's struggles. It was proposed that given the situation it might be possible to acquire Alton Towers, which would offer a more straightforward option than to create a new rival from scratch[191].

News broke in February 1990 of the negotiations for the park, with Broome reportedly looking for a cool £70 million+ to secure Britain's second most popular tourist attraction[192]. Tussauds were all too aware of Broome's financial struggles, and were seemingly willing to negotiate hard to get the right deal. The *Evening Mail* were reporting that Broome had taken out a £55 million bank loan to continue work at Battersea, which had stopped the previous year, and was even under time pressure to get the deal done to release funds before the end of March. By Friday 30th June the deal was done, with Tussauds parent company Pearson paying £50 million to take Alton Towers off John Broome's hands[193].

It was clear that the plan was to continue investing in Alton Towers to further boost its popularity and profitability. 28 year old Nick Varney was appointed as the park's new divisional marketing director, and he was happy to speak to the media about a bold new ten year plan that was being put into place. Varney told the *Evening Sentinel*[194]:

"If we are going to survive in this leisure business we have got to be the best – and we are. What we are delivering has to be something the public wants and it has to be the best, and be different from anything else."

Tussauds also shuffled their pack a little, bringing in expertise from Chessington to help the transition. Damian Varley, who had previously been development manager at the World of Adventure, agreed to take on the same role in Staffordshire. He was confident that Tussauds could up the standards across the park[195]:

> "I would say it is very much part of the Tussauds' concept of development that they believe at the end of the day quality will win out and it is quality parks which will succeed and ride out the recession"

One of Varley's final responsibilities at Chessington was to help deliver their biggest investment yet. After the success of the initial wave of theme park rides, they were now going to spend £8 million (equivalent of £18.5 million in 2020) on John Wardley's idea for a second phase, which consisted of a brand-new area containing two rides[196]. The *Transylvania* themed zone, included a suspended swinging coaster from manufacturer Arrow called *The Vampire* and a dark water ride called *Professor Burp's Bubbleworks*. It was a huge investment but the results were sensational. *The Vampire* was the first of its kind in the UK[197], but was more than a gimmick, offering a truly fun and exciting ride through the treetops, then swooping low and swinging riders side to side. The theming was sublime, with the roller coaster cars being large bats, and riders having to venture through a large graveyard as part of the queue experience. The pièce de résistance was in the dark, eerie ride station, where riders would be welcomed by the sounds of a large organ being played by a fantastically realised creepy animatronic figure.

The Vampire's atmosphere was impressive, and you might forgive planners for focusing on this and delivering a second lesser attraction, but if anything, the *Bubbleworks* exceeded it in every way. The boat ride centred on a tour around a fizzy pop factory, and was created by the man behind Thorpe Park's *Phantom Fantasia*, Keith Sparks[198]. It was in many ways the ultimate family ride, containing various rooms and set pieces, some naughty childish humour, and a small but thrilling drop followed by a sensational finale through a room full of colourful fountains. It was universally loved and admired. Even if Thorpe Park could somehow find the money to match such an investment, it was unlikely they would be able to recapture the innovation and imagination displayed by Transylvania in such a expertly realised way.

What Thorpe Park did have was £1.5 million to spend, and for the 1990 season they were going to spread it around a little. Colin Dawson was confident they didn't always need something on the scale of *Thunder River* or *Loggers Leap* to impress visitors, telling the Herald and News[199]:

"It's not the highest capital expenditure, but the impact on visitor attraction is greater than anything we have done in the past"

One of the changes made was an unexpected one to many. Since its introduction in 1984 *Space Station Zero* had been popular and seen millions thrilled by the cosmic themed indoor rollercoaster. With restrictions on developments at the park seemingly relaxed, it was now possible to run the Mack powered coaster outdoors. A spot was found in *Model World* and the coaster moved in its entirety to new surroundings a short walk from its old home. The reason given for the change by the park was that its previous indoor home left friends and family waiting outside bored, and unable to watch their loved ones on the ride[200]. With the space theme no longer appropriate new themed trains were ordered to match the new name of *The Flying Fish*, with the uncomfortable over the shoulder restraints replaced by basic lap bars. The friendly green fish would now race round the same track, with considerable work going into the surrounding landscaping. Beautiful gardens, waterfalls and rock pools were located all-round the track and freshly constructed queue-line. The entrance to the ride was marked with a beautiful old English style archway adorned with the ride's new name.

It's likely many were surprised by how small the drops were when they saw it in daylight compared to the darkness of the old location, however most members of the public were likely never even aware the ride was exactly the same one, believing the *Flying Fish* a completely new attraction. Television adverts featuring a cartoon *Flying Fish* train certainly positioned it as a brand-new ride. Regardless it was a big hit, and became something of a Thorpe Park classic in the years to come. Albeit rather unadventurous, it was still a rollercoaster, and by 1990 standards was quite an intense ride. Like *Loggers Leap* it was another attraction that families with older children could enjoy together and allowed Thorpe Park to keep their wholesome image whilst still offering a small but rewarding adrenaline rush. The setup for riders was similar to before, but with no pre-show or gimmicks, which was a mild shame.

The Flying Fish whips round the corner. Credit: Thorpe Park Nostalgia

Depending on how busy a day it was you could get several laps of the course, with the more enthusiastic ride operators teasing passengers by slowing down the train as they entered the station, only to then suddenly speed up and head out once again. Whilst this was usually on purpose, sometimes it would be necessary as the operator would need to line the train up perfectly in the station manually, and if they overshot the right spot, would need to let the train do another lap. Once finished riders would exit the opposite side to boarding and head out a bridge over the station. For some reason the ride operators would stringently enforce a rule of no lingering on the bridge, with the implication that some kind of apocalyptic scenario would play out if the ride were to operate with people watching from above.

Taking the place of *Space Station Zero* in the vacated 10,000 square foot building was a new medieval themed section called *Carousel Kingdom*. The centrepiece of this was the UK's only double decker carousel, which was a beautifully hand painted replica of a steam powered model from the 1890s. Decorated with hundreds of lightbulbs, it shone exquisitely in the dim indoor area. The ride itself was created by German specialists Peter Petz who, in addition to the traditional horses, added a number of other ways to ride. Most interesting of these was several miniature hot air balloons on the upper level, that riders could climb into and spin independently like the *Teacup Ride*.

Alongside the headline ride the new *Carousel Kingdom* also boasted a double decker soft play area for younger children, later called *Courtyard Challenge*. Joining the usual tunnels and ball pool was the *Castle Tower Helter Skelter*, which replaced a similar snake slide removed from another area and notorious for friction burns. Parents could watch over the young ones adventuring in *Carousel Kingdom* from a new catering unit which offered views of the whole area. Completing the new section was a fun house, including midway games such as the opportunity to fire rubber balls through clowns faces[201]. Bizarrely a new Clown Corner Shop was also added nearby. The entire package was a slightly peculiar mix, unlikely to draw anybody new to the park, but if nothing else it was helpful in spreading the crowds and offering a covered space during inclement weather.

The final new ride was *Drive in the Country*, replacing the space previously taken by the *Bronco Bikes*. The attraction invited young visitors to board one of 13 scaled down vintage Ford cars, and take a journey through a 1930s countryside scene. This involved replica ducks, lambs, rabbits and haystacks, as well as traditional British post box and phone booth. The cars followed an electric guide rail, and had space for up to four riders, most comfortably with two children in the front and up to two adults in the back. The front seats had replica steering wheels and horns for kids to play with. The whole concept was very similar to Chessington World of Adventures existing *Old Crocks Rally* which was sponsored by the AA. Both were likely inspired by Disneyland's classic attraction *Mr. Toad's Wild Ride* which involves a similar ride system and cars, but takes place in a more heavily themed indoor building. The outdoor Surrey versions have the flaw of struggling to work in wet conditions, leading to them being incredibly unreliable in the rain.

After the successful introduction of the Thorpe Park Rangers as mascots the previous year, they were to get their very own show in 1990, taking place in a small theatre at the back of the park. Unlike the entertainment in the *Palladium Theatre* and *Dome*, this was very much focused on children. This replaced a previous Mr Rabbit specific show which used large puppets to tell a story. Stephen Gold led on converting the theatre into something more suitable, and wrote a storyline that tied into a national anti-litter campaign and revolved around Baby Bear trying to capture a "litter lout"[202]. By the end of the 20 minute show the Rangers had successfully found the villain portrayed as a green puppet, and taught him the error of his ways, with the hope the message would get through to the audience too.

For the voices of the mascots, Gold turned to one of his most promising young entertainers. Tony Hall had been finishing up at drama school in Guildford when he was recruited by Peter Jennings to work as an entertainer in the park. Originally being led to believe he would be working as one of the street entertainers, juggling and entertaining the audience as himself, he was asked to dress up as one of the *Thorpe Park Rangers* and roam the park. Hall recalls his time inside the mascot outfits saying[203]:

"It was very hot, but once you got used to what you were doing, actually it was quite a laugh because you were there with a lot of young people, it was good fun. We were out there on our own, and we'd regularly just get punched by people. A few weeks into this we said it isn't safe, we're getting hit from behind, every day somebody got abused!"

Minders were introduced to walk alongside the mascot characters, which worked well as the Rangers were not allowed to talk, so they also doubled as a way to communicate with guests.

"We went up into the Dome and they had a load of costumes, like a Mountie, a native American and a clown. We got the costumes out and used them for the minders"

Hall soon took ownership of the Mountie outfit and his enthusiasm and wit went down a storm with the public. He eventually built a character for himself known as Chip the Handsome Mountie, which would stand and welcome guests for hours as they crossed the bridge every morning. Gold was a big fan of Tony's work[204]:

"Tony was the classic example of the perfect person to work in a park because he would come in when it was pouring with rain and the wind blowing, he'd go out his Mountie suit, and he would come back at the end of the day and say he'd had a great time. He was constantly positive to people, and people responded to it. People would come back at the end of the day and ask where he was. He was probably one of the best people we ever had"

Based on his performances Gold asked young Tony Hall to provide some vocals for the new *Thorpe Park Ranger* show he was creating. Mr Rabbit and Chief Ranger already had established voices from advertising campaigns, so Hall mimicked these, however he was given more freedom for the other characters[205]:

"We based the elephant on a careers officer at school called Mr Ellison who was always very forgetful. We had a lad we went to drama school with called Finchy who was a little bit like Kenneth Williams when he spoke, so we made the giraffe mimic him. For the monkey we weren't sure whether to make him a wide boy cockney style, but we ended up with a George Formby character"

In the show, costume characters acted along to a pre-recorded soundtrack, and it was a massive hit with the general public, with variants running in the theatre for years to come. To begin with Gold wrote these, refreshing them when necessary, however when he left Hall took over as lead writer. New entertainments manager Kevin Townsend wanted three new shows every year, and Hall created up to ten new shows with music by Steve Gallagher. These were updated and replaced depending on their popularity, with the characters given more distinctive movements and actions, rather than all physically acting the same way.

Whilst this was going on Hall was doing television acting work in the background under his stage name Tony Audenshaw, and would later be picked up by ITV soap *Emmerdale*. After initially appearing in a small role, his character of Bob Hope was extremely popular, and since 2000 Hall/Audenshaw has been watched by millions several nights a week for twenty years since. His character has been married a record seven times, not bad going for Chip the Handsome Mountie.

Another extension of the *Thorpe Park Rangers* brand was the introduction of a new membership club. For the cost of just £5 your child could be signed up for two seasons[206]. The perks included half price entry, a special passport, and a joining goodie bag. Inside the original goodie bag you would find a cavalcade of *Thorpe Park Rangers* branded items including three posters, felt tip pens, frisbee, pen, badge, giant paperclip, three fruit drinks, and a handy pocket comb. The original character costumes were great in photographs, including a photoshoot with comedy legend Ernie Wise, but impractical for performers so were quickly replaced. Despite the improved outfits, staff still had to put up with testing conditions for long hours, six days a week. Eventually one of the management, Chris Edge, offered to do a shift himself, and realised how hard it was. Some new measures were quickly introduced including more regular breaks[207].

Sensing an opportunity to put his music writing and performing skills to good use, having once been in a band with David Bowie, Gold recorded a number of *Thorpe Park Rangers* songs for an album which was sold in the shops. It featured classics such as *One Day in the Park, Picnic by the Sea* and *Up the Chimney*. A combination of the two albums that were released over the years can still be found on streaming service *Spotify*[208].

Another Stephen Gold initiative would go live during the 1990 season. *Thorpe Park Radio* would broadcast from a small studio based between the *Palladium Theatre* and the *Teacup Ride*. The station's output of pop music combined with updates from around the park could be heard throughout the existing speaker system, with pretty much every queue line and public space piping it out. It initially came from a desire to have a way to communicate information efficiently to all the guests, but sensing an opportunity to add some extra fun to the system, the station was born. On quiet weekdays this would be a pre-recorded soundtrack, but on weekends and holidays broadcasters were brought in to present live[209].

For the launch Chris Tarrant, star of the hugely successful *Capital FM Breakfast Show*, was invited along to present one of the opening hours alongside Gold. Some of the early DJs included Simon Doe, Michael Jackson (not that one), Trevor Marshall and David Wright. Several of which would go on to have successful broadcasting careers. At Thorpe Park they had the opportunity to hone their skills using a professional setup including a decent mixing desk and range of outputs such as vinyl and CDs. As well as background entertainment, Thorpe Park Radio also served the purpose of making important announcements, such as information on missing children, ride closures and of show times.

The music and talking was broken up by a number of specially created jingles for the various rides and shows. Presenters were given the freedom to construct the music for the shows as they wished, although a clever system allowed certain rides to bypass the main feed and play more relevant music to the area unless a presenter decided to override it. One of the presenters in the latter days of the station, Nik Rawlinson, went on to host shows on *LBC* and reminisced about his *Thorpe Park Radio* times in 2002 with *ReRide*[210]:

"There was nothing in the way of a playlist. No prescribed set of tracks to be played at a certain time, apart from a general edict that after four we should slow down the pace in an effort to encourage people out of the park.... The most fun was the half hour before the park opened up, though, when all areas except for the entry gates were fed direct from the desk, bypassing the tape machines. This was a chance to play loud tracks, as the team assembled at their positions and got ready for the day"

The station was a fine example of everything Thorpe Park stood for at the time, unashamedly cheesy family entertainment. *Thorpe Park Radio* continued to keep visitors entertained until around 1997, when it was deemed to be too much like a proper radio station, causing licensing bodies to demand a vastly increased fee to continue broadcasting. Given the extra costs required, the decision was taken to cut down significantly to get around the rules, until the plug was finally pulled shortly after.

Inflation and the new additions pushed the entry fee up to £7.99 per person[211] (£1 cheaper for children), which was marginally less than their main rivals £8.25 each[212]. Alongside entry fees and merchandise, food and beverage offerings were an increasingly significant part of Thorpe Park's income. During 1990 alone, they sold around half a million beef burgers, 250 tons of chips, and 200,000 cans of coke[213]. A new addition to the catering line-up was an 18-inch ice cream cone, claimed to be the world's largest, dubbed the *Eurocone*. It was an enormous creation, with each one containing a gut busting quarter a litre of ice cream.

All in all, whilst there was no eye-catching rollercoaster or water ride, it was yet another year of continued evolution. Speaking ahead of the opening on Saturday 7th April, Dawson was keen to suggest that regular change was a must:

> "We could not stand still and say that we have cracked it. There is always room for improvement"

Even Dawson would have to admit though that whilst Thorpe Park's latest developments were welcome improvements, Chessington World of Adventures had struck a major blow. The introduction of *Transylvania* and its associated rides was a terrific move, and one that would give the former zoo the edge for the next few years at least. That didn't mean that Thorpe Park couldn't thrive too, and their strong marketing continued, including supporting *Capital FM's Help a London Child* appeal. A specially arranged Clown Day on Easter Sunday helped raise around £10,000 for the charity, whilst an auction to go fishing at the park with Roger Daltrey and Chris Tarrant boosted the total further[214].

The three new rides for 1990 would all end up moving. *The Flying Fish* would remain for 15 seasons, before leaving its second home to make room for a major new attraction opening in 2006. *Carousel Kingdom* remained in place until the late 90s, before the main attraction moved to Alton Towers, becoming the *Cred Street Carousel*. *A Drive in the Country* was in place the shortest time, leaving the former *Bronco Bikes* site in 1994, but would find a new home in the park shortly after.

1991

The skating rink opened near the Dome a decade ago was now on its last legs, and deemed surplus to requirements. New plans were considered for this key section, likely to be the first and last every guest goes through on the day of their visit. Once again, an aquatic theme was preferred and (in a quite original move) the new area would include a man-made beach. For a theme park surrounded by quite so much water it does seem a little bizarre that the beach would actually be in the middle of the land, but the design allowed for greater control of the water, both in terms of its quality, and those enjoying it. The filtered freshwater pools by the sandy beach would be just nine inches deep, ensuring they were safe for families to relax.

Alongside the beach would be yet another new water ride, in the form of a 40-foot-tall, four lane waterslide. Created by a Belgium aquatics company, the attraction started high up, with riders having to climb to the very top via a winding staircase. Once there, riders are directed to one of four dinghy's waiting at the top of a slide, which can hold up to two people. Once boarded the dinghies are released by a raising platform and race down the slide. The slide itself is a completely straight line, featuring two distinct bumps in the middle, meaning there are three quick drops. At the bottom it's purely friction that brings the ride to a stop, with the boats having a long rough surface to eventually slide to a stationary position. The riders leave the boats at ground level, and the boats are returned to the top empty by a team member placing them on a central conveyor belt.

A total of £1.5 million[215] was set to be invested to create what was dubbed *Fantasy Reef*, but as always permission would need to be granted by the local council. Drawings were created to show off the proposed new development, revealing a fantastical underwater theme, complete with 120 suspended giant multi-coloured fish. Probably the most striking part of the plans was a huge yellow submarine, that would sit on top of the planned dinghy ride. The artists impressions didn't go down well initially, with Councillor Chris Fisher not impressed[216]:

> "The depths of vulgarity….This slide won't do anything for the view
> from St. Anne's Hill"

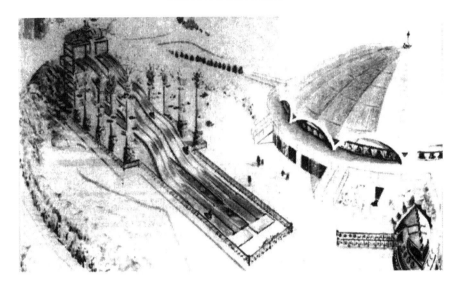

Despite Fisher's moans, the plans received the sign off required by January 1991. Not every councillor was against the introduction of *Fantasy Reef* though, with New Haw's Howard Langley more open to the work saying:

> "There is always some controversy with what Thorpe Park does but it
> does do what it sets out to do and that is to attract people to it"

Depth Charge was the name given to the new ride within *Fantasy Reef*, and with permission being received a little later than usual, the new area would not be ready for the opening day of the season. Construction did happen at quite a pace, and the submarine centrepiece was lifted into place just 48 hours before park opening[217]. This gave visitors at the start of the season an enticing glimpse of what was to come without being able to try it out themselves. In a quote to the press, Thorpe Park executive Marian Edge teased the new ride:

> "Those who enjoy the excitement and thrill of a free-fall drop in a rubber

boat – from over 30 foot into the splashdown zone below – will love Thorpe Park's new *Depth Charge* ride"

The yellow submarine arrives at Thorpe Park

An official opening ceremony for *Fantasy Reef* was arranged for Thursday 30th May, with once again the weather being far from ideal. Roped into doing the honours this time was the cultural phenomenon known as the *Teenage Mutant Ninja Turtles*, who were pretty huge in the early 1990s[218]. The assembled press watched the four costumed characters head down the slide, shouting their catchphrase "cowabunga". Reviews of the new ride were mixed, with Leonardo and Raphael apparently telling the press[219]:

"It was totally mondo to the max man"

However the returning Rosalind Renshaw was less impressed describing *Depth Charge* as[220]:

"Fairly tame"

In truth the new ride was mildly entertaining but rather a strange choice. It served much the same purpose of the superior *Loggers Leap*, but was not as entertaining, and had a much smaller hourly capacity. When riding you would get splashed a little on the way down, especially when sliding to a halt at the bottom, but never enough to warrant any kind of drying off. The racing element of having four lanes heading off at once was quite fun, but actually required the operator to press four individual buttons, more often than not meaning the winner was dictated by whichever button they touched first. The best ride experience possible is filling the boat close to the designated weight limit, meaning you fall faster, get some air time on the bumps, and fly further at the end. Its location close to the *Dome* led to the biggest queues at the start or end of the day as crowds pass by.

The popularity of the *Fantasy Reef* beach was understandably largely dictated by the weather. Herein laid a problem with the addition, as it was largely useless on overcast days, and too popular and not large enough when sunny. In fact, some were getting frustrated by the number of people in the park. In a tepid review, the *Evening Post* highlighted the queues that could dominate visits during the holidays[221]:

> "Millions have been spent on making this one of Britain's most successful theme parks. But in order to reduce the queueing, Thorpe Park needs either to be three times its size, or three times better organised, or preferably both. Or else another theme park could be successfully sprouted somewhere else in the Thames Valley"

This would turn out to be quite the premonition in the years to come. For now though, Thorpe Park was taking a look back to its origins for another new offering. Described as "aquafun" the lakes were again being opened up for new activities. The most interesting of these was the opportunity to go on the *Skyride*, which was a five-minute parasailing journey[222]. Visitors would be floated 100 feet in the air, before cleverly being returned via winch to the boat, without ever being in the lake. Surprisingly the activity was offered as part of the entry fee (now £8.50 or £9.50 on peak days)[223], and could be registered for on a first come, first served basis. It was a thrilling opportunity, and great value, but again suffered from a limited capacity.

Apparently being added to the options on Easter Monday was a space shuttle "borrowed" from Cape Canaveral for the day[224]. Advertising the temporary exhibition, the park promised the opportunity to book "Cut-price trips to space in 1999", and the chance to sit in the capsule and assess your suitability for space travel. However the date of the announcement, 1st April, revealed this was a hoax.

Another addition was typically 90s, an outlet where you could record your own professionally backed cassette tape. For those with a sweet tooth the new country kitchen would allow you to watch fudge being created, and then of course purchase it too.

Still chasing the lucrative school trip audience, a new *Education Centre* was created close to the farm to better cater for teachers' needs, with *Really Wild Show* presenter Chris Packham, invited along to perform the official opening[225].

Thorpe Park even signed up a former teacher as their new education advisor, and offered trips the chance to witness all sorts of farm work demonstrations including dry stone walling, sheep dipping and yarn spinning. Expanding on the offering Edge said:

"The emphasis is on practical activities at *Thorpe Farm* which cannot take place in the school environment, such as seeing a pig being weighed and perhaps watching the birth of a piglet, lamb or calf"

The park would again welcome over a million visitors through the gates, but one family would overshadow them all. Diana Princess of Wales was one of the most famous people in the world in 1991, and in March she made a surprise visit to Thorpe Park, bringing her young sons William and Harry for a day out[226]. Upon arrival she asked to be treated like any other guest, choosing to pay £26 for a family super saver ticket, and queue for any rides the boys wanted to ride. Tony Hall remembers meeting them as Chip the Handsome Mountie as they crossed the entrance bridge[227]:

> Chip: "What's your name young man?"
>
> Future King: "William"
>
> Chip: "Funny, that's my mother's name"

The iconic royals took on *Loggers Leap, Thunder River* and *The Flying Fish*, amongst many others. In an unexpected move for a Princess, Diana was happy to join her family and security on the rides, with *The Flying Fish* the only one she found too intimidating. Paparazzi captured their every move, and pictures of the happy and smiling young family flooded the tabloids the following days. They praised Diana's relaxed approach to the visit, and chastised her husband Charles for not joining her despite being a short distance away in Windsor.

It was the stuff of a PR manager's dreams, giving the Surrey park the royal seal of approval. Diana was a fashion icon, and anything she did would almost certainly lead to a flock of others following, with a huge boost in Thorpe Park's popularity shortly after. Diana would visit again the following year, trying out the now open *Depth Charge*, and for a final time in 1993[228]. The papers even started to run deals offering to "take your child free to the royal fun park". Colin Dawson accompanied Diana, William and Harry on their visits and was even invited to speak at her memorial event in 2007. One picture in particular became iconic for the Princess, a huge smile on her face whilst her sons laughed at the bottom of *Loggers Leap*. The notoriety of the picture led to one of the log boats being turned into a memorial garden for her, along with a plaque celebrating her life that was sadly cut short in 1997.

It seems that it wasn't just Diana who was impressed though, as Thorpe Park received the "Warmest Welcome Award" from the South East England Tourist Board[229], a credit to training manager Joe Petrou. He revealed the tactics key to getting the park's 1200 staff up to standard was specially filmed videos, a comprehensive booklet and lots of scenario role playing. Also singing the praises of the park was the *Gazette*, with journalist Amanda Holloway's review stating:

"The worst thing about Thorpe Park is trying to leave it. Ours were not the only children throwing major tantrums at the prospect of leaving all the fun behind. Only the promise of a return visit could persuade our youngsters to leave"

Depth Charge still entertaining guests in 2020. Credit: Alex Rowe

Whilst not a blockbuster addition, *Depth Charge* has remained surprisingly resilient over the years, and still stands unchanged thirty years later. Its longevity is in many ways down to the ride's simplicity, there's just not that much to go wrong, meaning no huge maintenance costs to keep it going. When change comes it quietly slips under the radar, and you wouldn't be entirely surprised if this rather run of the mill ride was to still be bringing smiles to younger guests in another decade. The beach remains too, and although the name has changed occasionally, the purpose remains the same. Paying an ever-increasing sum to visit a theme park and then just sitting on a beach might seem foolish, but it seems perennially popular with season pass holders and those who would rather relax, leaving queueing and riding to the other members of the family. The *Fantasy Reef* name was eventually changed to *Neptune's Kingdom*.

Despite the best efforts and improvements across the UK theme park industry, 1991 was a testing time due to a recession caused by high interest rates and falling house prices[230]. This left families with less disposable income, and parks struggled to hit their target numbers. Under new ownership Alton Towers managed to lose £3.5 million, but remained confident that they would continue to invest, promising further new rides. Thorpe Park suggested they would do the same, with the 1991 guide book stating[231]:

> "We carry out regular research to ensure that our new developments produce attractions that will offer our visitors maximum enjoyment. This policy continues to provide our visitors with the best value for money day out in the UK"

In reality the economic climate would see Thorpe Park scaling back their activity for a few years, until a new threat to the business made it necessary to up their game once again.

Credit: Thorpe Park Nostalgia

1992

Since the early days of operating, rowing boats and pedalos had been a classic part of Thorpe Park's offering to guests. The experiences would return for 1992, but with a makeover more in line with a modern theme park.

Joining the line-up in *Canada Creek* were the *Hudson River Rafters*[232]. These were pedal boats created by Metro Leisure and heavily themed with logs and multiple barrels to fit in with the surrounding area. Bright yellow canopies covered riders from the elements in 25 of these new boats, which could each hold up to five people. After a short time in Abbey Lake they were moved to the water in the middle of *Loggers Leap*, with a roughly defined course set out for visitors to follow, and all passengers required to wear a lifejacket. As the boats were completely powered and steered by the guests this could lead to some unpredictable rides, and races between competitive parents. Going at any kind of speed required a deceptive amount of hard work, and many would find themselves pretty exhausted long before they returned to the dock. One of the first to try the new attraction out was Prince Harry, who was seen laughing as he raced with a security guard.

In a similar vein, the *Viking Rowers* were added to a section of Manor Lake, accessed from between *Fantasy Reef* and the *Flying Fish*. The large replica Viking longboat that had featured in the *Invaders of Britain* exhibition was re-purposed on the water near the entrance, and joined by around 20 smaller new versions, each measuring about four metres. The newer boats were another Metro Leisure creation, not as well themed as the *Hudson River Rafters*, but still a nice improvement on the basic row boats that preceded them - including special dragon heads and tails at either end. Your group could take a boat out onto the lake, powered by a set of passenger operated oars. There was no specific time limit, so you could go around at your leisure, with buoys and ropes signalling the end of the defined rowing area. Presumably they were quite difficult to control, as I distinctly remember my father crashing into a nearby bank and having to push us back onto the lake with an oar, much to our amusement and his frustration.

Both attractions were interesting additions, with the management seemingly still having a desire to differentiate from the opposition and offer a leisure experience. Neither though would prove to be a massive draw, and had insufficient capacity to cope with a surge of visitors anyway. As a guest though it was a different type of experience, one where you felt truly in control of what happened, and a mild amount of peril due to the real possibility of you doing something wrong. A feeling lacking from nearly every theme park now.

Hudson River Rafters would only last until 1997 before being removed. In their final season they received some criticism when a group from Mencap were allowed to ride unattended, and were left stranded out on the lake. A speedboat was available to offer help-or perform an evacuation in these circumstances-but the staff member in charge of the ride at the time was not trained to use it. The incident was swiftly resolved regardless, but it did highlight some of the risks involved with operating the attraction. Once removed at least some of the rafts made their way to Flamingoland. The *Viking Rowers* lasted only one year extra, before they were removed for a new development. One of the boats was sold to Blackpool Pleasure Beach, where it formed a grand entrance to their extraordinary *Valhalla* water ride.

Elsewhere after the introduction of a yellow submarine atop *Depth Charge*, the park seemed keen to turn the entrance area into some kind of unofficial Ringo Starr tribute, by re-naming the children's ride area *Octopus Garden*[233]. This space had long been home to a number of popular off-the-shelf rides for some of the youngest visitors, and the new name and extra theming was to bring it in line with *Fantasy Reef* that had been introduced the previous year. New names included *Seaweed Line, Slippery Serpent, Swinging Seashells* and *Happy Halibuts*. Like the other additions, it seemed like a concerted effort to try and bring some of the previously un-themed rides and areas in line with the more modern areas. *Octopus Garden* continued to be popular and remained in place until 2010.

With no big new attraction to draw the crowds, the usual PR stunts were put in place to try and lure the public in. With another General Election in April, families were offered £10 off on election day itself, plus a mock election was held amongst the *Thorpe Park Rangers*[234]. Whilst John Major was the narrow winner in the real thing, Mr Monkey won the most votes at Thorpe Park thanks to his promise to offer more chocolate to everyone. Chief Ranger came second, with his pledge to lower Thorpe Park's prices apparently less appealing.

In June, for National Music Day, members of the public who could play an instrument were allowed in at a reduced price to help them set the world record for the "Wettest, Fastest, Scariest Musical Ride in the World"[235]. Whilst seeming like a completely fictional record, it was also used to promote the very real *Song '92* contest. The winner of which went home with £2000 worth of home recording equipment and the chance to lay down a track in Thorpe Park's studio. The contest was a pretty regular occurrence over a number of years, and at one-point broadcast on *BBC Radio* on a show hosted by Bob Holness[236].

The annual fireworks event was to return too, with the final two evenings of the season seeing £6,000 worth of fireworks being exploded in the sky around the *Dome*. Colin Dawson explained the reappearance in the local newspaper saying[237]:

"It has been some time since we held a fireworks display at Thorpe Park, we have had so many requests that we really had to respond"

1992 was also the first use of a popular advertising slogan that would be used in print advertising, and also television commercials[238]:

"Big, Enormous, Giant, Humongous, Great Thorpe Park"

It obviously went down well in the industry as Thorpe Park collected first prize in the *Brochure Advertising* category at the *Brass Ring Awards*, a ceremony that celebrates the high standards of excellence in marketing, advertising and promotion within the amusement industry. Speaking about picking up the award ahead of 400 entrants Dawson said[239]:

"We were up against some tough competition including some of the top theme parks in the USA. We beat Elitch Gardens in Colorado and Sea World of Ohio to the number one slot"

A continued aspiration and challenge of all UK theme parks is making good use of the attraction during the winter. Stephen Gold was keen to help by producing the very first pantomime in the *Park Palladium* theatre. In September DJ Bruno Brookes was at the park to reveal he would star in the production, set to run from the 18th December to the 9th January[240]. Adapting a script from a friend, Gold chose *Babes in the Wood* as the inaugural story, and wrote a number of original songs. To help create a festive spirit inside for guests, a neat nativity scene was created featuring a number of *Thorpe Farm's* animals[241]. Starring alongside Brookes was Gary de Carrington, Johnny Scott, Seb Craig, Ruth Donaldson and Tony Hall/Audenshaw. They did however have some troubles, in that Brooke's acting skills were not the greatest, described by Gold as "non-existent". Generally, the strong ensemble cast managed to help him out, but he was also pretty relaxed about his duties as Hall remembers[242]:

> "He had a monitor in his dressing room so you can listen to the show
> and hear all your cues (when to come on). One evening for a scene he
> just didn't appear, so I went on stage and did some marching around
> and ad-libbing whilst somebody went to find him. When they arrived in
> the dressing room he had turned it off because it was a bit noisy! Other
> times you'd tell a joke during the show, and he'd break character to tell
> you how funny you were"

Everybody who worked with him had positive words to say about
Brookes, he just wasn't a born stage performer. The panto was received
warmly by those who saw it, and was a modest success for Thorpe Park.
However with Gold keen for it to return the following year, management
delayed any decision until after the summer, which killed off any chance
of attracting a star or preparing properly[243]. This resulted in the
pantomime at Thorpe Park sadly remaining a one-off.

The biggest news in a rather quiet year for Thorpe Park, was about a
potential new rival. Windsor Safari Park, situated just seven miles away,
had been struggling financially and eventually had to close its doors to
the public. A huge effort went into re-housing the animals elsewhere[244].
The repercussions of the closure meant that officials were keen to find a
new use for the site. In July councillors from the surrounding areas
visited Billund in Denmark[245], after an invite from the Lego company
who had been running a successful theme park there. Rumours started
to spread that Windsor would be home to the world's second Legoland
park, with a figure of £60 million quoted as the potential budget for rides
and attractions[246]. If approved, the new attraction would leave Thorpe
Park placed slap in the middle of Chessington World of Adventures and
Legoland Windsor. The former aimed at younger children, and the latter
older children, leaving Thorpe Park marooned somewhere between
them. After trailblazing in the early 1980s, tough decisions lay ahead for
Leisure Sport and RMC on how to survive.

1993

As serious discussions continued behind the scenes about the best way forward, Thorpe Park opened as usual in 1993 with again no major new attractions. It was a quiet time for rivals Chessington too as a kind of major investment ceasefire continued following the successful introduction of *Transylvania*.

By May the Legoland Windsor rumours had been confirmed, with Maidenhead and Windsor councils backing the proposal[247]. Early details were being released of what visitors could expect in 1996 when the gates would open to the UK's newest theme park, with spokesman Clive Nicholls saying[248]:

> "What we want to do is something unlike anything else existing in leisure parks. You tend to find that most leisure parks are for young teenagers. There will be no white-knuckle rides here….essentially Legoland is for young children. They are our heroes"

Early plans promised a Lego miniland made up of world-famous landmarks in small-scale, a sofa ride taking families through a fairy tale land, a table which recreates the impact of an earthquake, and much more. The most intriguing part of the plans was possibly the promise of "a fantasy world where it is everyone's birthday all the time, with jellies and ice cream in constant supply". The aim was to attract 1.2 million visitors a year.

Back in Surrey one addition waiting for Thorpe Park visitors in 1993 was a very early example of Virtual Reality technology. The *Flying Aces Virtuality* allowed visitors to strap on a headset and try out this bold new world, which despite the early blocky graphics, was still revolutionary[249].

Whilst not ready for park opening, a deal was also struck to purchase a fairground style thrill ride. This would be a second-hand "troika" style spinning ride, the name originating from the Russian for group of three. This was because three arms protruded from the centre, each holding seven ride cars. At high speeds of 30 revolutions per minute, passengers could be flung around, with the sets of cars spinning in the opposite direction to the main arm. The modern versions of this ride were originally created by HUSS, but Thorpe Park had agreed to purchase a second hand *Fairmatt Tri-Star* model from Europe.

Permission was requested and granted in July 1993 for its installation in *Canada Creek*, and given the name *Calgary Stampede* after the annual rodeo[250]. It was a peculiar choice, appealing to more of a teenage audience than before, and with minimal artistic changes made to the ride itself. It remained covered in fairground lights, with a gaudy shiny paint job. A far cry from the immense effort that went into the previous *Canada Creek* attractions, although the tacky controllers console was covered up. The ride experience itself was more satisfying though, as it was a fun ride, with the cars flung to an angle of 34 degrees, and giving the impression you were about to crash into the surrounding fence before spinning away at high speed.

Calgary Stampede opened late in 1993, and remained in action for a decade. It has since returned to its more natural home of a travelling fairground. Chessington would re-theme their similar style *HUSS Breakdance* ride in 1996 to a similar premise, calling it simply *Rodeo*.

Another 1.3 million guests made their way through the gates during the year, which would turn out to be the last for the beloved *Treasure Island Railway*, and management were once again required to dust off their tuxedos to collect awards. This time Thorpe Park were handed the *Holiday Care Award for the Best Attraction for the Disabled*, and also the *SPCA's Merit Award for Best Communication Campaign*[251].

1994

A major battle was heating up in the north of England, with the travel industry dubbing 1994 "Year of the Rollercoaster"[252]. Blackpool Pleasure Beach, who had a long legacy of historic rides were preparing to open the world's tallest and steepest rollercoaster, the *Pepsi Max Big One*. Manufactured by Arrow and reportedly costing £12 million, it was being described by managing director Geoffrey Thomson as:

"The most significant structure in Blackpool since the Tower was built a century ago in 1894"

Over at Alton Towers they were preparing to unveil their most thrilling ride yet too, and one that would propel them to a new level of quality. *Nemesis* overseen by Tussauds' John Wardley couldn't claim any of the highest or fastest records that Blackpool's addition could. However, the Bolliger & Mabillard "inverted" coaster would win the long-term war, becoming one of the world's most revered thrill rides - thanks to its intuitive construct and detailed artistic design. The investment and scale of both rides was a startling example of how far the attraction and leisure industry had come, and how the stakes were getting higher.

Back in Surrey, Leisure Sport couldn't hope to compete with the steel giants that were appearing in the north. Focus remained on winning the hearts and minds of the families in the south, with a £2.5 million budget spread across a number of investments[253]. Ignoring the hyped coaster focused tourism push by the industry, Thorpe Park were ready to celebrate "International Year of the Family" instead. Explaining the philosophy Colin Dawson said[254]:

"We have spent the £2.5 million extremely carefully this year. It has been spread between the rides and attractions and improving visitor facilities. When you handle 1.3 million visitors each year, you have to look at customer comfort and satisfaction"

A huge £350,000 (equivalent of £700,000 in 2020) of this was spent on installing a new admissions and ticketing system, which was the same as the one being used at Euro Disney in Paris opened in 1992. Another big chunk of the budget was going on refurbishing the toilet facilities. The Leisure Sport belief being that quality would win in the long term.

With *Treasure Island* gone, all the rides and attractions with the exception of *Thorpe Farm* and wildlife areas were now situated in the main island area outside the *Dome*. These had been neatly split into three themed sections of *Canada Creek*, *Central Park*, and *Fantasy Reef*. A fourth was to be added in 1994 situated between *Central Park* and *Canada Creek* called *Ranger County*. As the name suggests it was to be based on the updated mascots introduced five years earlier, that had proved to be enduringly popular with visitors. Now their success was to be immortalised in a section that contained several bespoke rides and attractions, close to the existing small show theatre that opened in 1990.

Mr. Monkey's Banana Ride was a surprisingly exciting "swinging ship" ride. Created by German manufacturer Metallbau Emmeln[255], it replaced the traditional swinging ship hull with an enormous yellow banana vehicle that swung powered by a giant tyre. Riders sat in three rows either side facing each other, and would swing increasingly higher each side, until reaching around 30 feet in the air. The structure holding the ride in place was designed to look like logs, rather than the generic metal supports seen on other models. Sitting proudly atop this overlooking the boat was a giant replica model of Mr. Monkey who had a maniacal smile on his face. Whilst smaller than the version at Chessington it still packed quite a punch, and would give your stomach a fright, especially if you were seated in the back rows.

Joining the swinging ship was another carousel, this time an outdoor version by French company Euro Sujets ,with a completely bespoke makeover. *Chief Ranger's Carousel*, as it was named, replaced many of the traditional horse seats with replicas of other Thorpe Park rides. Guests could choose to sit in recreations of boats from *Viking Rowers, Loggers Leap, Hudson River Rafters* or *Thunder River*. Also appearing was a car from *The Flying Fish,* and the *Teacup Ride.* Fibreglass models of all the *Thorpe Park Rangers,* including two welcome recent female additions in Miss Hippo and Miss Frog, also featured, although you couldn't ride them as such. Any space remaining on the carousel was filled with the traditional raising and lowering horses. The characters and ride vehicles were developed by Design Workshop[256], who were also busy working on a project elsewhere in the park.

Completing the *Ranger County* line-up (for now) was a 900 seat outdoor arena. An impressively large bank of blue and yellow seats faced a large stage, a tall log wall surrounded the set-up hiding it from the outside. It was another ambitious attempt to offer all round family entertainment, not just rides, and added a large amount of capacity for shows, with the *Park Palladium Theatre* still hosting live performances too. The idea came from Dawson's visit to the *International Theme Park Convention* in Los Angeles[257]. There he picked up the rights to host an exciting all-American high diving show, with the aim of putting on breath-taking stunt shows five times a day in the peak season.

To entertainment manager Gold's surprise, he was asked to look after the show, despite having no experience in diving. The performance would require five trained divers coming over for the summer, ready to perform their well-honed routine. To prepare himself for the challenge Gold went to Europa Park in Germany, which already hosted a similar show, but found the experience a little sterile and lacking character. To counter this Gold, alongside Hogan and his technical director Kevin Townsend, went about writing and planning a suitable storyline around the stunts. When the divers arrived, they were perplexed as they would be asked to act, not just dive, but after a little hostility bought into the concept[258].

Hints of what was being planned for the summer were revealed publicly in May 1994 when permission was requested for a 90-foot-tall mast to be placed in the arena, making it the highest point of the entire park[259]. This would be made from a lighting mast from the nearby Heathrow

Airport[260]. Then as the premiere approached adverts began promoting the "US High Diving Team from Las Vegas". The *Stunt Spectacular's* original rough storyline followed a familiar environmental theme, with the cast trying to stop an "eco-lout" from dumping radioactive material on a beach. It was a fun show, with a variety of slapstick and small stunts. There were plenty of dives, with creative ways to try and make it relevant to the story including somebody being set on fire. The show would lead up to an incredible finale, with a high dive from the top of the new 90-foot mast into a pool of water just ten feet deep. Marketing claimed that this was the first time such a tall dive could be seen in the UK, although local newspaper[261] readers disagreed, with one writing in to say they had seen a one-legged stuntman called *Davedevil Peggy* perform the same feat, whilst on fire, and into just a barrel of water! Regardless, this was a quality show for all the family that would help suck up crowds from around the park.

The intimidating entrance to Wicked Witches Haunt. Credit: Thorpe Park Nostalgia

Phantom Fantasia was also given an upgrade this year, with the main focus on using dark light and neon paint in many of the scenes, which had become quite fashionable amongst such rides at the time. This was another piece of work done by Design Workshop, overseen by their managing director Peter Reaney[262]. No changes were made to the hardware, which retained its classic Mack Endless Transit System, but it was given the new name of *Wicked Witches Haunt*. In line with the new name, a number of animatronic witches were added, and some scenes underwent minor changes. A new soundtrack was created, and a giant new entrance sign added with an ugly large witch perched above the door, peering down over guests and pointing a bony finger at them. Former employee, and Thorpe Park fanatic, Phil West remembers being intimidated by the updated attraction as a child[263]:

"I remember seeing the cackling witch with the crooked nose above the entrance for the first time and being so intimidated, it made me cry I was so scared. Thankfully I plucked up the courage to go inside and try it out because it was actually a really good ride. My mum preferred the singing frogs on the *Magic Mill*, but *Wicked Witches Haunt* was my favourite"

Reaction to the revitalised attraction were mixed, with some preferring its original form, but at worst it was good to see some attention and budget given to a classic dark ride. Coincidentally Chessington would also spend their budget on re-working one of their dark rides this year, with significant changes being made to the former *5th Dimension* which became *Terror Tomb*.

The final addition for 1994 would once again see a classic Thorpe Park offering get an update. This time it was the crazy golf that would make a return in a new form, called *Jungle Zone Family Golf*. It was positioned close to the *Dome*, where some basic slides for children had to be removed, in-between *Depth Charge* and *Cinema 180*. It contained a pretty classic crazy golf set of challenges, which were given a general jungle theme complete with bright paintwork, the odd plant and piece of bamboo. As you would expect each hole had a different novelty way of getting the ball to the hole. The golf was included in the entrance fee, but no consideration seemed to be given to capacity, which was predictably terrible for such an offering.

With a new set of attractions for the family to try out, the entry fee was set at £11.25[264], with once more children receiving a pound discount. To celebrate the opening for the new season on 26th March, a massive Easter egg hunt was held with 20,000 chocolate treats given away to those who could spot large eggs hidden around the park[265]. Shortly after another quintessentially 90s event happened, when the Merlin sticker swap shop took place in the *Dome*. Helping kids to complete their *Gladiators* sticker book were Cobra, Falcon, Scorpio and Shadow who were also joined by mascots of other collections such as Captain Scarlett and Slick and Spin from the *Crash Test Dummies*[266]. Adding to the entertainment throughout the season was the returning *Thorpe Park Marching Band* led by Tony Carter[267]. The band added a real sparkle of magic to the park, really helping to raise the experience above the average fairground. Naomi Finn reminisced about an incident with the band in her youth:

"I was an incredibly shy young girl, and for my 10th birthday I was taken to Thorpe Park. We were near the band, when my mum snuck off and told them it was my birthday. Cue a full band rendition of Happy Birthday, which was extremely kind of them, but terribly embarrassing at the same time!"

The efforts to improve facilities and create special family days out didn't go unnoticed, with Thorpe Park again collecting an accolade, this time second place in the *Parent Friendly Awards*. This was presented to head of marketing Alan Randall by Ulrika Johnson - after a vote of 20,000 people from *That's Life* and *Tommy's*[268]. Yet, they were to be accused of going too far to protect the family atmosphere, especially when two schoolgirls were locked in a room for three hours after they were found to be queue jumping at *Thunder River*. Marion Edge explained the actions to the *Herald News* saying[269]:

"We have a lot of families with young children here and we have to protect their safety and enjoyment. Little children get very frightened if they see teenagers running around or using bad language"

The pair of 14-year olds were visiting as part of a school trip, and were eventually given some free tickets to return.

The new attractions would succumb to various fates in future years. An infamous incident in 2000 would see the end of *Wicked Witches Haunt,* but before that it would hit the headlines in 1995, when a 70-year-old called Michael Shannon died as a result of injuries sustained in the ride building. He was part of a group from a Hillingdon Mental Health Hospital who were trusted to go off and explore the park in small groups alone. Upon boarding he reportedly panicked and battled to leave the ride vehicle, but was mostly held in by the lap bar. Part of his body was crushed against a wall when leaving the station, resulting initially in a broken pelvis[270]. He would later die in hospital when blood clots from his injury blocked his heart and lungs. During an inquiry into Shannon's death it was claimed (by the hospital) that the visitors mistook the Tudor building entrance for a pub - however this was denied by other witnesses. Thorpe Park was cleared of any wrongdoing, and the health and safety executive concluded the ride was safe, although extra lighting and staff were added to the station to prevent a future repeat of any rider's sad demise[271].

The stunt show in the arena would go on to delight guests during the summer holidays for many years in different guises. From 1995 the show became known as the *Konica Splashtacular,* with the storyline now focusing on witnessing behind the scenes filming of a 1930s *Tarzan* movie. Tony Hall would occasionally act as a warm-up guy as the audience were settling in, until he thought he had found the perfect permanent replacement[272]:

"This guy was absolutely brilliant, a performer like Bill Murray, you just had to look at him and you'd laugh. We originally offered him a job as he was ace as an Italian policeman but unbeknownst to me, he hated the act, he hated me, and decided to just talk about Italian politics with people, so he ended up getting sacked"

Another issue arose the following year when the diving consultants used by the park decided to work exclusively with Legoland, meaning a scramble to source new ones[273]. By 1997 the show had become *Popeye's Pirate Adventure*, now created by Gold and Hogan's external company *Parkshow Productions*. The re-imagined *Splashtacular* show featured many of the same diving stunts as before with a new story and enlarged pool of water, plus of course a recognisable spinach chomping hero. Reviewing the show in the *Reading Evening Post*, Jeff Chapman concluded[274]:

"The plaudits must go the diving team which performs high dives and stunt jumps. It must be said that they were obviously employed for their aqua abilities and not their acting although they seem committed to the cause"

Popeye only stayed a short time before being replaced by the more generic *Safari High Dive Show*, which ran on and off for several seasons. In 1999 the Popeye show would be franchised to the United Arab Emirates, with the nine-metre pool, and 25-metre-high diving mast having to be shipped off to the Middle East. Ten actors and acrobats from the original show would travel to perform for the new audiences[275].

A new-look stunt show premiered in 2002, no longer a Parkshow production, but it featured one of the world's most popular superheroes instead. *The Amazing Spider-Man Show* swung into action that summer, however the Universal Shows and Entertainment production was more low budget Saturday morning TV, than big budget Marvel blockbuster. The cast would fight and mime to a pre-recorded soundtrack, with some underwhelming Spider-Man falls off buildings etc, as he attempted to rescue Mary-Jane. It also featured some truly cringeworthy singing and raps, which stuntmen and women tried their best to mime to. The show was re-worked the following year with a new storyline, becoming *Mystery of the Stolen Diamonds*. That was to be the last of the true family shows in the *Ranger County Arena*, although it would remain in place until 2014, when alongside *Chief Ranger's Carousel* it was removed for a major new addition opening in 2016.

The new carousel, swinging ship and arena were a strong start to the new Ranger themed area, with a second phase agreed, opening the following season.

1995

Joining the *Ranger County* line-up in phase two[276], was a couple of re-worked existing rides.

The *Magic Mill* had been a tranquil favourite of parents for over a decade, but its location right by the new *Ranger County* made it an easy choice for a quick re-theme. The boat ride would undergo some minor changes, with items added around the outdoor course to tell the story of how Mr. Rabbit recruited the other *Thorpe Park Rangers*. The indoor finale had Paul McCartney's familiar novelty song removed, and was changed to a more relaxed jungle scene, with some decorative pieces remaining and others being replaced with safari style elements and a waterfall. Also added was a model railway that made its way round inside. The boats received new jungle style coverings, and also had some fake steering wheels added so kids could pretend they were driving. The final result was re-named *Mr. Rabbit's Tropical Travels*.

A Drive in the Country, added in 1990, would need to be moved to make way for work beginning on a large new development for 1996. The track and cars were found a new home in the back of *Ranger County*, with the classic Ford cars receiving a suitable new look for a jungle-based expedition. It became known as *Miss Hippo's Fungle Safari*, although the now regular honking from horns would become a huge distraction right by the small *Thorpe Park Ranger* theatre. The nearby shop was labelled *Mr Giraffe's Fungle Store*, but poor Mr. Elephant was given the short straw, with only the nearby picnic area getting named after him. The most exciting thing ever to happen in an otherwise pretty mundane Mr. Elephant section was in 1998. Early one morning a World War One grenade was found in the picnic area[277], with the park having to be evacuated before opening. Eventually the all-clear was given, with the assumption being that it had been lost or left behind during one of the military air displays in the early 1980s.

The TV cameras were again at Thorpe Park in 1995 filming an episode of BBC's *Record Breakers*[278]. Presenter Mark Curry, and football commentator Tony Gubba presided over Thomas Lundman's attempt at the world record for heading a football. After an incredible seven hours and 17 minutes of continuous heading he was given his certificate, and presumably a headache.

It would now cost you £40 for a family ticket for the day at Thorpe Park, but with so many rides, shows and other attractions it was hard to argue that it wasn't good value for money[279]. An example of the extra lengths the park continued to go to was the *Thorpe Park Street Theatre Team*, who roamed throughout the day re-creating wild west shoot-outs and performing a pirate show. Gold also introduced a daily Disney style parade to visitors delight[280]. Unfortunately, the principles of the park were to come under threat, with news that longstanding manager Colin Dawson was to leave at the end of the year[281]. He was rumoured to be speaking to well-known showman and attraction owner Jimmy Godden about a new opportunity. Chris Edge would step up to replace him.

Dawson's resignation was far from ideal, especially just before Legoland Windsor was due to open, and Thorpe Park facing its biggest challenger yet. They were willing to take a massive gamble to retain their audience, with their biggest investment to date ready to be unleashed in 1996.

1996

After years of preparation and promises, the battle of the three major theme parks on the outskirts of London was about to begin.

Tussaud's Chessington World of Adventures was the current leader, welcoming around 1.7 million visitors annually[282], a lead of around 400k over Thorpe Park. Arguably their lead could have been even more significant, but their capacity was set at 15,000 which led to them turning away potential paying customers on a semi-regular basis. They had installed their latest big attraction in summer 1995, the HUSS *Top Spin* called *Rameses Revenge*, which was the first of its kind to include water fountains that soaked riders[283]. This had helped position them as a park that families with older children could enjoy, along with teenage groups.

The new contender was the Windsor Safari Park replacement, Legoland Windsor, who were targeting 1.4 million guests in year one. The opening selection of rides differed from the original promises, but some of the proposals remained. One of the most eye-catching was the Driving School, which allowed young children to drive an electric car and earn a driving license. Other classics like the log flume and a miniature railway, joined more original concepts such as *Miniland*, which featured famous areas recreated by millions of Lego bricks. Helped by the gorgeous surroundings, and healthy budget, the park looked beautiful, if a little underdeveloped compared to the more established rivals. The target audience was firmly families with younger children, with those over 12 unlikely to be too impressed.

This left Thorpe Park, which had always focused on families of all ages, in a fight with both. Chessington and Legoland were unlikely to be in direct competition with each other, but both would be looking to take a share of the market from the UK's original theme park. Keen to hold their ground against the fierce competition, a massive £6 million[284] was assigned to *Project X*, which they hoped would blow away their rivals. The entire budget would be spent on a state-of-the-art new rollercoaster, that they felt would be the ultimate attraction for 8 to 14-year olds, filling the gap between the two rivals target audiences. The ambition was that this ride would have the same overwhelming success *Nemesis* and *The Vampire* had for their respective parks.

Desiring something ground-breaking, Thorpe Park were intrigued by a new concept from experienced Dutch manufacturers Vekoma. They had a decent reputation in the theme park world, having worked with a huge number of attractions around the globe, including providing the hardware for some of Disney's most iconic rollercoasters. Arguably their most popular model at the time was a "boomerang" rollercoaster, but at Expo '93 in South Korea they had debuted a new product called *Enigma* that they hoped would be just as widespread in the future. The *Enigma* used the track system from their successful line of junior rollercoasters, this used a wheel driven lift rather than a chain, and didn't require the familiar Vekoma spine seen on their larger rollercoasters[285]. It was enclosed inside a building and used a number of block breaks and special effects to provide an experience that was just as much psychological as it was physically intense.

With Leisure Sport confident the *Enigma* was the unique offering that would destroy the opposition, they approached Design Workshop to create the specifics. Jeff Hill was lead designer on the project, and travelled to the USA to get ideas on how to enrich the experience further[286]. Planning permission was requested in November 1994, asking for the "erection of a new dark white-knuckle ride"[287], which was duly granted. Keen to keep specifics of the new attraction under wraps from the public, and quite possibly the opposition too, only vague details were revealed at first. The 1995 park map replaced the space left by the moved *A Drive in the Country* ride with a small teaser advert of a Thorpe Park Ranger making a shushing action whilst holding a sign reading "Project X 1996"[288]. Construction began by clearing the large amount of land required on the east side of the main island, which in the early days had previously also hosted the Go-Kart track and the Exhibition area. The original concept was for the entrance to be located between *Ranger County* and *Canada Creek*[289]. Later the plans were changed to switch the entrance to the other side, being one of the first things visitors would see as they entered through the Dome. A huge corrugated metal pyramid would enclose the entire attraction, but the coaster had to be built first before this could be put in place.

The rollercoaster wasn't the only thing the pyramid would be hiding though, as the attraction was to also include a long and ambitious walk-through section. When entering the building guests would need to make their way through a labyrinth of dark, narrow corridors before they reached the ride[290]. During the walk they would encounter a number of elements beginning with "'Laser Bays'" and a "'Decontamination Area'". These were pretty basic, but included loud industrial sounds, moving search lights, and robotic voices to crank up the weirdness. The next part of the queue was a classic spinning tunnel illusion, which often leads to people losing their balance, and the "Inverted Room" where items were upside down. My favourite section as an 11-year-old was the "Industrial Grinders", a number of room height rotating cog-like columns, made from strong foam material. You'd have to feel your way through these in the dark to find the pathway. The penultimate section was named the "Metamorphosis Chamber" and perhaps the best themed, using UV lights and vacuum technology to create weird sci-fi like moving figures protruding from the walls.

The whole walk-through section would take at least five minutes, and was quite a significant distance, with riders initially queueing outside before being sent through in batches. Before reaching the ride itself there would usually be a short final queue - before the final pre-ride experience - which was a fake lift. Riders would be batched into groups of ten and placed into a small shiny room by a host. The doors would close behind you and vibration effects would make you believe you were taken many floors higher/lower. During the fake lifts movement more 80s style computer noises would play, and a small spinning spotlight would move, taking turns to point at different people in the lift. Once finished, doors on the opposite side would open to reveal an empty rollercoaster train which the group could then board. Head of marketing

Alan Randall would compare the innovative walk-through section to two popular shows at the time[291]:

"Crystal Maze meets Krypton Factor"

Metamorphosis Chamber in the queue. Credit: Thorpe Park Nostalgia

The ride itself wasn't particularly big or scary, and much like *Space Station Zero* it would have to rely on darkness and mystery to create a larger sense of scale. The highest drop was just under ten metres high, and the fastest speed around 30 miles per hour. To add another layer of uniqueness and mystique to the already abstruse idea it was agreed that the Vekoma trains would be run backwards, which would be another novelty in the UK market. Riders would be secured with just a lap bar in the low seats that are slightly reminiscent of a Waltzer. The trains were also fitted with on board audio systems, which was extremely rare on rollercoasters. An orange rail on the otherwise black track provided the energy required, and allowed for sound effects to be triggered at key times during the experience. This was Thorpe Park's first non-powered rollercoaster, and the track layout was reasonably standard, with mild drops and helixes between each stop. The animated stopping sections of the *Enigma* allowed riders to experience wind, mist and sound effects. The train could also roll slightly forwards and back, before proceeding to the next section. With separate stations for unloading and boarding, plus the various stops, the ride could in theory run five trains at a time each holding ten people. Although in practice this was impractical.

Instead of opening with the rest of the park at the start of the 1996 season, the launch would be during the main battleground of the three competing parks, the prime school summer holiday period. To help brand and promote their biggest ever investment, Thorpe Park commissioned external agency Davies Little Cowley[292]. Creative director of the agency David Little came up with a concept he felt would appeal to the new generation of computer literate children who would be visiting the park. The idea was around a computer virus, and the name would reference the DOS operating system and the unique walk-through element, becoming *X:\ No Way Out*. The name was revealed in January, but other details remained under wraps, with Rebecca Avard teasing readers of the *News & Herald*[293]:

"It will be the only place in the whole world where you can experience this ride, but visitors will have to wait until the summer to experience it"

Knowing that price would be a key consideration for visitors choosing where to take their families, a big deal was made out of the fact that Thorpe Park were freezing theirs. A family ticket remained at £49, £5 cheaper than the new Legoland and £10 cheaper than Chessington[294]. Another move was to open two weeks earlier than usual, with the hope that this would give them an early advantage. Spokesperson Marian Edge took a diplomatic approach when pressed about the new competition:

"We welcome another theme park into the industry, and hope people can find time to visit both"

New general manager Chris Edge was more pragmatic:

"The UK leisure market is becoming increasingly competitive and we
have decided to take a bullish attitude and fight them head-on by cutting
our prices. It can only be good for customers. We have no doubt that we
have to fight for the British family's leisure time by offering the very best
value for money. We have had an encouraging start to the new season
and attendances are in line with previous years"

The Independent covered the battle between the three parks. Legoland
were confident they had a superior product, with head of marketing
Joanna Oswin claiming[295]:

"Our target market is ABC1 families. We have put in an investment of
£85 million so it will be quality product. It is not our policy to discount at
all. We have very few sales promotions. We would rather add value to a
day out"

Meanwhile Chessington World of Adventures Virginia Sudakiewicz
refused to compare the parks and get involved in a pricing battle:

"The competition is based on what we are planning to do, not on other
people. We set our prices at good value for money"

Another looking to join the battle later in the year was SegaWorld, billed
as an indoor theme park in the heart of London, based in the Trocadero,
Piccadilly Circus. Also on the periphery was the prospect of film giants
Warner Brothers opening a £225 million joint studio and theme park
called Movie World, which they had applied to be constructed in
Hillingdon House Farm[296]. This was just 25 minutes from Thorpe Park,
and claimed to be targeting two and half million visitors a year. The
intense competition and huge capital being spent piled the pressure on
X:\ No Way Out performing upon opening.

With lower than expected visitors the previous year, a new major
attraction to fund, and forecasting less entry income, many departments
found their budgets slashed. This included a massive 50% cut to the

entertainments budget, meaning the end to many of the performers and sporadic shows that had made Thorpe Park in the early 90s so special. Looking back at the decision to heavily reduce the budget entertainments manager Stephen Gold was disappointed[297]:

> "A ride is a big investment but then only needs one or two people to operate, whereas a live show is people centric and I guess when they look at the bottom line that's an easy cost to eliminate"

He would remain at Thorpe Park for only a short time longer before leaving to work independently for a number of other theme parks including bitter rivals Legoland. He would marry his long-time partner, and show collaborator, Penny Hogan in 2002. Gold describes his career, including his many years at Thorpe Park, in the entertaining autobiography *Unparallel Careers.*

The X:\ No Way Out pyramid. Credit: Thorpe Park Nostalgia

Prior to the new rollercoaster opening Davies Little Cowley started to step up the promotional work, and details started to be released about what the public could expect. To fit in with the computer theme the first ever Thorpe Park website was launched[298], and it was revealed this would be the world's first backwards in the dark rollercoaster, with the word "Blackwards" created to describe the new innovation. Adverts in print contained unrivalled levels of hyperbole[299]:

"Once you enter there's No Way Out! Using a series of illusions and optical tricks which distort your perception, the pre-ride experience creates interest, fear and tension while queueing! Total darkness allows mind and sense manipulation with special effects and a deafening on-board sound system. Thorpe Park promise THE most adventurous X-perience of '96"

In press interviews the new attraction was positioned as "The most expensive theme park ride to open this year", and the cost didn't stop at the ride itself with £1 million of the budget for promotion. A major TV advertising campaign had been agreed to run for ten weeks, which would consist of a 40-second-long advert costing £200,000[300]. The advert was directed by Ian Sharp, who had just two years earlier earned critical acclaim for his work on the opening sequence on the James Bond film *Goldeneye*. Unfortunately, the advert, which had been produced by David Little and Richard Tennant, was not to be amongst his finest work. It depicted a couple of SAS style soldiers being lowered via helicopter into the new ride building, and then finding themselves on it, viewed via some kind of night vision which didn't really show much at all. The advert finished with the seemingly *Wayne's World* inspired slogan:

"Kids Stuff. Not"

Whilst deliberately vague, the advert did a rather poor job of whetting the appetite of potential visitors, with most likely bemused by what they were being shown. Agency director Don Cowley explained:

"Theme park ads used to consist of just a video showing people enjoying the rides, but we've managed to do something new and different"

A further promotional video was commissioned that promoted the ride, featuring a number of people involved in the project speaking about their work. This included Peter Bobst from Vekoma[301]:

"The first ride we proposed to Thorpe Park, and the one you see here now, are completely different. I believe personally, that this will be a milestone in the history of amusement rides"

Finally, after years of planning, and a lot of publicity, *X:\ No Way Out* was ready to open to the public at the start of July, just as the country was coming down from a wave of *Euro '96* euphoria. A flashy opening with dancers signalled that visitors could now explore the mysterious new ride[302]. Finishing touches had been added throughout, including the addition of helicopter noises during the ride to match the advertising campaign. Outside the grand new blue and terracotta metal pyramid was a number of cylinders that sprayed mist over those approaching the building and queueing outside. Added to the exit corridors inside the building was a large display showing a giant alkaline style battery, the signage of which purported to be the Thorpe Park Power Supply.

The final attraction was interesting, but undoubtedly a bit of a mess. It was an enjoyable enough experience for the target age bracket, but underwhelming given the level of hype and expectation. The many stops proved to be frustrating and confusing, losing all momentum from the ride. Even the staff at the park found it a little baffling, as one of the ride supervisors at the time Graham Clatworthy explains[303]:

"Even when it opened and we had our first rides we really didn't understand what it was. You didn't know what you were going on, you walked down these long corridors, you didn't quite understand what you're meant to be doing. You got on the ride, it went backwards, I don't think it was particularly good backwards. It was all a bit strange"

David McCubbin was a theme park enthusiast, and landed a job at Thorpe Park where he operated *X:\ No Way Out*. It was an intense job, with keeping guests moving through the attraction vital. If the next train didn't leave promptly, the other three on the track at the same time would stop and back-up. He was more of a fan than other staff, becoming mesmerised by the ride's experience[304]:

"The sound effects were so loud from the helicopters and weird noises. When you were on it, and you had the sound coming out of the speakers and it all worked properly, it took you over, you were in the zone. Although, they spent so much money on building that massive pyramid, and all the queue line. You look at these things and in hindsight think what else could have been done"

The public seemed largely indifferent to the new experience, and it was soon clear this major investment had neither the quality or pulling-power of a ride such as *The Vampire*. In fact, for many *Loggers Leap* remained the most intimidating attraction the park had to offer. Thorpe Park had gambled all their chips on *X:\ No Way Out* being an outright success, but the bet on the strange new concept had not paid off, leaving the attraction side of RMC's business in serious bother.

A picture of the Vekoma track with the lights on. Credit: Thorpe Park Nostalgia

In the years that followed some small changes were made to *X:\ No Way Out*, with much of the walk-through queue line section either being scaled back or removed entirely. It never seemed to match the popularity of some of the other headline attractions, but the Vekoma coaster remained reliable and the core ride transport system remains to this day.

The name and concept had been slightly dated from day one, with MS DOS already on the way out, but it lasted until 2007 when the story was changed to "X Laboratories" although the name remained until 2013. Riding backwards, and the dark confusing surroundings left many guests feeling nauseous and being sick, so as a trial in 2010 the lights were left on, revealing the coasters layout to many for the first time.

One of the early changes was the removal of the sound effects, as McCubbin remembers:

"It was a maintenance nightmare keeping the sound system going, so it was decided to switch it off and it was not maintained. You really noticed it wasn't there anymore, as you realised there was nothing else going on, and nothing to see"

Unsurprisingly only one other Vekoma *Enigma* was ever ordered, by Dream Park in Giza, Egypt. When *Dark Ride* opened in 1998 the coaster section was identical to Thorpe Park's version, but the trains ran forward. There was also no walk-through, with visitors instead queueing in a more traditional way before the station.

In its first year Legoland Windsor attracted 1.4 million guests. Despite the best efforts of Thorpe Park to overshadow its debut, there was no doubting that a theme park relying completely around little plastic bricks had upstaged them.

1997

The money spent the previous year left little to invest in 1997. However, keen to celebrate their 18th birthday, a party was held on Saturday 24th May. As part of the celebrations 40 mascot characters were invited from all walks of life, with the meet-up becoming the cartoon character equivalent of *Avengers Endgame*. Bart Simpson, Spider-Man, Postman Pat, Popeye, Dennis the Menace and many more came together for guests to meet, with the *Mercury FM* roadshow broadcasting live[305]. Joining them was a new character that Thorpe Park had created that was getting increasing prominence in their marketing.

Harley was described as a "Cool Cat", wearing a backwards baseball cap, jeans and a leather jacket to cover much of his distinctive pink fur. His demeanour was that of Fonzie reborn as a feline, specially designed to appeal to that mid-range child audience the park was now trying to attract. Whilst the *Thorpe Park Rangers* continued to appear, and of course had their own bespoke area of the park, Harley became the front man. Popular comedian and actor Paul Whitehouse was enlisted to voice Harley in adverts[306], which once again Tony Hall would mimic for park use. Harley even commanded his own show in the centre of the dome, where he would perform guitar solos because, you know, he was cool. Hall wrote a number of these shows including one that saw him change the words to Robbie Williams track *Let Me Entertain You*:

"Mums and dads, grandpas and grans. Boys and girls and Harley fans..."

Some have compared Harley's addition to that of Poochie in a famous Simpsons episode centred around the *Itchy and Scratchy* cartoon. It's a wickedly cruel but somewhat warranted comparison given the overt desperation to appeal trendy to young teenagers.

Overseen by Randall, the marketing now always referred to "The Great Thorpe Park", plus a couple of additional slogans were introduced reminding the public of the park's achievements to date[307]:

"Britain's First, London's Greatest"

"Britain's Favourite Family Leisure Park"

Randall also signed a deal to be sponsor of an *ITV London* weekend programme hosted by Emma Forbes and Andi Peters. The presenters would also film a promotional video trying out the rides as part of the agreement. Previously 90% of his £1.5 million budget had been spent on traditional TV adverts through Davies Little Cowley, but after their failures the previous year, Randall told *Campaign* they would be taking a new approach[308]:

> "The fragmentation of both the TV and leisure markets means that it's increasingly difficult to maintain our profile. Sponsorship gives us a lot of exposure throughout our season. We intend to be a lot more promiscuous with our budget from now on"

A large poster campaign was also in place targeting Kingston, Reigate, and Watford. Unfortunately, despite efforts to make the park trendy using backwards rollercoasters and a baseball cap wearing cat, the country was riding the wave of "Girl power" thanks to the all-conquering Spice Girls, and one of those was ready to stick their stiletto deep into Harley's heart. Victoria 'Posh Spice' was quoted in the national news saying[309]:

> "I had a few dumb boyfriends who thought it was a good idea to go to Thorpe Park with a load of mates on an August Bank Holiday. I'd go along and think how much better Disneyland in Los Angeles was. I didn't like Thorpe Park with all its ridiculous dancers and people going round dressed as silly cowboys. Eating candyfloss and queueing up in the rain for three hours just didn't really impress me, it's not my scene at all"

Randall hit back at Posh stating:

> "In this case I would suggest that she's out of touch with the millions of children who come to the park every year and enjoy themselves"

Take that Victoria. Another international pop sensation was seemingly more open to the park, with Michael Jackson apparently popping in to watch the diving show, sign autographs for several hours, and then visit the local Magna Carta School[310]. However bizarrely this was all a hoax, which turned out to be a lookalike, leaving duped kids and teachers mortified.

The Thorpe Park entrance in 1997. Credit: Thorpe Park Nostalgia

1997 was of course the year that the nation was shocked by the death of Diana Princess of Wales. Thorpe Park had been the backdrop for some of the most iconic pictures with her young family, and the decision was taken to close the park out of respect on Sunday 6th September[311], the day of her funeral.

As an updated firework show signalled the end of the season over two weekends[312], the future of the park was in the balance due to another year where it had made a financial loss. Rumours started to fly after the Warner Brothers Movie World project failed in Hillingdon, that they would instead turn their attentions to Thorpe Park, and find it easier to convert the existing attraction into a new-look studio park. RMC would decide to sell their experimental leisure project the following year, however it wasn't Warner Brothers who would get the keys to the gates.

1998

Enrolling the huge number of seasonal staff to run an attraction such as Thorpe Park is always a challenge, and in 1998 this hit a new low when only two suitable candidates showed up for the annual recruitment day[313]. In total ten had attended, significantly lower than the 700 that would arrive earlier in the decade. In the late 1980s the park had made great efforts to keep their best staff, even introducing a creche that would allow new mothers to return to work[314]. With the backdrop of New Labour coming to power, and a fresh-faced Tony Blair leading the country, Runnymede had reported the highest level of employment in the whole country. Press officer Rebecca Cable was bemused by the lack of interest:

> "I just can't believe it. We have increased our pay to £4 an hour, we are giving training qualifications, paid holidays, discount admission to the park and out-of-hours activities and hours to suit. It's such a sad thing. We are a local company. People need jobs. I can't believe they are all in work"

An anonymous letter to the local paper from a former team member suggested that shoddy treatment of the entry level staff was to blame for many of them not returning[315]. The letter sighted having to work twelve hour shifts during the summer with only one 45-minute break, being forced to work additional hours without warning, and claimed that sub-managerial staff were not respected by higher management. They also highlighted some even more concerning safety fears. Claiming that some rides were being operated by under the minimum number of staff required due to shortages, and that others simply didn't open occasionally as nobody was available to run them.

It was a testing time for the management team all-round, not helped by the fact that their closest rivals were both opening new coasters for 1998. Legoland were adding the well-themed family *Dragon Coaster*, whilst Chessington's *Rattlesnake* was a compact Maurer Söhne "wild mouse" that offered more thrills. Thorpe Park's additions were underwhelming all-round, as they scratched around to offer more attractions on a tight budget.

Returning this year was another classic from the early 80s, the bumper boats. They were positioned in an area close to Thunder River that previously housed remote-control models, and re-branded as *Dino Boats* for no particular reason. Each two-person boat was powered by a small engine, and riders could control them for several minutes, inevitably choosing to bash into other guests. On a similar theme the old *Cinema 180* building (which had stood empty for a couple of years since the experience finally left) was used as a home for some bumper cars, called *Dare Devil Drivers*. Both rides would only last a few seasons.

Dino Boats close to Thunder River. Credit: Thorpe Park Nostalgia

The most striking addition was a new trio of water-slides on the *Fantasy Reef* beach, in the shadow of *Depth Charge*. They were similar to what you would find at a waterpark, and were neither particularly long nor tall, but were a solid upgrade to the beach area. It unfortunately faced the same issues as the beach itself, in that the attraction was only useful on the nicest of days, which were reasonably rare in the UK. Seemingly in a reference to the Scottish pop band known for *Love Is All Around*, the slides were named *Wet Wet Wet*.

The other side of *Depth Charge* on a patch of grass near the *Dome*, was possibly the most embarrassing attraction to ever be promoted as "new"[316]. *Slides by Slides* was simply a few sets of playground equipment. Probably better than you'd have in your garden, but not as great as your local park. It was, to say the least, rather random.

With enough staff found to start the season, and the first Spice Girls movie set to be released (featuring Thorpe Park mega fan Victoria), the double decker Spice Bus from the film came as part of a promotional tour[317]. At the same time, a new promotional stunt was planned for the Bank Holiday Weekend. The proposal was to create the world's first 24-hour amusement park, by opening at 5am on the Bank Holiday Monday, and remaining open throughout the night[318]. Unfortunately, traffic chaos and reports of trouble inside the park led to the experiment being cut short, shutting at midnight instead. Despite these problems Thorpe Park would still remain open until midnight on many weekends during the summer with no further issues[319].

In the background discussions continued around the future, and Tussauds had been quietly eyeing up the competition, considering whether it was worth making a move themselves. Alongside his colleague Gill Britain, Chessington and Alton Towers ride mastermind John Wardley made an incognito visit to Thorpe Park to report on their offering[320]. Likely aware of Leisure Sport's financial troubles at the time, and seeking somewhere new with potential to grow, Tussauds decided that Thorpe Park fitted the bill. Their parent company Pearson agreed that an offer could be made to purchase the park, providing that Tussauds sold their 40% stake in Spain's Port Aventura[321], which was duly acquired by Universal. In June 1998 the deal was done, with Tussauds paying £15 million to purchase Thorpe Park in full[322]. This ended over a decade of rivalry between Chessington and Thorpe Park, as the two were now under the same umbrella, along with Alton Towers, which was the UK's leading theme park at the time.

The sale ended 19 years of ownership by Leisure Sport and RMC, a brave gamble that was ahead of its time, but had been outgrown by its peers. The £15 million was a fraction of the money invested over the years, but given the financial difficulties, a price that represented where the visitor attraction found itself. In a RMC press release they stated[323]:

"The intended purchase price means that the transaction is not material in relation to RMC Group's assets or turnover"

Tussauds hinted towards backing their new acquisition with further investment, Michael Jolly telling the *Staines and Ashford News*[324]:

"This is a great opportunity to develop our visitor attraction business in the UK and we are very excited at the prospect of Thorpe Park joining the Tussauds Group. We plan substantial new investment to make the park even more attractive to visitors"

As always, the Residents' Association were keeping an eye on the news, and Jolly's quote pricked up their ears, with Hugh Papworth replying[325]:

"I am sure it has big plans for the park. I am just worried about the consequences"

After talks with the new owners and local residents, Chris Norman who was leader of Runnymede Council was keen to sit on the fence:

"The park has some ideas to get it back on its feet, but the main aim is to allay any fears residents have about expansion"

Before any plans could come to fruition, another surprise would come a few weeks later, when the news broke that the ownership was set to change hands again[326]. Pearson had decided to offload a selection of their assets to help fund their core business which they saw as media, and specifically the *Financial Times* and the new *Channel 5* television station that had launched the previous year. The leisure side of their business was sold to an investment fund managed by Charterhouse Development

Capital for a reported £350 million, with the deal going through by October[327]. The timing of the Thorpe Park purchase was suspicious, and unlikely to be coincidental. Was the purchase a term of the deal? Should Warner Brothers have purchased Thorpe Park, it would have severely dented the value of Chessington World of Adventures, so this could have been a defensive move to protect another of their core assets and secure the deal.

Tussauds now held somewhat of a monopoly on the UK theme park business, and every good Monopoly player knows at this point you start building hotels on what you own. The process had already started at Alton Towers with a hotel freshly opened, and plans were being drawn up for Chessington World of Adventures too[328]. The expanse of land on offer at Thorpe Park meant it was a prime contender for a future dabble in the overnight market.

First though Tussauds were keen to sort out how best to differentiate the two Surrey parks they now owned less than nine miles apart, and they had a plan that would transform Thorpe Park forever.

PART THREE

THE TUSSAUDS YEARS: RISE OF THE GIANTS

1999

Contrary to what some people might think, theme parks cannot build whatever ride they like. Many parks, especially in the UK, are strictly limited - not by their imaginations but by local planning laws.

Tussauds had become experts in making the most of their parks in difficult circumstances, coming up with creative solutions to build thrilling state-of-the-art machines that were almost impossible to see or hear from outside the boundaries of their land. The latest of these to open was *Oblivion* at Alton Towers, which required a massive hole to be dug into the ground to allow for a 180-foot drop when it opened in 1998. This was a far more expensive process than simply building the ride higher, but one that allowed the park to circumvent the rules and keep the beautifully natural skyline. The situation at Chessington was similar, with no rides allowed to appear over the treeline, and in fact the *Rattlesnake* rollercoaster was partially dug into the ground to ensure it kept within the strict rules.

The location of Thorpe Park is slightly different, and although it is still susceptible to the local planning laws as they found in the early days of the park, improved relationships suggested they would now be allowed greater flexibility. The reclaimed land sits in a more open environment, close to already loud motorways, and with only a smattering of local residents nearby. This gave it great potential for future expansion, and the prospect of building rides that simply wouldn't be possible at the other UK parks that Tussauds owned. Therefore, the decision was taken to significantly change the target audiences of the two southern theme parks. A plan was put in place for Thorpe Park to become the home of older families and teens, slowly relinquishing the family friendly title that they had worked tirelessly to create for the previous 20 years. The prospect of being able to build taller and faster rides than ever before with little complaint was just too tempting. In return Chessington World of Adventures would begin a process of becoming the traditionally wholesome family park, which would be less of a jarring makeover, with a more gradual change to the atmosphere. This fitted the park well, as it was still home to some excellent family attractions, plus the historic zoo.

Knowing that Thorpe Park had an awful lot of catching up to do if it was to be taken seriously as the UK's home of thrills, a huge war chest was signed off that would allow numerous major investments to be introduced over the coming years. Planning was underway quickly, with the objective to introduce several monster rides in consecutive years to make a statement of intent (Chessington would largely suffer from this, receiving little in the way of major new investment for a while). Although work was already underway, the first of these new statement pieces would not be ready to open until 2000, so the first post-Leisure Sport attraction was something a little quicker to install.

Monty Python legend Eric Idle had written a short movie script for an American company called Iwerks[329], which had been set up by a couple of former Disney employees in the late 80s. The proposal was that the 15-minute film would be shown exclusively in advanced theme park theatres, that were capable of synchronising a number of special effects with the action happening on screen. The concept was sold to Seaworld Ohio and Busch Gardens, allowing production to begin. Idle would star in the film himself, alongside deadpan comedy supremo Leslie Nielsen, and experienced child actor Adam Wylie. The film was directed by Keith Melton, who had experience working on the high budget *Terminator* theme park movie shown at Universal parks.

The storyline of the film was based around that ever-reliable theme park topic, pirates. Young cabin boy Davie (Wylie) has been betrayed by Captain Lucky (Nielsen), and sets up a number of booby traps to stop him and his crew recovering treasure he has buried on Pirate Island. Think *Home Alone* meets *Pirates of the Caribbean* and you get the picture. The various traps allow for a selection of crazy situations, which set off the special effects (escaping bees send the audiences' seats vibrating, cannons firing sent out a burst of fog with air jets, and pigeons pooing would send a sprinkling of warm water on your head). The whole movie was shot in 3D, which heightened the effects further, but required the audience to wear polarised glasses. The overall experience was an example of 4D, the effects making up the extra dimension, which wasn't a particularly new invention. It had been used in theme parks as early as 1984, when Landmark Entertainment's *The Sensorium* had played at Six Flags in Baltimore. Iwerks updated use of the technology would be titled *Pirates 4D*.

Thorpe Park were able to secure the rights to be the first attraction outside of the USA to show the film, but with no cinema currently at the park, would need to install the correct hardware. The decision was taken to refurbish the *Park Palladium Theatre*, which had been the home of many family variety shows for a decade, with the space being an ideal fit for the attraction. Planning permission was requested in October 1998 to change the classic façade outside the theatre[330], and both Advanced Entertainment Technology and Technology Design Associates worked to install the required systems inside the building. This included over 500 advanced new seats and a high-quality screen in place of the original stage. The interior was decorated like a Caribbean fort, and a large penned waiting area created outside where visitors could wait for the next showing. The entrance of which was signalled by a huge ship's mast, with the opened sail displaying the attraction's logo, and a large hole appearing like a cannon had been fired through it.

A press release[331] from the park teased the new show ahead of its launch:

"Visitors will be invited to sit back, put on special 3D glasses and be transported to the fourth dimension. It's an experience so new and so adrenaline pumping that you'll never trust your senses again"

This was accompanied by advertising in the press proclaiming the slogan[332]:

'You have to FEEL it to believe it'

Being able to draw on the vast experience of the creative teams at Tussauds was already showing its benefits, with the attraction looking significantly better quality than the other additions in recent years. This included the addition of one of the most memorable parts of *Pirates 4D* at Thorpe Park, an animatronic wise cracking parrot. Justa Parrot, named after a recurring gag in the movie itself, spoke to the audience both outside in the queue and once inside the theatre building. His pre-recorded repertoire included terrible jokes to keep those waiting entertained, and was an intuitive way of conveying key information to guests without relying on the performance of a team member. One of the challenges associated with the ride was having hundreds of pairs of glasses ready for each performance, with team members using an industrial cleaner to disinfect them after each showing.

Despite a relatively short turnaround time, *Pirates 4D* opened smoothly on Saturday 27th March. Early reactions were positive, with many finding the storyline and jokes a little cheesy, but the special effects adding significantly to the experience. It was loosely aimed at families, but there were reports of younger children finding it a bit much, with tears often following some of the more intense surprise effects. In her review shortly after opening Carey Pullen stated[333]:

"Don't get me wrong, the overall effect is quite dramatic but not quite as innovative as all the advertising would have you believe"

Whether by accident or design, the new attraction had done a good job of slowly starting the major changes planned for the park. It didn't completely disregard the existing loyal audience, as it was an attraction the whole family could experience together. Instead it was a showcase of the high quality that Tussauds were capable of, with an edge of intensity and tech that would have been missing from the usual 'safe' shows that had been common since the mid-1980s.

Behind the scenes, changes were also taking place to help introduce best practices across both Surrey parks owned by Tussauds. This meant some cultural tweaks and learnings across the board, which Graham Clatworthy found to be a positive move[334]:

"As things progressed we ended up with a south parks concept, with one management team across the two parks. A lot of people moved across from one park to the other, and that team spirit worked really well, because we were getting best practice across both parks. Two parks operating efficiently, and dropping the best bits into the other one"

Clatworthy would become guest experience manager for Thorpe Park, a new role introduced allowing him to be duty manager the five days a week he was in, rather than it being constantly split between different department managers. Explaining what that involved he said:

"Dealing with any issues that come up during the day, so it could be anything from an ice cream freezer breaking, to a major ride breaking down or a first aid incident. That's what I thrived on because you never knew what you would be faced with, but you had to work it out on the spot, working on what resources you had, how you could fix it, what the repercussions would be, and how to recover and get back on track"

It was a role he flourished in and enjoyed immensely, especially as working in any theme park ensures a lot of variety:

"There was no average day, every day was different. Some days could literally be a stroll in the park, and other days real pressure. Most of the time though at the end of the day that was it, nothing carried on to the next day really"

It was also rewarding for a couple of reasons:

"I used to go and stand on the exit to the park at the end of the day and watch people walking out, seeing a smile on a little kids face, and thinking we did that, and that's what it is all about. It's no secret that I used to go out and have a good few drinks with people in the evenings and have a brilliant time. It was all about camaraderie. Work hard, play hard. One team putting on a brilliant experience"

In the years to come 1999's new addition *Pirates 4D* would become a bit of a cult favourite, with many finding the cringeworthy jokes and familiar characters a welcome break from the more intense attractions elsewhere in the park. Naturally over time some of the effects deteriorated, leaving your experience a little hit and miss depending on where you were seated. This type of attraction tends to have a shorter life in theme parks, and so it did well to last until 2007, when it was replaced. Justa Parrot went on to find a new home at Alton Towers, where he entertained visitors to their *Mutiny Bay* area.

Those paying their £17 each[335] to enter in 1999 might have been drawn in by *Pirates 4D*, but when they reached the entrance their eyes were likely taken towards work beginning on a massive new ride that was being promised for the following year. Thorpe Park were planning to make a big splash....

2000

Before work had even started on *Pirates 4D*, plans were in place for a significant new water ride to open alongside the park in the new millennium. An area of space that housed the *Viking Rowers* was identified for development, which meant the boats were to leave the park at the end of the 1998 season, after a planning application to build the tallest ride to date was submitted in September that year[336].

The park had purchased a popular concept from water ride specialists Hopkins OD in Florida. Commonly known as a "Shoot the Chute" boat ride, this followed a very basic layout, with a large flat-bottomed boat being taken directly up a chain lift, before performing a tight U-turn and going down a steep drop to the bottom. Here the boat is stopped quickly and effectively by an expanse of water, which due to the large force from the vehicle sprays high in the air. It was an unusual choice of ride, as Thorpe Park was already home to a number of water drop rides, including *Loggers Leap* and *Depth Charge*. However, this would be taller and significantly more intense, again nudging the audience towards a more grown up future without completely abandoning everything they knew.

Although the ride itself would seemingly take place on the water, the area of Manor Lake previously home to the rowing boats would need to be filled in. This would be used to create a new artificial lake where the water could be self-contained to ensure it was clean. The sheer amount of water passengers would be subjected to meant that using it directly from the lake would be unacceptable. Also cleared ready for construction was another part of *Model World*, the Eiffel Tower replica leaving the park after 20 years. Construction took place throughout 1999, with large fences surrounding the new site promising "Europe's Tallest Water Ride" arriving the following year. At a height of 85 feet this was surprisingly tall for a ride of its nature, with most similar models reaching around 50 feet (about the same as *Loggers Leap*). The true scale of the new development became apparent when the drop was installed, reaching into the sky at a seemingly near vertical angle, towering over every other ride at the park and visible from far and wide.

Although Tussauds Studios had worked on *Pirates 4D* the previous year, this was their first chance to really get their teeth into a project on a Thorpe Park ride. The initial concept was to go with a pirate theme fitting in with the new 4D cinema close by, with early artwork showing the ride's station being inside a large classic pirate ship, with another abandoned ship in the middle of the artificial lake[337]. The idea was pretty impressive, although it was rather similar to the area that Legoland's log flume sat in. Eventually a new, more original, plan was created for the area based on the huge splash the ride makes. This was around a 1960s New England fishing village which had already suffered at the hands of a major tidal wave, with the buildings and surroundings ravaged by flooding and water damage. The creative team played with this concept magnificently, producing a bespoke layout for the land that would feature a number of distinctive components. The ride itself would represent a second hit, and was thus simply called *Tidal Wave*.

The surrounding area would become known as *Amity*. The boat station was re-imagined as a sinking building with every aspect out of kilter. In the middle of the ride's lake was a sunken church spire, from which you could still hear the bells. A giant aged traditional water tower proudly displaying the Amity name would dump tons of water at irregular intervals. Possibly best of all was a large gas tank, that would occasionally "explode" firing flames into the sky, from which you could feel the heat from quite a distance away. Each of these interactive items were built and installed by the technicians at special effects company Artem[338]. The entrance archway seemed to be created by an electricity pylon and a advertising sign collapsing on each other. The queue was scattered with debris from the disaster, with wrecked buildings and animated features such as an overflowing toilet. Everything was done to the highest standards, with countless small touches and attention to detail, making it without doubt the best themed ride in Thorpe Park's history.

Theming arriving during construction. Credit: Thorpe Park Nostalgia

Tidal Wave under construction. The drop installed first. Credit: Thorpe Park Nostalgia

The underwhelming *Carousel Kingdom* was also removed to make way for additions to the new area, with the interior changed to a KFC which was also impressively themed. It had lots of nice links to *Amity*, including a sail boat coming through the deliberately wrecked ceiling. The space not taken up by the fried chicken restaurant was then used for a pretty run of the mill arcade.

The most eye-catching part of the whole attraction was not the huge drop, or the immaculate theming, but the incredible splash it created as each boat hit the water. Each time one of the 3,000kg boats got to the bottom 4,292 litres of water are thrown into the air[339], with a huge amount falling on the riders soaking them thoroughly, but also spraying far and wide around the area. It was the ultimate spectator ride, engrossing anybody who walked nearby, begging for their full attention. The novelty value remains no matter how many times you see it, with the mixture of spectacular visuals and the threat of a personal soaking impossible to ignore. There's also the evil pleasure of watching those who have just been soaked in the boat recover, which is especially enjoyable if you can catch a first timer. To add to the fun the exit bridge is built over the splash zone, allowing people to wait directly in front of the wave of water. Designers seemingly underestimated just how forceful the falling water would be, with the roof of the bridge having to be replaced during the first season as it became damaged.

David McCubbin remembers watching the construction of the project[340]:

"The whole area was completely transformed, it really was a big statement. *Tidal Wave* was a complete gamechanger, it was a huge thing. It was amazing because we were used to watching *Loggers Leap* and seeing the usual splash at the bottom, but then *Tidal Wave* and this massive wave was incredible. I remember watching it for the first time and the wave coming over Pier 13 (the exit bridge) and thinking oh my god, people are going to choose to get soaked"

As a full-time member of staff, he was one of the first to try out the ride:

"I rode for the first time the day they were filming the TV advert. There was a balance between commissioning the ride and the theming artists doing their work, so quite often testing happened in the evening. I didn't fully appreciate that you'd get soaked like you do. We went round about five times and didn't want to get off"

The announcement press release ahead of the opening in April teased the interactivity of the new ride for all[341]:

"…This is one ride from where there will be no escape…the phenomenal impact of the ride and its real life setting will ensure that spectators share in the thrill"

This was one piece of marketing hype that McCubbin felt was right on the money:

"A lot of attractions end up being that unless you're in the queue for it, you're not part of it. With Tidal Wave you could be a part of it, even if you didn't want to go on the actual ride"

The creative Tidal Wave entrance sign. Credit: Alex Rowe

Tidal Wave was an instant hit with visitors, with the whole package delivering far more than the sum of its parts. The British weather didn't seem to deter guests either, with many finding a twisted pleasure in riding during downpours. Others were happy parting with a few pounds to get an official branded poncho before boarding. Vending machines were even installed in the queue line to cope with the demand for them. Understandably though the biggest queues were reserved for the warmest days, with crowds keen to cool down in the most spectacular of manners. The ride system itself used three boats, each with five rows of up to four riders, with each row held in place by one giant lap bar. The short nature of the journey gave *Tidal Wave* a high capacity allowing it to crunch through the queues.

The huge splash as the boat reaches the bottom. Credit: Alex Rowe

Those who did have to wait were in for a treat though, as speakers located throughout *Amity* blast out the specially created *WWTP Radio*. This is actually a pre-recorded loop, but is performed as if broadcasting live from the local *Amity* radio station. The station plays a surprisingly wide selection of tracks from the 50s and 60s, including the *Beach Boys*, *Little Richard* and *Johnny Cash*. After each song the presenter Big Bob updates listeners on the impending floods, with the odd amusing fictional advert in-between. The script throughout is witty and entertaining, and the songs chosen help create the fun and captivating atmosphere.

The experience as a passenger is pretty basic. You start by being taken straight up to the top of the lift, where you start the short turn round to the drop. The surprising thing about this is, that unlike other boat rides, there is no water at all in the top. The boat uses wheels to roll round to the drop, which again doesn't need any actual water to work. The water you see falling on the drop is merely for aesthetic purposes, and the angle of the 85-foot straight drop is quite gut wrenching, but over quickly. Once you hit the water there are a few glorious seconds where you can see the sheer magnitude of water flying into the air, before gravity returns it downwards and onto your head. The weight of the water falling is actually quite significant, and it's not an understatement to say you get absolutely drenched. The heavier the boat, the bigger the splash, so you might want to keep clear if the local rugby club is queueing in front of you. After the shock of the splash the boat floats slowly back to the station. Graham Clatworthy remembers some guests misjudging the ride when he was park manager[342]:

"When it's sunny it's fantastic to get wet, but sometimes people would go on their first ride of the day at 10am, get soaked to their skin, and then it would be rainy and cloudy and they'd have a difficult day"

With their new star attraction performing well things were looking positive for the park heading into the summer holidays, but another disaster was about to strike, and this time it wasn't a fictitious one. On Friday 21st July 2000 at around 3PM a fire broke out by the *Mr. Rabbit's Tropical Travels* ride. The flames quickly spread through the surrounding buildings, and the park was hastily evacuated, with thankfully nobody being injured. Huge blazes shot into the air signalling massive destruction, with 100 firefighters across 15 vehicles called to battle it[343]. By the time the blaze was brought under control it had destroyed an area in the middle of the park, which included the indoor portion of the *Tropical Travels* ride, and the entirety of the *Wicked Witches Haunt* dark ride. Confectionary shop *Sweet City* and the new KFC were also affected.

Remembering the day well, McCubbin thinks the early stages of the fire might have been brewing for a while:

"Whenever you worked on *Wicked Witches Haunt*, because it was an indoor ride, you were well trained to take reports of smells of smoke seriously. This would happen quite often, and it would be thoroughly investigated. On the day of the incident on the radio I heard engineers called over two or three times because of the smell of smoke and nothing was ever found. Eventually it became apparent that there was a significant fire, but at the time there was no suspicion at all that it had started at *Tropical Travels* next door. There were no reports coming from *Tropical Travels*, nobody got off the ride saying they could smell smoke."

Staff were rightly praised for their professional evacuation, and ensuring nobody was hurt, although McCubbin admits it was a scary situation:

"It was unbelievably shocking. I remember everybody was radioed to be told this was now declared a serious incident, and we were going to have to evacuate the park. It was the first time this had happened since I'd been there. We had thousands of people from all the different rides and queues, and we had to get everybody off without trying to create panic. Although when the fire took hold, there was this massive plume of smoke in the sky, and people were saying you could see it 20 miles away. It was crazy, you couldn't quite believe this was happening. It sounds cheesy, but the whole time I worked at Thorpe Park safety was the number one thing. You spent so much time training people, assessing people, practicing evacuations twice a week"

Addressing the press at the time Glenn Earlam confirmed the damage:

"The *Tropical Travels* building has collapsed due to the construction - it is a timber-framed building. The fire subsequently spread to other buildings and rides, one of the rides being *Wicked Witches* (Haunt)"

This was especially sad news for the latter, as Tussauds had just begun planning a new life for the Mack transit system inside. Wardley was looking at ways to make better use of the concept, which he felt wasn't ideal for a ghost train style ride, the issue being that the cars were so close together and the reactions of the riders in front spoilt the surprise for you. He planned a re-fit of the attraction, giving it a more fun and joyous atmosphere, in line with the much admired *Bubbleworks* at Chessington. His assumption was that he would reunite with Sparks, bringing the prolific partnership back together after huge successes with the World of Adventure and the *Haunted House* at Alton Towers. The destruction in July 2000 ended any hopes of what would have been a highly anticipated re-working, with Wardley admitting the process had just begun[344]:

> "I'd just started getting some ideas together and the damn thing burnt down"

Wicked Witches Haunt destroyed by the fire. Credit: Thorpe Park Nostalgia

Pictures of the flames ravaging Thorpe Park had been on every television news report that evening, thrusting the park into the public's consciousness once again in unfortunate circumstances. The reaction from the team was sensational, amazingly managing to get the park open again the following day by cordoning off the large affected area. To compensate for the loss of two attractions the entry fee was reduced by £2. The combination of the publicity and the discount sent attendances soaring that weekend, with the public seemingly having a morbid fascination in viewing the very real destruction just metres away from the romanticised version.

With less rides to soak up the queues for the rest of the season, an additional ride was sourced at short notice to help. Located close to the Dome this was a second-hand HUSS *Enterprise* where riders sit enclosed in small capsules arranged in a circle with a metal gate locking them in. The ride starts to spin at high speed, with gravity forcing the gondolas outwards almost at a right angle. The whole ride is then raised 90 degrees by a hydraulic arm, spinning passengers 59 feet in the air and turning them upside down, centrifugal force pinning them to their seats. It was a familiar site at fairgrounds around the world since its creation in the early 1970s, but also at some theme parks including Alton Towers. It was a completely different type of ride to the ones it was deputising for, and probably the most intense to ever grace Thorpe Park to that point, also being the first to invert visitors. With little time or need to brand the ride it was simply called *Enterprise* (the original name a Star Trek reference) and it retained the air of a fairground ride with no theming.

Wicked Witches Haunt was gone forever but *Tropical Travels* returned briefly the following year, albeit with the most interesting indoor section gone. Rumours about how the fire started suggest it was a discarded cigarette in a queue line, a faulty smoke alarm, or both that led to the fire raging out of control.

Tidal Wave was a big hit and remains one of the most popular rides on a warm day. It has aged remarkably well, appearing younger and more advanced than its twenty years and counting. Although, over time many of the special theming pieces have stopped working for various reasons and look unlikely to ever be replaced. Thanks to its "refreshing" nature it has attracted several sponsorship deals, including the likes of Original Source, Dr. Pepper, Oasis (the drink not the band) and Fanta. The successful implementation of Amity would see the area grow and evolve in years to come. "Shoot the Chute" rides are seen in many places around the world, but possibly most successfully implemented at Universal parks with *Jurassic Park/World: The Ride*. This version is superbly realised, finishing with the same 85ft drop as *Tidal Wave*, but with a huge tyrannosaurus rex attacking you. The European record for tallest water ride was taken by *Hydro* at Oakwood in 2002, measuring around 100 feet tall.

Whilst work continued on ambitious new headline rides for the future, the events of 2000 meant some unplanned changes would be required, and some new additions to the line-up for 2001 were hastily arranged.

2001

With a large charred hole now sitting in the middle of the park, and money already committed for a major attraction in another location set to open in 2002, solutions for what could replace the rides destroyed in the fire were discussed. One of the early thoughts was to hastily install a Vekoma launched rollercoaster on the site, with plans drawn up, but the timelines just didn't work. Instead a second rollercoaster would eventually adorn much of the land but not for a couple of years. Keen to keep the momentum going and add further new thrilling rides for the start of the season, the best answer given the short timescale was to seek off-the-shelf flat rides that could be purchased and installed quickly.

Already at the park was the HUSS *Enterprise* introduced after the fire, and it was decided this would stay in a more permanent location where *Cap'n Andy's Revue* used to perform. The generic name was ditched with it instead becoming *Zodiac*. Joining it nearby would be a brand new KMG *Afterburner*. This was a type of "frisbee" ride, with guests sitting in one of eight four-seater gondolas facing each other in a circle. Once the over the shoulder restraints have been locked, the floor slowly drops, leaving legs dangling unsupported. The gondola starts to spin moderately fast and then begins swinging like a giant pendulum gradually getting higher, eventually reaching up to 65 feet in the air. It's an exhilarating experience that combines several classic ride troupes into one quite nauseating experience. The *Afterburner* was given the fitting name of *Vortex*. Like the *Enterprise* it had a reputation for appearing at travelling fairs, but Thorpe Park were the first to install it permanently, and willing to go the extra mile to blend both the new attractions into the park.

Situated close together on the east side of the park close to the *Dome*, the additions would be the first of another new themed land. The *Lost City* was based around the remains of a not particularly specific ancient civilisation, but with strong Aztec vibes. The area was decorated with pebble dashed pathways, aged rockwork, and luscious plant life. It was far less developed than the glorious *Amity*, with a more generic feel and no set piece interactive items, but it worked in evoking an ancient ambiance with consistent surroundings.

Vortex up in the air. Credit: Alex Rowe

A rousing soundtrack helped provoke feelings of adventure and impending doom without needing to be as on the nose as *WWTP Radio*. The rides themselves were treated to an aqua and maroon colour scheme that would become the standard for the area, and decorated with a number of relevant props. *Vortex* would have a large naval style protractor to the side, whilst *Zodiac* received astrological style markings including a sun that would rotate in the centre of the wheel. Although technically *Zodiac* had been introduced the previous year, it was understandable that both would be promoted as new attractions for 2001[345].

Zodiac spinning fast. Credit: Alex Rowe

Joining them would be a third new thrill ride, which would sit on the former home of *Wicked Witches Haunt*. Short term permission of five years was granted to install the tallest ride to date, a drop tower reaching 115 feet. Tussauds Studios had already been working on a similar ride by S&S, that would launch riders up a tower, with plans submitted to place this on the site of what remained of *Model World*. Instead this alternative tower ride would come from Italian manufacturer Fabbri. The ride allowed twelve people at a time to sit in around the tower, facing outwards, and again with legs dangling. Pulled up to the top by a catch car, it would give riders a bird's eye view of the surrounding park, lakes and M3 Motorway (depending on where you are positioned). Rather than just letting go at the top, the ride is held and a countdown played, before being thrusted downwards by pneumatics. This creates a force greater than gravity, raising everybody out of their seats, but held in by the over the shoulder restraints. The drop is over very quickly, but it's surprisingly powerful, apparently hitting a massive G force of over +5.

Like *Tidal Wave* that preceded it, the plan was to align this with the *Pirates 4D* cinema nearby. One proposal was to place a large skull at the very top of the ride, but eventually this was reduced to some barrels and cannons on ground level. The name of *Detonator* was a good fit for the ride experience and offered a subtle pirate-y link. There was more good work on the soundtrack front, creating an atmospheric background for the ride that helped rack up the tension before each drop.

With three new rides to promote, the marketing team created a campaign focused around the tagline "Sensory Overload"[346]. With the rides not ready for any filming, a creative approach had to be found to make the accompanying television advert, with actors and graphics used to represent the latest additions. When it came to opening day though, visitors expecting to try out the three new additions were left disappointed. *Detonator* was ready and firing, but the two *Lost City* additions were not, with the spot were *Vortex* should be just an empty pit. Despite extensive promotion it would take seven weeks for all three rides to be operational, leading to complaints[347]. *Vortex* opened with some theming missing, and without its bespoke coloured restraints ready, instead beginning operation with pink ones KMG had available.

Despite a phased opening all three new rides were welcome additions and popular with the public. Whilst none of them offered a particularly high capacity, they helped spread the crowds around the park a little more. Of the three *Zodiac* became the most troublesome, constantly suffering from maintenance issues and spending long periods closed leading to frustration. Being a common ride meant that spare parts could be sourced but the regularity of the breakdowns was concerning. Problems came to a head in September when a corroded bolt caused one of the gondolas to come loose, sending teenagers Gemma Clark and Scott Reeves into danger[348]. The ride operator did their best to perform an emergency stop, but the carriage struck the surrounding infrastructure. Both only received minor injuries of bruising and whiplash, but it was a major incident that could have ended in tragedy. Taken to court, Thorpe Park were ordered to pay a total of £100,000 in fines and costs[349].

After the incident new safety procedures were put in place, and the ride spent a large period of time closed. By 2006 the decision was taken to completely replace the ride, when a similar model became available. Drayton Manor sold their *Enterprise* to Thorpe Park and it became the new version of *Zodiac*. Disappointingly little was done to bring it into the *Lost City* atmosphere, with a more generic paint job and no theming visible.

Whilst having spells of downtime, *Vortex* has become a modern classic Thorpe Park ride, although it has attracted some sensationalist headlines in recent years. In 2017 it was briefly closed as a precaution after a death on a similar ride at the Ohio State Fair, but was swiftly re-opened[350]. The following year a smartphone caught the moment something flew from the ride, with the video going viral with speculation about what had happened. In reality it was just a bit of foam from an out of use chair, but it highlighted the danger and speed that social media can have on reputations. A Thorpe Park statement cleared things up[351]:

"This was a non-critical part of the ride and came from a chair that was out-of-service during the ride's operation. Vortex was promptly stopped whilst further safety checks took place and re-opened 15 minutes later"

Detonator ended up extending its initial planning permission to become permanent. Possibly surprisingly considering the fate of other rides to follow, all three 2001 additions remain part of the attraction line-up 19 years later.

Signs of Tussauds re-branding of the park were now unmistakable, with such a sudden surge of adrenaline fuelled fun meaning some of the previous family friendly entertainment was on its way out. The logo was updated, which meant a version created by Leisure Sport including a splash for the 'O' only lasted a year in 1999. A smooth modern version was introduced with rings/infinity symbol in the background. Harley was quickly dispensed of, presumably taken out the back and put down, with his body somewhere at the bottom of Abbey Lake. The *Thorpe Park Rangers* were going to be a little more difficult to remove, as their bespoke area in the middle of the park was largely still intact. They would instead be slowly phased out over time, initially being removed from new materials as they were created. Models of each Ranger outside the entrance are actually now bizarrely sunk like ancient ruins underwater, which you can find if you visit the Diving Centre in Chepstow[352].

Duty manager at the time Graham Clatworthy was already starting to see the impact of the re-branding, with visitors often being more boisterous[353]:

"Towards the end of my time there was a definite swing because of the thrill rides. Instead of families from Surrey, there were gangs of kids from London, with that came additional issues. As a park manager expectations were higher, and if people didn't get what they wanted the complaints were more aggressive. Rather than families wanting to have a quick word, it was people wanting to square up to you"

The 2001 season concluded with a four-night fireworks and laser spectacular, but in truth every event and ride introduced during the year had been overshadowed by the prospect of what was coming next. During the season an incredible monster had begun to rise that would be a massive statement of intent of Thorpe Park's future ambitions.

2002

Since bringing Thorpe Park into their portfolio Tussauds had been working towards this moment. Delayed a year later than they initially envisioned, *Project Odyssey* was to show their true plans for the future. Whilst the previous two decades had seen consistent investment from two owners, and the introduction of so many adored attractions, this was on a completely different scale and had the budget to match. This was to be the first rollercoaster at the park since *X:\ No Way Out*, but for sheer significance there was simply no comparison.

A large area on the east side of the park had been identified as the ideal spot for the new project. This ran parallel to Abbey Lake, running from the new rides in *Lost City* and all the way down to *Canada Creek*. It was a previously underutilised piece of land that had hosted a simple pathway and *Trappers Trail* (which had become known as *Fort Ontario*). When it came to choosing what type of rollercoaster to install there were a few main considerations. The first was time. This needed to be constructed as quickly as possible to signal the thrill revolution at the park. The second was the space available, which was in theme park terms a pretty generous sized rectangular piece of land to work with. The third and possibly most important to senior management, was the need to offer an experience that would blow the communal public mind. This couldn't just be a very good rollercoaster, it had to have the wow factor to draw in a new audience to the park. Afterall, the proposed eight figure budget needed to be justified.

Having been responsible for the hugely successful coaster installations elsewhere in the group, John Wardley was asked to consider what might work[354]. A number of different manufacturers put forward proposals for the available space, reportedly including Swiss giants Bolliger & Mabillard, and heritage Italian brand Pinfari. However, it was an idea from Intamin, the same company who had installed the rapids in 1987, that caught the eye. They had built a coaster at a Brazilian park in 1998 that they felt was the perfect fit for the location. Wardley and his colleague Alan Brown agreed that it was an impressive prospect but were wary of proceeding before having experienced it themselves. With the clock ticking to get *Project Odyssey* underway, they took an overnight flight to the Terra Encantada park in Brazil, which was home to the *Monte Makaya* rollercoaster that Intamin had created. After requiring three different flights to get there, Wardley and Brown only had time for a quick ride, before turning around and taking three flights back. The exhausting journey had been worth it as Intamin's proposal had the potential to fit all three of the key criteria.

Monte Makaya stood a little over 100 feet tall and contained a then record equalling eight inversions. These were a large loop after the first drop, followed by a small but effective "bunny hop" into a cobra roll which twice turns riders upside down. After this the train manoeuvres through a couple of corkscrews, three heartline rolls, and a final helix back to the station. Keen to not just match the record, but to beat it, discussions continued with Intamin about how some extra inversions could be added to the layout for Thorpe Park's ride. After doing some stretch calculations it was deemed completely possible to add a couple more heartline rolls onto the design by extending the ride area slightly and removing the helix. Whilst this wasn't going to change the ride experience massively for those on board, it would of course ensure that Thorpe Park claimed that all important world record for most inversions. This was about making a big statement, and breaking the record was going to ensure Thorpe had a PR story that would hit the mainstream media in the UK, and be on the radar of enthusiasts around the world.

This was a massive declaration of intent for the direction Tussauds saw the park going in, and nothing like Thorpe Park or the UK had seen before. In fact, "seen" is the optimum word in this instance, as this huge expanse of twisting steel was highly visible, a pleasure Tussauds had not been able to indulge in before for their UK parks. Both Alton Towers and Chessington World of Adventures had impressive coasters, but classics such as *Nemesis*, *Oblivion* and *The Vampire* had been hidden from the public until they were actually pretty close to them, certainly not visible from across the park, and definitely not outside. *Project Odyssey* was different, helped by the aesthetically pleasing twisted nature of the track. It practically begged to show off as soon as you entered the car park, which was located just the other side of the lake. It was more reminiscent of something you might see at Blackpool Pleasure Beach or at one of the chain of Six Flags parks in America.

Thorpe Park's manmade island gave them the pleasure of reduced restrictions, but possibly at the cost of some creativity. There's no doubting that one of the core reasons that *Nemesis* has been such an enduring hit for nearly thirty years is its unique layout, with the park having to dig huge excavations into the ground to accommodate the demands of the ride. This led to a ground hugging layout, that offers a sensational experience for riders. Should Alton have been able to take the easier option, with restrictions reduced, it's extremely likely we would have seen something far more generic. This would have been a lot cheaper at the time, but almost certainly not the iconic rollercoaster it became, bringing riders from around the world that have the pleasure of still riding to this day. So, whilst Thorpe Park's more relaxed restrictions allowed it to create a striking statement from a distance, it was almost certainly at the cost of some imagination.

That's not to say that creativity didn't go into the project as a whole, far from it. Wardley had noticed that the land available would allow for the track to be slightly sunk into the ground, which would lead to a less generic and more enthralling experience. The Brazilian original was also well hidden, with the ride coaster track well away from park visitors, basically in a big field. Wardley described blocking the substantial piece of land off as[355]:

> "A terrible waste of capital in a theme park"

He set about investigating how the audience could better interact with the new giant they were creating. To do so he cut out paper copies of the planned layout, and using bits of foam worked out how pathways might interact with the ride itself. Experienced landscape architect Andy

Nicholls helped work wonders with Wardley, together planning a winding set of carefully placed pathways making up spectating and queuing areas. This allowed close up views of every imposing twist and turn the coaster had to offer. To get to the entrance you'd literally have to walk through one of the corkscrews, and if timed right, the train would pass very close to your head. This would allow for a far more enjoyable wait whilst you were either queueing for the ride itself, or just killing time whilst others in your group were.

This was a big opportunity for Intamin in the regional market too. They were already a major player supplying rides to titans such as Disney and Six Flags, but had relatively little presence in the UK apart from working on the uncomfortable *Shockwave* at Drayton Manor almost a decade earlier. Installing a ride of this nature is always a huge construction project, but they were helped by the presence of the previous design, and pre-existing technology. This meant any issues would have been identified during the construction of *Monte Makaya*, and likely eradicated for future versions. At exactly the same time Tussaud's were developing *Air* at Alton Towers, (a world's first flying coaster) which experienced a fair dose of its own teething problems. But that's often the price you pay for ingenuity.

Although opening after *Vortex* and *Zodiac*, the plan was always for this to be the headline attraction in the *Lost City* area of the park. The artwork was in line with attractions added the previous year, but on a larger scale. Fitting in nicely with the work Nicholls & Wardley had done, the cobra role was to sit in a pit filled with water, with ancient facades working as fountains. Additionally, the ride station, shop and pathways would have *Lost City* touches added to them. It suffered from many of the same deficiencies as the rest of the land, in that it wasn't anywhere near as inventive and entertaining as *Amity*, but it largely worked. A bigger issue was finding a suitable colour and name for the ride. A few different colour proposals were bounded around, including matching it to the X pyramid which stood snuggly nearby, but the final decision was a turquoise track with pale yellow supports[356].

As it was such a statement piece, giving the ride a suitable name took on far more significance. Thorpe Park's only two previous rollercoasters had been named by a nine-year-old and a marketing company, both of which were questionable. Proposals at first included *Helix* based on the heartline rolls appearing to be like DNA, or possibly *Atlantis*, fitting into the ancient civilisation theme. In the end suggestions were welcomed from park staff, and it was guest experience manager Graham Clatworthy who came up with the winner, with his proposal of *Colossus* being chosen[357]:

> "The marketing team said let's have a competition to name the ride. I don't know how many entries there were, but I called *Colossus* because I thought, apart from the fact it means big, all the loops would work well in the logo. On the day of the all-park presentation when the whole team gets together, they announced the winner and my name was called out. I got a bottle of champagne and a hug from (park manager) Glenn Earlam"

Construction begins with the lift hill being installed. Credit: Thorpe Park Nostalgia

With planning complete and contracts signed, work finally began late in 2000 on clearing and preparing the site ready for construction. When visitors began to arrive for the 2001 season they found a huge site boarded off, and the previous direct route to *Canada Creek* from the entrance gone, along with the Fort Ontario play area removed. Large banners along the fences promised the "World's First 10 Looping Rollercoaster" which was kind of true. It would of course only feature one actual loop, but the British public were obviously deemed too ignorant to understand what an inversion was, so the marketing focused instead on the word "loop", which was regarded as an adequately dumbed down substitute. Eighteen years later the ride would still be referred to on the official website as "one of the most looping roller coasters in the world"[358]. Along with these large proclamations, viewing holes were cut into the construction fences to allow visitors a peek at what was going on.

The model that promoted the arrival during construction. Credit: Thorpe Park Nostalgia

Additionally, a pretty cool scale model of the planned attraction was added to help promote what visitors could ride the following year. This helpfully had the ten inversions identified, to help ease any confusion for children and adults about why they couldn't see ten massive loops. Incidentally when *Colossus* opened this model was then moved to Chessington World of Adventures, where it sat near *The Vampire* promoting Thorpe Park. Once the initial promotion had died down this was moved backstage at Chessington, and sadly one day I saw it destroyed when the roof of the viewing case it was sat in collapsed. A real tragedy, as I'm sure had they auctioned it off, it would have sat very happily in a geek's shed frustrating their partner for years to come.

As somebody who was knowledgeable about rides and attractions around the world, David McCubbin knew this was going to be a big deal[359]:

"To know that this massive rollercoaster was coming was amazing, and you knew it was going to put Thorpe Park on the map. This was the first time we would be competing with something like Alton Towers, and many of the people who would normally go there might come to Thorpe Park to ride *Colossus*. This wasn't like Alton Towers who kept things under wraps with their secret weapons, this was a real big, brash statement. We're getting a ten looping rollercoaster and you've got to come back for it"

Walkways and track being placed during construction. Credit: Thorpe Park Nostalgia

Initially construction was slow with a large amount of landscaping work required ahead of the main build. This included the addition of some huge hollow concrete blocks that would eventually work as the tunnels and walkway bridges, along with all the usual footers and foundations that have to be placed for a project of this nature[360]. It was nine months after construction work began until the first pieces of coaster track started to arrive and were then put together in July 2001. By October the entire ride layout was in place, revealing the magnitude of the creation. *Colossus* was Gulliver in Lilliput, the sheer scale making everything else in the park seem half its previous size. However, there was still months of landscaping, theming and testing to be done before the project was ready.

An early test run of Colossus. Credit: Thorpe Park Nostalgia

Getting the marketing right ahead of the launch was imperative, and a chunk of budget was set aside to promote the loopy new attraction. A television advert was shot which featured a number of people unable to walk straight, revealed to be due to the disorientating nature of the ride. It finished with the tagline "It Never Leaves You"[361]. To capitalise on the intrigue, return tickets had been offered in 2001 to come back the following year for the reduced price of £12.50[362]. The website was also embraced as a marketing tool with a computer simulation of what the ride would be like, although this was an early example of the technology, with the blocky recreation taking an age to load on dial-up internet connections.

In good time and ahead of the new season the first test runs on *Colossus* took place, with generally the process going pretty smoothly. After the usual tests with a slow pull-through and sending the cars round with just weighted dummies, humans could try it out, revealing for the first time what it was like to be turned upside down ten times on a rollercoaster. The experience received the thumbs up, although early riders were surprised by the highlights of the ride. Many cited that it wasn't any of the many inversions that gave them the biggest thrill, but the small "bunny hop" taken at high speed after the initial loop, which then dives under the shop creating a head chopper element. The world record might bring in the punters, but the Intamin machine was showing that it had a little more to offer than just that.

David McCubbin had been involved regularly in the project representing the rides and attractions team, and when a staff night to try the rollercoaster was arranged, he couldn't wait to finally ride it[363]:

"I wanted to be on the first train, so I managed to engineer a situation because quite a few of us had been trained by Intamin on how to operate it. Everybody got to go round and round as much as you wanted. It was amazing, I remember thinking how good it was, and it really was an amazing ride. That first season it was smooth as glass wherever you sat, it wasn't rough. I only had one disappointment which was when you go over the bunny hop and under the shop, I remember wishing that drop under carried on for another 100 feet."

Just a week before the season began, an opportunity arose to heavily feature on BBC television programme *Tomorrow's World*[364]. This special episode was filmed "as live" at the park and saw willing participants split into two groups. The first would ride having not queued at all for *Colossus*, with the other waiting in line before getting their turn. The purpose of the experiment was to measure which group enjoyed the experience more, and to show if queueing for a ride actually enhanced the experience, with heartrates and other measurements taken. Conveniently for Thorpe Park and every other attraction out there, the experiment showed that queueing was actually beneficial to your experience. Forevermore giving theme parks a reason to justify long queues.

The first inversion, a massive loop. Credit: Alex Rowe

The project was on schedule and the finishing touches could be added before the start of the season. This included a bespoke epic soundtrack created by experienced attraction composer Ian Habgood which played throughout the station and queue line. Appropriately huge signage was created at each end of the area, situated on impressive tridents and revealing the new logo. Foliage was strategically added in areas that would allow for it to grow and add to the aura in years that followed. As you would expect, a gift shop was added that offered a plethora of merchandise and the customary on-ride photos. A *Guinness World Record* certificate was proudly displayed by the entrance, proving to all that this was the first of its kind.

The official *Premiere Screaming* launch night was held on Thursday 21st March, just before the start of the new season. A number of celebrity guests were welcomed to be among the first to ride *Colossus* along with a number of annual pass holders. Notoriously events for new rides can be a gamble as they are likely to experience teething problems, or construction delays. It was a huge credit to this project that everything was delivered on time, and the ride launch went very smoothly. *EastEnders* actor Dean Gaffney was joined by, not-yet-but-soon-to-be, *EastEnders* actor Shane Richie to try out *Colossus*, and of course feature in pictures provided to the media.

A corkscrew over a walkway, just as John Wardley wanted. Credit: Alex Rowe

Colossus was opened to the public successfully on Friday 22nd March, but would the massive new investment be a hit? Well initially the consensus seemed to be yes, it was obviously a huge step up in scale, and riders were loving the experience. The four heartline rolls in a row seemed in particular to capture the public's imagination, and the uniquely twisted track in that section became a photo favourite when captured from the far end looking through. The project had reportedly cost over a whopping £13,000,000 to complete (just shy of what had been paid for the entire park a few years earlier), but the early signs were that it was looking like a sound investment.

When the gates opened for 2002 *Colossus* wasn't the only noticeable difference though. Over the closed season changes had been made to stone cold Thorpe Park classic *Thunder River*, as part of a partnership with Ribena soft drinks. The new look *Ribena Rumba Rapids* was largely the same ride as before, but with many of the rapid's elements tamed down. It was given a bright new purple and green colour scheme in line with the soft drink's branding, some new music and some berry creatures added in a partially re-built tunnel.

The most notable change was the boats, which had been completely replaced. Gone were the original *Thunder River* boats with the large handlebar in the middle, replaced with brightly coloured versions with nothing in the centre, just small handles by each seat. They looked to the untrained eye, like a tacky downgrade to the originals, although maybe that's just nostalgia misleading fair judgement. The advantage the new boats did have was a couple of extra seats each, raising the capacity of the ride. The Ribena partnership covered both this and the *Berry Bouncers* at Chessington and lasted until the end of 2006. At this point the Ribena branded items were removed, but the other changes remained.

The new boats turning Thunder River into Rumba Rapids. Credit: Alex Rowe

Next to the re-branded rapids, in the old *European Square* section, a new Caribbean restaurant opened called *Sleepy Joe's Rib Shack*. It was a pretty unremarkable, if slightly above average theme park food option. It is memorable to me as I visited it on opening day, and as I sat down, immediately fell through the chair as it shattered into pieces. Being around nine stone at the time, I can only assume it was the hasty assembly of the furniture, rather than my immense weight, that caused the incident. Staff kindly offered some free fries when my brother-in-law had stopped laughing.

Back on the other side of the park at *Colossus,* an obvious issue from the beginning was the design of the trains that riders would board, which were different to those used on *Monte Makaya.* They were tight, and required guests to crouch very low down to get into them. Larger riders would especially struggle to squeeze in and pull the over the shoulder restraints down to the required level. This sometimes delayed dispatching trains and held up the queues. Then it became apparent that the train design potentially allowed riders to get their legs outside the car whilst in motion, so metal sections were hastily added to the sides to prevent any accidents, but added further discomfort for riders. These were eventually removed a few years into operation when new restraints could be fitted that blocked the movement of the legs.

Small gripes aside the ride was a hit with the public, and with word getting around about this rollercoaster unlike anything seen in the south of England before, attendance boomed.

Colossus certainly delivered the statement of intent that was desired and would become synonymous with the Thorpe Park experience for many years. Unfortunately, though the ride has not aged particularly well. The already uncomfortable trains gradually became rougher during the ride, causing many to experience something known as "headbanging", where your head quickly whacks the restraints either side of you. In addition, the cars quickly began making a loud screeching noise as they made their way round the track, equivalent to a tube train pulling into an underground station. Attempts were made by the maintenance team to try and find solutions to these, but the issues were not possible to completely resolve. Entering the 2020s the ride remains a more unpleasant experience than it once was, but still popular with the public.

The world record for most inversions was retained until Alton Towers installed *The Smiler* in 2013 which had an incredible 14. A near identical version of *Colossus* was purchased by Flamingo Land, North Yorkshire which was due to open in 2020 but delayed to the following year by the COVID-19 pandemic.

As other giants started to rise around the island, *Colossus*'s failings were to be further highlighted. Regardless it was a massive turning point, and the undisputed king of the park in 2002, but visitors were not going to have to wait long for a contender to its throne. Before that though, a new seasonal event was in the pipeline that would transform Thorpe Park's calendar for years to come.

Colossus as seen from the car park in 2020. Credit: Alex Rowe

FRIGHT NIGHTS

Chessington World of Adventures had been home to an annual *Fright Nights* event in the 1990s. It was an opportunity to give the park a boost at the end of the season, capitalising on the double whammy of Halloween and the October half-term school holidays. Awareness and popularity of the event had been growing for a number of years, and in line with the audience at the time, it tended to attract large groups of young people.

With Thorpe Park now very much aiming for a teen and young adult audience, *Fright Nights* made the switch across in 2002, leaving its former home at Chessington. Replacing it at the World of Adventure would be a more family friendly Halloween event called *Hocus Pocus* focusing more on pumpkins, magic and hay bales than full on frights. Family friendly characters with spooky connections were also introduced, such as *Scooby Doo*, and later a deal was struck for *Star Wars* shows. Meanwhile, the Fright Night event at Thorpe Park would focus on scaring the living daylights out of visitors, becoming one of the most successful moves in the history of the park.

Late night Halloween events at theme parks had become a big deal in the USA, with Universal Studios leading the way with their *Halloween Horror Nights* since 1991 (originally going under the same *Fright Nights* name). They had found success by adding a number of walk-through haunted house attractions to the line-up, alongside specially produced shows and roaming characters based on their feature films. Being filled to capacity has meant the events in Florida and California are each now over a month long, with the park open as usual during the day, and then transforming into *Halloween Horror Nights* for a different set of guests in the evening. It's a sensationally realised event of the highest quality, acclaimed for its creativity and professionalism.

Thorpe Park's new event would be in a similar vein, initially taking place over just four consecutive days from Thursday 31st October until Sunday 3rd November 2002, preceded by a fireworks event the previous weekend. Each night the rides would remain open until 9pm, with a number of scare zones introduced with roaming actors, and two walk-through mazes introduced specifically for *Fright Nights*. Promotional material for the new event was clear this was not for kids:

"Hideous, terrifying monsters will be around every ghostly corner…This petrifying fright-fest promises to scare the living daylights out of the most fearless"

One of the original mazes was called *The Freezer*, which unusually for this type of attraction was an actual maze that would require guests to work their way out. It was themed around an industrial freezer, complete with impressive large double doors at the entrance that emitted smoke each time they were opened to let a small group through. Roaming inside were a number of actors, usually well made-up to look like they had been frozen inside for a long time. Smoke and lighting effects were used alongside a number of mirrors to provide plenty of jumps. *The Freezer* was located at the back of *Ranger County*, with those who made it out alive exiting through the small theatre that hosted the *Thorpe Park Ranger* shows.

The other original maze was *Freakshow 3D*, located in the now unused long sections of *X:\ No Way Out's* indoor queue. As the name suggests visitors were required to wear a pair of 3D glasses throughout, which interacted with a number of paintings and set pieces. Groups of five or six would be asked to walk through together in a line, with their hands on the shoulders of the person in front. Each group's journey would begin with a stern reminder not to touch any of the actors, who were dotted around the attraction waiting to jump out and surprise guests. This is always incredibly effective, with the intense atmosphere including horror soundtrack creating a nerve-wracking environment.

The very first *Fright Nights* (for the first few years spelt *Fright Nites*) also included the *Fright Zone*, where actors would generally mix with visitors as they made their way through to their next adventure. The new event was an instant success, with crowds flocking to try out the new experience, and willing to wait in long lines to walk through the mazes. David McCubbin remembers the original event well:

"It was a completely different thing for us, so to have the *Fright Nights* was amazing. It was really, really successful so they immediately knew it would come back the following year"

By 2003 *Fright Nights* was expanded to a full week, with the closing time extended until 11pm, and the mazes returning. In addition a selection of clips from horror films was being shown in the *Pirates 4D* theatre under the title *Ultimate Horror Movie Bites*. This was less well received than the walk-through mazes, and was replaced just one year later in 2004 by *The Carnival of the Bizarre*, where circus style artists would interact with dangerous creatures and perform curious skills such as stretching skin and contortion. The show was performed by a travelling group called *The Circus of Horrors*, who toured the UK with their act year round, and would become a staple of *Fright Nights* for several years. There was also a less successful attempt at a scary movie created by the in-house team, called False Sense of Security. The film was due to be projected onto a large piece of material around *Ranger County*, but quickly caught the wind and blew down, maybe it was truly cursed.

The first shake up of the horror mazes took place in 2005, with the decision taken that after three years in action the original walk-throughs would be retired. The chilly *Freezer* theme was replaced by *The Asylum*, based on being trapped in a mental hospital, complete with patients in straightjackets ready to accost groups trying to make their way out. As the annual event grew in popularity, *The Asylum* became a huge favourite, returning a further eight times until 2013. Replacing *Freakshow 3D*, was the reassuringly two dimensional *Hellgate*, with the garish multi-coloured walls becoming the halls of an intimidating mansion. As the reputation of the event grew, more dates were added to accommodate the popularity, and by 2006 a third maze was added to spread out the crowds. The latest walk-through *Seven* was based around the deadly sins, located in the *Ranger County Arena* where the stunt and diving shows had once taken place.

Whilst effort was made to distinguish each different attraction, the basic premise of the mazes remained the same. Visitors would walk round an intimidating environment, with loud noises and disgusting scenes well placed to make everybody jump. The constant risk of a terrifyingly costumed actor jumping out at you cranks up the adrenaline, as does the regular screams echoing through the halls from other groups. The successful recipe was repeated with other additions such as *The Curse* (2008-2012), *Dead End Terror Zone* (2010), *Experiment 10* (2011-2012) and *The Passing* (2012). These are located creatively in otherwise underutilised spaces around the park.

Whilst a huge financial success for Thorpe Park, the event was not without its issues. *Fright Nights* tend to attract more trouble than the regular season, with frequent reports of anti-social behaviour. Management have responded with heavily increased security and checks, but at times the event has been tinged with a nasty intimidating atmosphere, and not the kind of exaggerated fun horror mood that is trying to be achieved. On a more practical note, much of the expanse used for the rides and attractions is not pre-prepared for opening in the dark. This means a large number of temporary lights and generators have to be brought in to safely operate.

On a more positive note *Fright Nights* tend to attract high profile guests, giving Thorpe Park precious column inches in the mainstream media. This is partly fuelled by their own PR, with an annual launch night now held with television stars and influencers invited to attend to help raise awareness, but often celebrities will attend on a normal day and try to keep a low profile. A mere snapshot of those who have been spotted at *Fright Nights* include (in no particular order) Kate Moss, John Boyega, Cara Delevingne, Maisie Williams, Katie Price, Michelle Keegan, Ant McPartlin, and of course Linda Robson. You can also seemingly hardly move for cast members of *The Only Way is Essex* or *Love Island*.

By 2013 *Fright Nights* were a core part of Thorpe Park's annual business, and the park was increasingly relying on the event to pull in the visitors to reach their hefty targets. Despite now offering five mazes in addition to the other rides, the popularity had seen capacity being hit on a regular basis, and the marketing team were focused on making the now month-long event a complete sell-out in advance. To help achieve their goals a deal was agreed with film company Lionsgate to license several of their horror film brands, which would be used to create a number of updated mazes. The new relationship saw walk-throughs for several years based on the feature films *The Cabin in the Woods, The Blair Witch Project,* and *My Bloody Valentine.* Following the end of this deal in 2017, a similar one was agreed to bring mazes based on the cult TV show *The Walking Dead* in to largely replace them.

Huge credit must go to the creative team behind all these temporary attractions, as the effort that goes into them is mightily impressive, often outdoing what's seen around the permanent attractions. Creating a good scare maze is an artform in itself, and the increased popularity of the concept across the world has seen a hardcore following develop who passionately discuss the many examples now operating across the globe. This extends to organisations who hold annual conventions, including *ScareCON* who issue annual awards to who they deem the best. Thorpe Park have picked up several awards over the years, as have Alton Towers, who have developed a slightly more family friendly annual Halloween event called *Scarefest.* Elsewhere the burgeoning industry has seen several other scare events become hugely popular, most notably *Shocktober Fest* at Tulleys Farm, which is located less than an hour's drive from Thorpe Park near Crawley in Sussex.

In recent years you can expect around six scare mazes at *Fright Nights,* including the additions of original creations such as the circus themed *The Big Top* (2015-18), and use of the discarded original rides in *Canada Creek* for *Platform 15* (2016 onwards) and *Creek Freek Massacre* (2019 onwards). To deal with the relentless crowds that now attend from late September onwards, some regular shows such as *Terror at Amity High* and *Screamplexx Cinema* have been on the line-up too. Thorpe Park have also dabbled with a pay extra option in the shape of an escape room called *Containment*, which has received strong reviews, but is only available to a small number of guests.

Fright Nights is now very much a staple of the Thorpe Park calendar, and account for a huge part of the annual ticket revenue, being almost as crucial as the summer holiday period. It's come a long way from its small four-night test event in 2002 that David McCubbin worked at[365]:

> "It has kind of taken over the park, it's such a huge part of the season now. It was such a tiny thing to begin with"

After *Colossus*, it was a second game-changing debut for Thorpe Park in 2002, and there wasn't going to be a long wait for the next, as another rollercoaster was rising on the horizon.

2003

Before *Colossus* had even finished construction, Tussauds were already preparing to double down on their investment, with the funds released to add a second major rollercoaster just twelve months later. Thorpe Park was receiving investment on an unprecedented scale in an attempt to banish the public preconceptions about it being somewhere for young children. Rumours suggested the next project would be situated on the abandoned area previously home to *Treasure Island*[366], but *Project Calypso* would instead sit on a space at the back of the park which had been partly damaged in the major 2000 fire.

Once again John Wardley was asked to work on the project, and would this time return to collaborate with a company that had already given them a trio of hits at Alton Towers, Bolliger & Mabillard. Commonly known as B&M. They specialised in high quality rollercoasters and had an exceptional reputation both in the industry and with enthusiasts. They were well known for designs that offered an extremely smooth ride experience, and a high level of reliability for parks. They were a premium option, but a safe bet for delivering something that would be a quality piece of work for years to come. Wardley had built up a great rapport with their founders, and the strong relationship had ensured Alton Towers got to debut several of their new design types, with both *Oblivion* and *Air* being world exclusives.

Keen to again offer something that would be both rare and make headlines, management asked for a stand-up coaster to be created[367]. One actually already existed in the UK, with Drayton Manor's *Shockwave* the lesser known launch in 1994 during the "Year of the Rollercoaster", and reviews were mixed at best. Stand-ups had been one of the earliest B&M specialities, but Wardley wasn't convinced. A small team travelled to test out various examples but were left sceptical at the ride experience, believing it offered nowhere near an enjoyable ride as you might expect. One of the problems was the comfort of passengers, which required you to balance on what was basically a saddle. Reluctantly accepting that standing probably wasn't the way forward, another look at the B&M range saw them come at the dilemma from a different angle.

Instead of looking for a new novelty, they could instead return to the inverted style that had given them a critical and financial hit in 1994 with *Nemesis*. The inverted coaster sees riders sit underneath the track with legs dangling free. It was also a safe bet with B&M having already sold and constructed 22 inverted rollercoasters in the previous ten years to rave reviews across the world. As well as the aforementioned beast in Staffordshire, high profile installations included the *Duelling Dragons* (later *Dragon Challenge*) at Islands of Adventure in Florida, and a series for Six Flags parks themed to the *Batman* franchise. Instead of concocting a new gimmick they would deliberately market this as a sequel playing off the success and acclaim of the original. Tussauds did have concerns that installing another inverted rollercoaster would detract from the Alton Towers ride, and also *The Vampire* at Chessington which had a similar seating style installed in 2002, but with Thorpe Park such a focus it felt warranted.

To help sell the *Nemesis* idea to the general public the marketing team were set on giving the new version an identical name, which upset Wardley[368]:

"I was absolutely horrified and asked them to seriously reconsider"

Nemesis was his masterpiece with a world-famous reputation, and he felt this should be something different altogether. After all, the name wasn't just evocative of the coaster model, it was the unique landscaping and layout that had set it apart from the competition. Eventually a compromise of sorts was agreed with the name *Nemesis Inferno* being locked in.

With a longer timescale available than *Colossus*, Wardley had the opportunity to design an original layout for the ride, featuring some elements that were proving popular on B&M's other inverted coasters. The journey would start from a raised position, a quirk Wardley enjoyed as it allowed a more efficient use of energy later in the ride. The starting height would allow the train to make the short drop straight out of the station and into action rather than immediately hitting the traditional lift hill. From here the train would directly enter a tunnel 95 feet long with some mild turns before reaching the lift to the maximum height. The layout from the top included a loop, inline twist and interlocking corkscrews. Additionally, a number of banked turns and helix at high speed would add to the thrills, with the layout spread over 2,500 feet.

Nemesis Inferno's loop being constructed in 2002. Credit: Thorpe Park Nostalgia

The theme developed for the new ride would be around a Caribbean volcano, with the train loosely representing the lava. The elevated station would be set inside the volcano itself, with a grand façade being created featuring fake rockwork, which guests would have to venture through to reach the loading bays. The tunnel the train passes through at the start would be enhanced by red lights, and mist machines. Seeing no issues with the plans Runnymede Borough Council gave permission for the project agreeing the maximum height of 95 feet tall, just shy of *Colossus*'s peak, was acceptable[369].

To accommodate *Nemesis Inferno*, *Mr Rabbit's Tropical Travels* were sadly over, after surviving a stay of execution after the fire in 2000. *Dino Boats* were made extinct, opening up the space required in the south west corner of the main island. Clearing of the area started late in 2001, and by the time the park opened with *Colossus* for the 2002 season, the next big thing was already being promised on banners and on the park map. Never to be accused of modesty, the marketing team had decided to promise "The world's greatest coaster experience" was set to arrive[370].

Andy Nicholls was again responsible for the surrounding landscaping, and bought into the concept adding a number of touches to really bring the Caribbean atmosphere to Staines. Like *Colossus* there was plenty of opportunity for visitors to see and walk round every aspect of the coaster. This wasn't a surprise hidden inside a building, you knew what you were signing up for before joining the queue. Due to their proximity the new rollercoaster and *Rumba Rapids* would form a colourful new area of the park called *Calypso Quay*, giving somewhat more justification to the rapids bright makeover the previous year.

By August 2002 the fiery red metalwork had arrived, with installation starting shortly after. B&M's chunky track is known for eliciting a distinctive roaring sound as the train navigates the course, so to reduce the potential of complaints from local residents some sections were filled with sand which dampens the noise somewhat. Soon the name was also revealed, causing some predictable hysteria in the enthusiast community. By the 18th of October the last piece of track was put into place, and the project was well on schedule to open the following spring. The top piece was added to the impressive volcano structure in time for the inaugural *Fright Night* event, with lights added around the project site in order to show off the new addition, working as the perfect advert to the thrill-seeking audience, and whetting their appetite for what was to follow. The *Fireworks Spectacular* was also used as a marketing tool, with rockets and lasers being fired from a replica volcano floating in the lake, teasing the new attraction.

Nemesis Inferno half complete. Credit: Thorpe Park Nostalgia

As with other inverted coasters (and *Vortex*) a special lowering floor would be installed in the station. When raised to usual floor height this allows riders to easily board and disembark the ride vehicle. Once in place, and the over the shoulder restraints locked down, the floor then lowers from beneath riders to ensure their legs dangle rather than being dragged along the ground. The station would also be fitted with an impressive sound system, capable of pumping out a specially composed soundtrack featuring deep bass sounds triggered when each train leaves. Bespoke wheel coverings featuring flames were added to the trains, making them look really rather smart.

With the rapid transformation of the park showing no signs of slowing, *Nemesis Inferno* wouldn't be the only new attraction to debut in 2003. Two other rides were being added, provided by *Detonator* manufacturer

Fabbri. Both would be located in the *Lost City* section near the main entrance. *Quantum* was a minor thrill ride, basically a smaller version of the "magic carpet" style attraction that had been in operation at Chessington and Alton Towers in the late 1980s. Its basic motion propelled riders, who sat opposite each other in several rows, forward and backwards in a circular motion half a dozen times. It was a pretty unremarkable addition but added another option for visitors and possibly soaked up some people from other nearby queues. Some nice theming and finishing touches were added to hide its more traditional fairground origins, including a gyroscope in the centre of the ride vehicle. Although some of the features added to the far ends of the gondola had to be removed shortly after opening as they were deemed unsafe.

Quantum's entrance sign. Credit: Alex Rowe

The other addition was a peculiar one. *Eclipse* was an 82 foot tall traditional Ferris wheel which seemed to go against Thorpe Park's new thrill-centric image. It offered people a gentle ride, with some views of other attractions from above, as well as an excellent view of the car park opposite. With interest low from visitors, *Eclipse* was only to last for two seasons before taking the short 16 kilometre journey to Chessington, where it would stand in the same spot the *Magic Carpet* once did in the

Mystic East section, being re-named *Peking Heights*. Apparently the original name requested to management of the *Peking Eye* was rejected due to similarities with the *London Eye*.

Eclipse under construction. Credit: Thorpe Park Nostalgia

Undoubtably though, the main addition for 2003 was to be the shiny new B&M rollercoaster on the other side of the park. Before Christmas the trains had been delivered and completed their first complete circuit of the track, signalling everything was on time. Marketing of the new ride stepped up with a press release playing up the connection with the original stating[371]:

"One of the world's hottest roller coasters just got hotter"

&

"One of the world's top ten roller coasters PLUS volcanic effects and theming"

The wording used seemed to be suggesting that *Nemesis Inferno* would be even more intense than the original:

"...turns the awesome original suspended coaster into a seriously white hot thrill. With all the gut wrenching, raw adrenaline of Alton Towers' legendary *Nemesis*, *Nemesis Inferno's* volcanic theming and effects turn it into a scorching, feet free, legs-dangling experience that gives new meaning to 'hot footing it'!"

The official opening was set for Saturday 5th April, with the usual media and passholder *Premier Screaming* event taking place shortly beforehand. Early reactions were extremely positive, with admiration for Thorpe Park pulling off the installation of two such significant rides in successive years. There was some criticism of the seemingly irrelevant connection to *Nemesis*, with others feeling that it was enthralling but the intensity overegged. It was one the last additions during David McCubbin's time, and he instantly knew it was another winner[372]:

"There was a lot of hype at the time about the ride starting up in the air, and the drop into the volcano. I thought it was a brilliant ride. I think it's a fantastic ride and very different to *Nemesis* at Alton Towers, and I really like the volcano aspect. It's just a shame there are so many comparisons with the original"

The drop out of the station into the tunnel. Credit: Alex Rowe

Opening on time, and for an estimated cost of £8,000,000 the new addition was a hit. The classy B&M manufacturing worked seamlessly, and offered riders a comfortable and thrilling experience, plus it achieves the classic Wardley trait of getting better as it goes on. The final two helixes arranged in a figure-of-eight, able to pack just as much of a punch as the first drop. Having a Bolliger & Mabillard coaster in Surrey that everybody over 1.4 metres tall could ride was a real coup for Thorpe Park, and showed that it valued quality, not just gimmicks. You'd have to think that this is a ride, that if Tim Hartwright could see sitting on the site of his original concept, he'd be pretty delighted with.

The interlocking corkscrews. Credit: Alex Rowe

The distinctive tunnel at the start that the train drops straight into looked wonderful when combined with the effects. However, during the early days of operation it was clear the mist could be too powerful at times, with the blowback from the trains managing to cover much of the surrounding area in a haze! Thankfully this was one issue that was easy enough to fix.

As you leave the ride there is an absurdly long walk to get out, the pretence of being inside a volcano is abandoned as you are led out the back door of a shell structure to a metal walkway. Several minutes of walking and about 200 feet later you reach the classic ride photo booth and merchandise shop, which in turn eventually kicks you out by *Mr.*

Monkey's Banana Ride. Documents show this was a late change, with an exit originally planned near the volcano. However, the building eventually used for the shop already existed, so this was presumably a good way to save budget and re-use an existing structure.

In the years since its introduction, *Nemesis Inferno* has aged well. It has been an incredibly reliable ride, continuing to rate well with guests visiting the park despite two decades in operation. Very little has changed, mainly because there has been no need, which is a credit to all involved. The plants around the area have swelled helping to sustain the pleasant aesthetic. The volcano itself is surprisingly resilient, but the mist is rarely used which takes something away from the experience.

In May 2004 Thorpe Park decided to utilise the ride for its latest publicity stunt[373]. After already owning one certificate from Guinness to celebrate the record breaking ten inversions on *Colossus,* they were out to earn another. This time students were enlisted as part of rag week to try and set a new record for most naked people on a rollercoaster. Unfortunately, the day of the attempt saw rather chilly weather, but they succeeded, although this has now been surpassed several times. Then in 2008 British viewers of a certain age would have seen *Nemesis Inferno* (and Thorpe Park as a whole) feature in a typically funny and cringeworthy episode of the sitcom *The Inbetweeners*[374]. The ride is a core part of the plot where Will gets into an argument over riding in the front seats.

Nemesis Inferno is undeniably the lesser of the UK's B&M inverted coasters, but it doesn't stop it being a hugely successful in its own right. *Inferno* likely suffers from the name association with the original, but the marketing opportunities of linking the two, with the brand perception goals that Thorpe Park were trying to achieve, makes the decision understandable. From, a business point of view, if not a creative one.

The original *Nemesis* was closed at the end of 2022 to receive a complete re-track, likely extending its life for another few decades. If *Inferno* has the same expected lifespan, Thorpe Park will have a decision to make around keeping it in 2030.

Detonator, with Nemesis Inferno's loop behind. Credit: Alex Rowe

2004

The gamble on the massive outlays was proving to do the trick, with a huge number of new visitors discovering the once relaxed leisure attraction, now home to two world class rollercoasters. After investing over £20 million in a short period, there would understandably be a more affordable addition in 2004.

Chessington World of Adventures had introduced *Samurai* in 1999 to rave reviews. It was a *Top Scan* ride manufactured by Dutch company Mondial who specialised in flat rides for amusement parks and travelling fairs. A *Top Scan* is possibly best described as a giant whisk, with a large support arm spawning six smaller gondolas where riders are seated with their legs hanging. The support can spin in a circular motion, taking riders up to 62 feet in the air, with the smaller gondolas also being able to independently spin a full 360 degrees. This results in an unpredictable and highly thrilling ride experience lasting a couple of minutes and producing g-force of up to plus four and minus three.

Whilst queueing for the ride in Chessington's *Mystic East* area, signs would claim that you would get a unique ride every single time. This was to an extent true, as although the ride predominantly ran on a number of pre-set programmes, the spinning of the gondolas was dictated by the velocity of the ride's movement, and weight of the riders in each. This meant you could be turned upside down and thrown in different directions a completely different amount each time. The most thrilling seats were of course the outside of the five in each gondola, as this would fling you the furthest distance.

Despite the success of the ride at Chessington, Tussauds deemed that *Samurai* was a better fit for the new thrill-centric image they were trying to portray down the road at Thorpe Park. Therefore, in the summer of 2003 signage started to appear around Thorpe Park promoting that "an intense thrill ride" would be coming the following year, alongside an unmistakable picture of the ride from their sister park. *Samurai* was one of the jewels in Chessington World of Adventures crown at the time, so the removal of the ride was a surprise, even taking into account their attempts to become less thrill-centric.

Samurai in action at Thorpe Park. Credit: Alex Rowe

The new addition at Thorpe would be taking the place of the *Calgary Stampede*, which occupied a similar sized footprint, now wedged between *Colossus* and *Loggers Leap*. It had been one of the most extreme rides Thorpe Park had to offer in the 90s, but as the park progressed it no longer had a place. Transition of *Samurai* would be reasonably simple, unlike a major rollercoaster there would not need to be months of groundwork, footers and construction. With some basic preparation you can position a ride of this nature into your chosen spot quite easily.

Before that happened though *Samurai* would be sent for a service and paint job to fit into its new home. Whilst the public perception would be that the ride had simply made the 25 minute trip down the road between seasons, it had actually been sent all the way to Holland where Mondial would completely strip it apart and totally refurbish the five year old ride. Gone was the distinctive red and black, to be replaced with the generic *Lost City* colour scheme. The allocation into the *Lost City* area was a peculiar one, as *Calgary Stampede* had always appropriately sat in the *Canada Creek* area of the park. The look of a *Top Scan* is inherently saw like, making it a perfect fit next to the existing log flume, especially as the other *Lost City* flat rides were a fair walk away. Nevertheless, the ride would be the same regardless of the themed area it sat in, all that was required was the new name.

Some consideration was given to what this new name might be, but the decision was made to keep *Samurai*, even though this really didn't fit into the *Lost City* theme. For the second time in consecutive years the brand association with another Tussauds park was deemed preferable to something more fitting. The obvious benefit of keeping the *Samurai* name was the opportunity to convert fans of the ride from Chessington. In the days before social media, news like this travelled slowly, so unless you were a theme park enthusiast this would not have been on your radar. The easiest way to send the message that *Samurai* had moved to Thorpe Park, was therefore to call it *Samurai*. After all, if it looks, swims and quacks like a duck, it probably is a duck.

The refurbished *Samurai* opened for the 2004 season in its new home, although with understandably less fanfare than had welcomed *Colossus* and *Nemesis Inferno*. The ride was a modest hit and added another high-quality thrill ride to the quickly expanding line up. With the popularity of the park rising, it also helped spread out the crowds, reducing some of the queues elsewhere. Like all rides of this nature it does have its limitations. It can hold thirty riders at a time, but with loading riders, checking bars etc the number of riders per hour can be limited, and the queue slow moving. The safety measures in place also cause it to shut down and be reset sporadically, which can cause further delays.

It is a popular belief that since the transfer between the parks, *Samurai* has been less extreme, which seems generally warranted. The ride can be set to different pre-programmed routines of various intensities, so it can fluctuate, but the belief is that the less explosive options are now recommended. This reportedly helps reduce the wear and tear, helping to minimise downtime. Travelling versions of the *Top Scan* also offer a manual programme option, where the operator can choose to control the ride themselves, although if this is available at Thorpe Park, it is rarely used.

At the time of writing *Samurai* is still standing strong. Parts have been sent back periodically to Mondial for refurbishment and the aging attraction has experienced a few periods out of action whilst it required maintenance, but nothing out of the ordinary. It did eventually get an official move out of *Lost City*, however this was just in designation on maps etc, and no aesthetic changes were made to the ride. The *Top Scan* really is a top-quality flat ride, offering extreme thrills within a reasonably small package. Something that Thorpe Park would try to replicate again soon after, with mixed results...

2005

There was to be no let-up in Thorpe Park's race to add as many thrills as possible, with Tussauds allocating additional budget to purchase another two high adrenaline rides for the 2005 season.

Utah based S&S Worldwide, named after founder Stan and his wife Sandy, had begun life in the early 1990s creating bounce-based sports equipment such as trampolines and bungee experiences. They quickly diversified into air powered amusement park rides. Their *Space Shot* model which fired riders up a tall tower had quickly become a favourite in the United States and around the world, which had led to Thorpe Park planning to install one before the hasty addition of *Detonator*. By the late nineties two had been installed in the United Kingdom, at Blackpool Pleasure Beach and Fantasy Island. High profile examples also appeared at Universal's Islands of Adventure in Florida, and a vertigo inducing version at the top of the Stratosphere in Las Vegas. S&S had been busy developing new prototypes to diversify their product range and invited a Tussauds project team out to their factory to see their progress[375].

On the visit they were one of the first to try out a new concept called the *Screamin' Swing*, which they already had a working eight seat prototype for. The premise of the ride was simple, riders are strapped into a giant version of your traditional playpark swings, and propelled fast and high in the classic S&S way by compressed air. The safety harness was minimal, holding you in by the waist rather than the more intrusive over the shoulder restraints seen on many other thrill rides. This combined with your legs swinging free, left riders feeling delightfully exposed, with more freedom than they were accustomed to on a high velocity attraction. As this was just a prototype, it was promised that bigger, faster and higher capacity models could be provided to suit the needs of the park if required.

Alongside this S&S had a couple of other new concepts that had been revealed in 2002, but yet to build momentum amongst buyers. The first was a revolutionary new rollercoaster type called the *Screaming Squirrel*.

This was designed for parks with little room to play with. The idea saw riders seemingly reaching the end of a straight piece of track, only to go over the edge and continue underneath it. It was compared to a classic wild mouse rollercoaster, but with the usual sharp turns at the top turned vertically.

The other concept was called a *Sky Swatter* and was garnering a lot of attention from theme park enthusiasts. This machine looked like a giant set of scales, or seesaw, with 24 riders (18 on the prototype) sitting either side to balance it out. This was then raised high into the air by two supporting towers, and then the two ends allowed to flip over the top of each other, turning riders completely upside down. It seemed quite a slow machine when watching from afar, but whilst riding it packed a punch despite S&S peculiarly promoting it as a family thrill ride.

Management approved the acquisition of both a *Screamin' Swing* and *Sky Swatter* for Thorpe Park. Only one park in the world, Six Flags AstroWorld in Houston, already owned the latter so this striking new concept would be a European first. Knott's Berry Farm in California had introduced a version of the *Screamin' Swing* at the end of the previous year, but as a low capacity upcharge attraction. The full size 32-person version arriving at Thorpe Park in 2005 would be a world's first.

With *Eclipse* departing after a short spell in the *Lost City*, a perfect sized footprint for the *Screamin' Swing* opened up, which was labelled *Rush*. Located close to *Vortex*, *Zodiac* and *Quantum*; this would add another thrilling flat ride to the area.

The *Sky Swatter* would need a larger area to operate, and a space in a previously underutilised spot where part of *Trappers Trail* once stood behind *X:\ No Way Out* was identified. Accessed through the *Canada Creek* area of the park it would become known as *Slammer*, complete with a fiery logo that evoked a somewhat Lord of the Rings feel, the trilogy of films having just been completed at the time.

Construction of the new S&S rides largely took place during the period the park was closed after the 2004 season[376]. *Slammer* was up and running by the end of March as the park was gearing up for the busy Easter weekend. It was met with lukewarm reviews, including *Theme Park Insider*[377] writing:

"With a max height of 105 feet and a top speed of 30mph, it isn't exactly the best ride for those new to the wonderful world of flat rides. But for those of us looking for a pretty intense thrill, it shapes up quite nicely"

Coaster Kingdom's well written review was also a mixed bag for the new addition[378]:

"The *Sky Swat* looks great. Well... kinda. You see, while it looks great in terms of majesty, it is a very, very ugly ride"

"So, is Slammer everything we could possibly want from a spin ride? Definitely not. It is better than you'd expect from a looping machine, and a meaty addition to Thorpe's line up, but we will have to see whether or not it maintains popularity"

Rush however was proving more problematic, and delays meant some last minute headaches and problems to be solved by the project team during the testing phase. This larger version developed by S&S would have two swings operating at the same time and moving in opposite directions. It would also reach heights of 72 feet in the air by propelling you over 40 miles per hour[379]. International specialists Ride Entertainment Group were brought in to assist, with an opening date eventually set for Friday 27th May, two months after *Slammer*.

For the launch of *Rush* the marketing team played up the simplicity of the ride's concept, proudly presenting it as "the world's largest swing" and having adults dressed as schoolchildren welcoming the first visitors[380]. Teething problems struck though as the ride broke down minutes after the grand launch, as problems that had arisen during the testing process, persisted.

Teething problems were to continue, but reliability did improve. The feedback from riders was generally positive, albeit with many criticising the relatively short ride time, with the swings only reaching full height a few times before quickly slowing down and becoming stationary. When in motion the ride would make a distinctive loud whooshing noise, caused by the compressed air used to propel it.

Rush at close to full swing. Credit: Alex Rowe

As with many rides that are the first of their kind, it would suffer some issues, and at times queues would build due to one of the two large swings being out of action, halving its capacity. Some felt that the thrills offered didn't match up to those on Thorpe Park's other recent acquisitions, but most complemented the ride experience and saw it as a solid addition to the rapidly evolving theme park. It did hit some minor headlines in 2008 when a piece of the ride fell from near the top, hitting the swing and landing nearby[381]. Nobody was hurt, but changes were made to ensure maintenance could be conducted more thoroughly, leaving *Rush* closed for weeks.

With the flurry of new rides having a positive impact on the attendance figures, a couple of extra seasonal activities were also introduced. *Stuntz Mania*, a show in the *Ranger County Arena* where "wacky and funky stunts"[382] would be performed. These included circus skills such as the "space wheel", and motorbikes performing 360 loops inside a cage. The second was the *PlayStation 2 Freedom Weekender* between 1st and 4th September. This combined the chance to try out the computer games console, followed by live performances from high profile bands such as Faithless, Feeder, and Razorlight[383]. The new attractions, big events, and odd news story saw the awareness of Thorpe Park amongst the general public rise sharply, and 2006 would see that skyrocket further.

The *Screamin' Swing* would go on to be a modest success for S&S, especially in the US where approximately a dozen have been installed. Most are still in operation, along with Rush which still emits the distinctive swooshing noise all these years later.

The *Sky Swat* concept would be less successful. Despite much excitement and positivity amongst the industry, S&S failed to ever sell another model to a theme park, and the product was officially discontinued in 2010. Six Flags New England, that had taken possession of the only other one produced, closed their version in 2013, leaving *Slammer* as the only operating version in the world at the time.

What happened to *Slammer* at Thorpe Park? It had a difficult existence having some severe maintenance issues, being out of action for long periods, and causing headaches for the maintenance team. Engineers battled against the issues with limited success, but the consensus was the design was fundamentally flawed. Over many years they struggled to fight the issues with different facets causing concerns about safety and reliability. This might go a long way to explaining why the *Sky Swat* failed to get much momentum elsewhere. After long closures each season, most notably in 2013 where the ride was removed from the website and signage taken down, *Slammer* was eventually officially swatted from Thorpe Park's line-up in May 2017[384], killing off the world's last remaining *Sky Swat*.

2006

With attendance numbers and awareness soaring, Tussauds were confident their ambitious masterplan to transform Thorpe Park was working. This helped untie the purse strings once again, with a third major rollercoaster in the pipeline and set to open in 2006. The persistent desire to finance the once ailing park was exciting for all involved.

The planning team continued to keep their eyes on the latest developments in ride technology, and across the pond previous collaborators Intamin were starting to hit the headlines again. Their new concept known as a *Rocket*, or *Accelerator Coaster* had first been installed at Knott's Berry Farm in 2002 to great acclaim. This powerful launched rollercoaster fired riders off at over 80 miles per hour, and straight upwards into a 200-foot vertical climb. After a 90-degree twist, the train coasts over a "top hat" element, before gravity sends everybody hurtling down the vertical drop the other side. The original called *Xcelerator* then completed a couple of high-speed banked turns, before strongly breaking and returning riders to the station. The whole experience is quick, over in 25 seconds, but packs an exhilarating punch and is visually spectacular.

Whilst the journey to opening *Xcelerator* at Knott's Berry Farm in 2002 had some hiccups, the end result was enough for other orders to come in. Cedar Point in Ohio was known for its wide selection of coasters and was in a continuous battle with its rivals such as Six Flags Magic Mountain to be known as the rollercoaster capital of the world. The hydraulic launch system used on Intamin's new product opened up the exciting prospect of going higher and faster more efficiently, which they were keen to take advantage of. They decided to plant a massive punch on their opposition by using the fledgling Intamin technology to break the world records for both speed and height on a coaster. *Top Thrill Dragster* would open in 2003, boasting a sensational top speed of 120 miles per hour, and a maximum height of 420 feet. That's approximately the height of the *London Eye*, and whilst the capsule on that takes fifteen minutes to get to the top, this would be roughly ten seconds from a stationary position.

By this time Thorpe Park had a much stronger relationship with the planning department at Runnymede council, with development proposals submitted roughly every five years. These were general outlines of how the park would like to develop in the future. These plans don't give them permission to go ahead and build necessarily, but offers both parties a chance to scope out any potential issues, saving time and money on expensive design and planning applications down the line. Permission had been given for plenty of new attractions, all of which had been kept under a ceiling height of around 100 feet tall so they didn't significantly impact the skyline. When it came to the next plan they were going to push that, asking for one off permission to build an iconic new rollercoaster for the park, twice the height of anything previously on the site.

The Intamin *Rocket* was the obvious way to go, but before committing John Wardley and Glenn Earlam took a trip to Knott's Berry Farm to try the original out for themselves[385]. After experiencing *Xcelerator* first hand Wardley created an elaborate layout for a Thorpe Park version, with a substantial amount of track after the showpiece top hat element. His track configuration was designed to make the best use of the speed and momentum created by the massive launch, feeling that blasting into the brakes at high speed was a terrible waste of energy. Confident that this would likely be the best of its type on the planet, Wardley remembers submitting the idea to be considered internally:

"The news came back that the plans were too expensive, and they wanted a much more basic design. I was so disappointed. This would have been a world beater"

A much-simplified proposal was put together and by late 2004 a full application to bring a *Rocket* coaster to Surrey, codenamed *Project Stealth*, was put to Runnymede council[386]. Despite being scaled back it was still set to be the fastest rollercoaster of any type in Europe, hitting over 80 miles per hour, and topping out at a height of 205 feet. However, Blackpool Pleasure Beach would keep the height record, with the *Big One* standing just eight feet higher. Although a substantial layout would have been incredible, the real thrill of this coaster is the powerful launch and phenomenal height you reach so quickly. It was definitely going to be something rather special.

Surprisingly, *Stealth* would not be the first Intamin *Rocket* coaster to launch in the UK, as Tussauds had struck a deal to also bring a version of the ride to Alton Towers. *Rita: Queen of Speed* was being fast-tracked to open in 2005, and the name wasn't the only peculiar thing about it. Due to Alton Tower's strict height restrictions the ride would forfeit the usual top hat element, and instead stick much lower to the ground, making high speed tight turns close to the park's iconic *Corkscrew* ride. The launch speed would be a nippy 60 miles per hour, but only ever reach 60 feet high. It was a certainly a thrill, but *Rita* was without doubt the little sister of the pair.

To make way for *Project Stealth*, an extensive amount of space would be needed, and that meant saying goodbye to a couple of classics at the end of 2004. The last part of *Model World*, one of the few surviving originals from the 1979 opening, was removed. Also making way was one of Thorpe Park's 90s icons, *The Flying Fish*. Significantly the waterbus service to *Thorpe Farm* was also stopped, with the jetty previously being accessed through *Model World*, now blocked. The *Canada Creek Railway* would be the only transport to the farm now. Surprisingly one feature that still remains to this day is the *Sunken Garden* area that was located right next to *Model World*. This space is not advertised, and is a little fiddly to find, but offers a moment of respite for those who need it, although you'd be hard pressed to claim it was peaceful due to its proximity to other rides. The landscaping team who care for it have always done a fantastic job, and it's obvious they still take great pride in caring for this little spoken of corner of the park.

Plans for *Project Stealth's* site revealed it would be designated inside a new extension of the *Amity* area of the park, which was so terrifically realised for *Tidal Wave*. The new part would be themed around a fifties or sixties style racetrack. As part of this an impressive sized grandstand was to be built alongside the launch track, which ingeniously would double as the queue for waiting riders. Unfortunately, this clever set-piece was to get the chop, to be replaced with a more traditional floor level winding line. Many of the other planned retro American decorations remained however, including the rollercoaster trains themselves being hot rod cars. Original plans for the area would also see another thrilling flat ride added in the space underneath the main top hat, but this was eventually deemed unnecessary.

As was usual by this point, much debate and speculating happened online about what name would be given to this new icon of the park, with much conjecture about *Hot Rod* or *Burnout*. Two names were under very serious consideration at different times in the project, with a decision being delayed until very late in the day. The plan was to name the attraction either *The Edge* or *Johnny Rocket*, with the former close to being confirmed. Concerns were raised during the project about clashes with brands of similar names. *Johnny Rocket* would have been the ideal fit for the tone and theme, but potentially the restaurant chain of the same name was the stumbling block. Eventually, and quite underwhelmingly, it was decided that the project name would do just fine, and was kept as the final name of the attraction.

Construction on *Stealth* began a year before the planned opening[387], with the land previously taken up by *Model World* and the *Flying Fish* cleared and flattened. This left the space required running from the far side of *Tidal Wave*, to the *Rumba Rapids*. David Jones, who had been the engineer in charge of installing *Rita* at Alton Towers the year before, was again called upon to oversee *Stealth*[388]. Whilst the layouts of each ride varied greatly, there were many similarities between the construction of the two. Most obviously the hydraulic system required to launch the coaster at great speed, which is housed at the end of the launch track.

Many of the launched rollercoasters from the twentieth century used linear induction motors (LIM) on the track to speed them up, which use an enormous amount of power. The Intamin technology mostly takes place in the innocuous building at the end of the launch track. Inside are two large tanks containing 14,000 litres of hydraulic oil. Through the force of three enormous hydraulic pumps, the oil makes its way into numerous nitrogen accumulator tanks which pressurises the nitrogen inside to 50,000 PSI. Eventually a valve opens, forcing the fluid into 24 powerful motors, which in turn power a winch drum. Attached to the winch is a rather long and strong cable, that in turn is attached to the ride car about 25 metres away. The cable pulls the rollercoaster car at great speed for 18 metres, before releasing it to complete its circuit.

The entrance to Stealth. Credit: Alex Rowe

Not being an engineer, I can't pretend to fully understand all of the above paragraph intricately, but put simply a large cable uses hydraulics to catapult the rollercoaster forward. Many of those queueing for *Rita* or *Stealth* assume the multiple large metal parts on the track that lower quite loudly just before each launch are part of what propels the ride forward. These are in fact just a safety feature, as they are magnetic brakes. On occasions despite the hefty launch, the train will not have enough momentum to make it over the highest point, in *Stealth*'s case the top hat element. If you have ever watched or ridden *Stealth* you'll notice it crests the highest point at quite a slow speed. This is deliberate, as you wouldn't want to be flung over the top at high velocity, it would be a deeply unpleasant experience. This means that on rare occasions, usually due to an extreme gust of wind or a brake popping up too quickly, the ride will make it nearly over the top but not have enough momentum to make to the other side. Gravity kicks in, and the ride starts to return where it came from, falling backwards. This was exactly what happened on Wardley and Earlam's visit to Knott's Berry Farm, with the pair granted permission to ride before park opening. The train failed to make it over the top and started tumbling backwards. Not aware of the system at the time, Wardley had a fright[389]:

"I had no idea this was supposed to happen, it's the only time I have been genuinely scared on a rollercoaster. The staff were very casual and said it happens at the start of the day all the time, I just wished they had told me!"

To stop the car returning to the station and smashing into the next load of unsuspecting riders, the magnetic breaks automatically ease everyone to a gentle stop. It's an incredibly safe and reliable system. These so-called "rollbacks" are incredibly rare, but do happen sporadically, especially on *Rocket* coasters with top hat elements. In fact, many enthusiasts are desperate to experience one, seeing it as a badge of honour.

The first few months of construction were mainly taken up with the usual ground preparation, including creating footers and foundations, but with little to see for curious guests who were being promised a new rollercoaster for 2006 on the park map. Construction of track itself started in September 2005, and quickly rose high into the sky. The scale of this new ride was suddenly apparent, towering over the Thorpe Park skyline, and visible not just from every part of the park, but from miles around. The ground level track was navy, but the colour transitioned to white as it rose into the sky, possibly to limit the impact from a distance. The final part of the track, the distinctive top hat element 200 feet high, was put into place by a giant crane on 26th September.

Stealth with the train cresting over the top. Credit: Alex Rowe

Unmissable to guests who visited for the remainder of the season, including those attending *Fright Nights*, *Stealth* was the perfect advert for itself. To help with the promotion giant lights were installed to illuminate the intimidating top hat. Advertising throughout the year had also used giant charts to illustrate the height compared to Thorpe Park's other rides such as *Nemesis Inferno* and *Tidal Wave*, with *Stealth* rising high out of the billboard due to its unrivalled altitude. With a decision on the name being delayed, no branding was ready, so a generic slogan of "Are you ready to scream?" was used instead alongside specs of the ride.

As work continued to test the complicated ride systems, another team were busy bringing the *Amity* theming to life, including an enormous car tyre that would signal the entrance to the queue. The popular *WWTP Radio* was back with a new selection of catchy pop classics from the likes of *Buddy Holly* and *The Beach Boys*, plus of course those memorable presenters like Big Bob. Grand prix style lights above the station helped build anticipation before each launch, along with light smoke machines that are supposed to replicate tyres burning. The area inside the rides circuit was paved to create a kind of public piazza, with distinctive American style corporate logos added to buildings and carefully weathered to add an aged feel. Away from *Stealth* work was also going on at the entrance to the car park, where the previously mundane gates were having a makeover. Giant pieces of fake rollercoaster track similar to the corkscrews on *Colossus* were added ensuring the feel of the park was unmistakeable from the moment you arrive.

Testing of *Stealth* was underway in early 2006. During the construction process the team had embraced some modern marketing methods, and had featured a developer's diary throughout the process[390], showing off their new baby as it grew in size. With things seemingly on track the next stages of the promotion kicked in, including offering fans the opportunity to be ride testers, and experience *Stealth* weeks before the gates to the park would officially open. Thousands entered for the chance to win, but the latter stages of testing the ride was showing up some problems. The delays were causing headaches for the promotion of the ride, and with the project falling behind, there was no guarantee Stealth would be ready for the new season.

After some hectic late testing and training of staff, Stealth did hit the deadline of opening along with the rest of Thorpe Park for the new season on Wednesday 15th March 2006. Those who had won the competition to be the first to ride had the promise honoured, and although it was only moments before other guests, they were the first members of the public to experience *Stealth*. On the same day the park experienced a major power cut knocking many attractions out of action, but thankfully *Stealth* was not impacted to the joy of those who had travelled specifically to experience it.

Keen to get creative, the PR team asked Father Michael Hereward-Rothwell from St Mary's Church in Thorpe to come along and bless the new ride, which he happily did in front of the assembled media[391]. From the off, riders were enthusing about the sensational experience of riding *Stealth* with early reviews of the £12 million project extremely positive, including *Theme Park Insider*[392]:

"*Stealth* is easily the best ride at Thorpe Park. Many people are put off of it purely because of the height, and the fact it lasts roughly 15 seconds. They don't know what they are missing"

Many citied the launch, top hat, and final bunny hop as all massively enjoyable. It might be a short ride, lasting only a matter of seconds, but it didn't seem to be putting people off.

The park had banked on this being a big hit, so a DJ station was added in the centre of the queue to entertain crowds who might have to wait two hours or more to take their turn. Despite the short length two trains were in action, with separate station areas for those boarding and disembarking to increase the capacity. The new attraction was doing the business the park wanted, with capacity for the entire park being reached on Easter Sunday, and visitors turned away when over 15,000 tried to get in[393].

Those who were getting to ride *Stealth* were raving about the experience, however many visitors who flocked to try it out in the early days were left disappointed due to a number of closures. The explosive hydraulic launch was the main culprit, with engineers working hard to limit the glut of issues from which *Stealth* suffered. Counterparts from Alton Towers who had experience working on *Rita* were called in to help get operations working consistently. This wasn't a problem unique to *Stealth*, with many Intamin *Rocket* coasters suffering hiccups, including launch cables snapping.

The following year many of the teething problems had been ironed out, and *Stealth* had apparently received a slight upgrade to now launch to 80 miles per hour in under two seconds. In the years since it has remained temperamental at times, but still a huge favourite with visitors. The scale of the ride, and its appeal to the public, can only position it as a huge success. Another enormous investment by Tussauds had paid off, and Thorpe Park's popularity was at an all-time high.

After initially being a hugely lucrative model, the Intamin *Rocket/Accelerator* rollercoasters reached their peak during that decade, with a total of 15 being built being 2002 and 2010. The largest of which, *Kingda Ka* in New Jersey's Six Flags Great Adventure, still holds the world record for tallest rollercoaster in the world at 456 feet. More recently the craze for this model has quelled with only one further installation opening in the last decade.

The hydraulic launch system used by these models continues to be problematic, with linear synchronous motor (LSM) launches now preferred for newer styles of rollercoaster. Some older Intamin models are now having their launches retrospectively switched from hydraulic to LSM, with every chance *Stealth* might be updated in the future.

2007

With a procession of new and ingenious high adrenaline attractions making their way to Thorpe Park, they were now promoting themselves as the nation's "thrill capital"[394]. The demographic of the visitors had been shifting drastically, and in fact if anything the transformation of audience had been even more dramatic than initially thought possible. A little concerned that groups of teens and young adults alone were not enough, Tussauds still wanted to ensure that families with children who were maybe slightly too old for Chessington World of Adventures, still had a place at Thorpe Park. It was mixed messages possibly, but like any theme park, pulling in revenue dictates the next move.

Therefore, after sitting in storage for a couple of years, the classic old favourite *Flying Fish* would be making a return for the 2007 season. There were rumours that buyers were being sought for the still working attraction after its removal for the *Stealth* project, but with no nibbles the fish remained ready to be called back into action. Once the highest adrenaline ride at Thorpe Park when installed in 1984 as *Space Station Zero*, it now fitted the bill when seeking something additional for the family market.

With the spaces previously taken up by this classic Mack ride now occupied by *Stealth* and a KFC, another location between *Tidal Wave* and *Depth* Charge was found. Effort was put into revitalising the coaster, including a new train that replaced the classic green fish with a bright orange look. Additionally, the *Flying Fish* received a new logo and smartly designed entrance area to fit in with the nearby Amity look and feel. Optimistically it also received a Fastrack queue line for those wishing to pay to jump the queue, and a ride photo booth.

With a classic ride returning, it was also time to unceremoniously say goodbye to another important part of Thorpe Park's history. *Thorpe Farm* which had been open to guests since 1982, had closed the previous summer with the assumption that it would return the following season. However, an announcement was made to confirm the permanent closure early in 2007[395], claiming a decline in interest since the introduction of more modern attractions. The animals had been re-homed with no opportunity for nostalgic visitors to say a final goodbye. For the first time in its history, the entire Thorpe Park experience would now be confined to the one central "island".

With no farm to transport guests to, the *Canada Creek Railway* was largely surplus to requirements, and the majority of the kilometre long track was cut off, leaving a much smaller circuit. This followed only the last section of the ride around *Loggers Leap* and acted more as a gentle scenic ride without a practical purpose.

The Flying Fish in its new home. Credit: Alex Rowe

Controversially a short-lived charge for the park map was also introduced in 2007, with visitors having to pay 50 pence for a copy if they wanted to find their way around, leading to awkward conversations for the poor admission staff. Also making a brief appearance was a *SingStar* area in the former *Thorpe Park Ranger* show building, allowing visitors to sing their hearts out in public, and try out the karaoke style game that had proved a huge hit for returning sponsors PlayStation.

Behind the scenes more significant changes were happening at the top.

In 2005 Tussauds had been quietly sold to Dubai International Capital for £800 million[396], with very little altered to the setup and running of the organisation. This was part of an investment project, which would prove worthwhile in 2007 when Tussauds would again change hands, this time for an increased figure of roughly £1 billion[397]. Investment management organisation the Blackstone Group were the new owners, making the purchase through majority-owned Merlin Entertainments. Already controlling the likes of Legoland Windsor and many Sea Life centres, Merlin would add all Tussauds' current attractions to their line-up. This formed what they claimed was the second biggest leisure group in the world behind Disney. With Legoland, Chessington World of Adventures and Thorpe Park all now overseen by the same owner, the three parks who had been at loggerheads in the 1990s were now all on the same team for the first time.

Merlin would be taking complete control in managing the new company and a familiar Tussauds face would be returning to oversee the future of Thorpe Park from the very top. Merlin Entertainments CEO Nick Varney was the fresh face marketer brought in to help rejuvenate Alton Towers in the early nineties. He had significant theme park pedigree, but despite this saw most potential in increasing the bottom line of the company through other means, telling *Reuters*[398]:

> "If we were sitting here five years from now, I think we'd be disappointed if we weren't operating 10 businesses, from three now, under three different brand names in America...all those things point to a stock market flotation in three or four years' time. That is probably the most likely outcome"

The passion emitted from the new enlarged company seemed to be around creating a number of city centre franchises that could be replicated cookie-cutter style around the world. Explaining to the *Financial Times*, Blackstone's senior managing director Josepth Baratta said[399]:

> "These are venues in the city where parents can take their children for 3-

4 hours. There aren't enough of these"

Thorpe Park, just ten years ago the solitary theme park run by a concrete company, had now changed hands several times to become a small fish in a very large multi-national pond. The buyout meant that several longstanding members of Tussauds senior management were soon to be leaving, and after being the golden boy since the turn of the millennium, the future of the park was once again thrown into uncertainty.

PART FOUR

THE START OF MERLIN'S SPELL

2008

With new owners getting their feet under the table at the former Tussauds offices near Chessington, there was to be no immediate change to the plans for Thorpe Park. After the initial splurge to get the park on track at the turn of the century, a blueprint had been put in place to add a major new investment every three years, and between that gap to subsidise with cheaper alternatives. This meant the next big ride was due in 2009 with progress continuing behind the scenes. In the meantime, a more affordable new attraction was to be introduced in 2008, and just Tussauds first addition nine years earlier, it would be a film.

Gardaland in north east Italy was a popular theme park, attracting around three million visitors a year, that was also under the ownership of Merlin Entertainments. It was in many ways not too dissimilar to Thorpe Park in that it shared a similar level of rides and theming. In 2007 Gardaland had debuted a new 4D cinema, which featured a specially created computer animated film called *Time Voyagers*. The premise of this eight-minute movie was that a couple of drone-like robots called Bix and Ting travelled through time to explore a pyramid containing items of archaeological interest, or something to that extent. In line with other 4D attractions, effects would be triggered by certain actions. So, seats buzzed and water was splashed to great ilarità.

After nine seasons in operation and an estimated 16,000 showings, it was time to say goodbye to *Pirates 4D*. Leslie Nielsen, Eric Idle and company's corny jokes were to be retired after what should be considered a very successful run for a cinema show. Unlike a rollercoaster, there's probably a limit to the number of times you can re-ride a 4D theatre attraction. Rumours were intensifying that R.L. Stine's *Haunted Lighthouse 4D*, which was already running successfully at Busch Gardens in America, would be coming to Thorpe Park as a direct replacement. It certainly fitted the existing theme. In this, *Back to the Future's* Christopher Lloyd starred in a tale of two young ghosts trapped in a lighthouse for 100 years, when new kids arrive to explore the building.

When Thorpe Park opened their gates for the 2008 season there was a surprise, as instead of a new nautical themed adventure, guests would instead get to experience *Time Voyagers* fresh from Gardaland[400]. The original being in Italian meant some new voiceover work was added, but nothing else would be changed, even the credits still featured the Italian park's logo. For Thorpe Park putting an existing film from a Merlin park in their current 4D theatre was a low-cost way of offering a new attraction for guests. The *Haunted Lighthouse* film would instead end up at Flamingo Land in Yorkshire the same year.

Ahead of the new attraction opening some minimal changes were made to the cinema surroundings, with the memorable, if somewhat polarising, Justa Parrot gone. The new film was a bit of an odd fit to its environment, mixing the science fiction adventure with the remaining pirate architecture. The film itself was shorter, less amusing and entirely forgettable. In fact, whilst researching this I was confident that I had never viewed it, until an Italian video on YouTube[401] jogged my memory. James Salter reviewed the attraction on his website *Theme Park James*[402]:

"The film was very dull and the storyline was almost incomprehensible"

In an otherwise quite quiet year for Thorpe Park, one of their security guards hit the headlines when he decided to change his name by Deed Poll. After years of hating his birth name, Stephen Edmunds changed his name to Animal Stephen Leonidas Floyd Mayweather McManus Edmunds. Animal/Stephen had set up a Facebook group offering to do it if he received 5,000 followers, but decided to do it anyway when he reached 1,178. Explaining the choice to *Surrey Live*[403], Animal said:

"After biting a child at school when I was about 10, my friends gave me the nickname Animal and it stuck"

Time Voyagers lasted just four seasons at Thorpe Park before being removed quietly due to a lack of popularity. At Gardaland the film remained running until the end of 2017, before being replaced by the action-tastic *San Andreas 4D Experience*.

For those seeking new thrills it had been a quiet couple of years for Thorpe Park, but a terrifying new attraction the following year was about to change all that.

2009

With the next major investment now due, a team was assembled to consider what this might be, with the project given the name *Dylan*. After trying to take a break after his illustrious career, John Wardley was coaxed out of semi-retirement to once again work as a consultant. After the success of *Colossus*, *Nemesis Inferno* and *Stealth*, a fourth rollercoaster was the default choice. However, Wardley was keen to identify something that was different to what the park already had to offer.

Creating a new wooden rollercoaster in the UK had long been an ambition of Wardley. A space close to *Canada Creek* was identified for the new project, and it seemed a perfect fit for the concept. He created one layout for a twin racing coaster to be manufactured by Great Coasters International (GCI) that would be a real crowd pleasure. The concept included LIM launch boosters, that would allow for the race to be fixed, and keep the winner a secret throughout[404]. Another wooden design went even further with GCI working up detailed proposals for a 27 metre high ride, featuring a number of thrilling sections. These included a high-speed dip under the station and thundering through the *Loggers Leap* tunnel, creating a neat crossover between the two rides[405].

Despite confidence this would be a fantastic ride, ambitions for the wooden coaster struggled to advance further. There were serious concerns from senior management about how the general public would perceive such an attraction. The fear being the same one that had prevented Alton Towers installing a "woody" for two decades. Research showed they were deemed old fashioned and dangerous compared to the newer steel counterparts. Frustrated by the rejection of a GCI creation, a new alternative had to be sought. The fresh idea was to find a coaster system that could offer a dark ride sequence where riders would be able to watch part of a story unfold, before the more traditional high-speed sections kicked in.

German company Gerstlauer had been grabbing some attention in the amusement industry with their innovative *Euro-Fighter* rollercoaster product. When entering the rollercoaster market, they had specialised in steel *Bobsled* models. The new Euro-Fighter design used a similar track, but with some more revolutionary elements. In fact, a couple had already been installed in the UK, with Oakwood's *Speed: No Limits* opening in 2006, and Adventure Island in Southend opening *Rage* in 2007. The most distinctive part of the *Euro-Fighter's* capabilities was the "beyond vertical" main drop, that would take riders even further than 90 degrees.

A world's first vertical drop had been a major selling point for Alton Towers in 1998 when they opened the B&M manufactured *Oblivion,* and technology had already advanced. Offering a vertical drop on any rollercoaster requires you to have much shorter trains than other designs to stop extreme forces being felt, which often leads to wider cars to maximise capacity. *Euro-Fighter's* offered cars with two rows of four seats, which also allowed for more compact and flexible designs. This meant parks could fit more rollercoaster elements into a small space. The short cars and flexible design fitted the bill for what Wardley was seeking for *Project Dylan,* so the system was put forward as the new preferred option[406].

With a ride type selected, plans were created by Wardley for the new rollercoaster on a site somewhere between *Loggers Leap* and *Colossus,* just behind *Samurai.* However, where the main station building was to be located was currently part of Abbey Lake. Very early preparation work started at the beginning of 2007, over two years before the ride was due to open, to fill in the part of the lake required[407]. This would give the land time to settle before serious construction began.

Creative director on the project was Candy Holland, who had been using her famous imagination for Tussauds/Merlin parks for over a decade. Her team decided they wanted to create a horror themed attraction, taking place in a seemingly abandoned warehouse, using the initial dark ride section to add some genuine frights before the thrills began. It was also agreed with Gerstlauer that they could make a small amendment to allow the new coaster to be the steepest to date by a few degrees, allowing them to claim a world record of sorts. This was something that appealed to Nick Varney's marketing instincts, with him personally requesting that each major new addition had an easily understandable tagline and killer marketing image. Holland's visuals were impressive and convinced Merlin's senior management to press ahead.

Planning documents submitted in November 2007[408] revealed publicly what the park had up their sleeves for the 2009 season. Permission was officially granted in January the following year with a triumphant official press release stating[409]:

"Located in the *Canada Creek* area of the Park, the new ride will offer thrill hunters an experience of a lifetime, creating a darker atmosphere never seen before at THORPE PARK"

The release also confirmed that the yet unnamed ride would stand 100 feet tall, have four inversions, and last one minute and 40 seconds. A considerable time compared to something such as *Stealth*. Interestingly it also stated that 30% of the ride would take part inside the building, teasing an unknown surprise that lay hidden. Also released was the artist's impression of the planned station, with imposing vertical climb and 100 degree drop next to it.

Construction of the new ride began in earnest in spring 2008, with a couple of small changes required to allow work to happen. The (shorter than original) *Canada Creek Railway* which would pass closely by would be closed for the season, and *Colossus* would have some of its extended queue line changed. With vertical construction of *Dylan* due to begin, a late amendment was made to the design, removing a set of the mid-course brakes which were deemed unnecessary, replaced with a stomach lurching airtime hill[410].

Whilst work continued to bring the project to life on the site, the marketing team were busy planning a campaign to raise the profile of the ride. With the horror theme already identified they opened discussions with Lionsgate, owners of the *Saw* film franchise, about potentially working together. *Saw* had started as a low budget horror film in 2004, which massively exceeded expectations by bringing in over £100 million in revenue from a £1.2 million budget. Its huge success meant a sequel was immediately greenlit, and a hectic production schedule was to follow with *Saw* branded films being released annually every Halloween.

Created by James Wan and Leigh Whannell, the *Saw* films centre on a serial killer known as Jigsaw. This psychopath doesn't just like killing though, nope, he enjoys psychologically and physically torturing his victims by setting them "games" which offer them the chance to escape. He is known for communicating with his victims by using a puppet called Billy, who has distinctive red spirals on his face, and appears both in videos and in physical form. Each of the films had generally been panned by movie critics, but continued to pull in the punters. It was a very recognisable brand, with Billy especially becoming iconic in certain circles.

In the middle of 2008[411] a deal was agreed for the new rollercoaster to become *Saw - The Ride*, with the horror franchise fitting the already under construction attraction's general theme well. This also allowed Candy Holland's creative team to work with Lionsgate and Twisted Pictures to add *Saw* elements to aspects of the journey through the experience. Plans for the dark ride section were amended to include Billy, and in addition special media would be created to be played before riders boarded the train. Although this was a reasonably late addition to the project, enough time was available to turn everything around.

Track pieces arrived towards the end of the summer holidays, and were put into place at a fast pace, with the entire 2,362-foot circuit being completed in around five weeks. Much work was still to be done creating the large station building, with some ambitious theming to be added before the ride could open. As construction work ramped up, so did the marketing efforts, with teaser videos being released on the 13th of each month to create hype.

On the 13th October in the midst of the annual *Fright Nights* event, Thorpe Park issued a press release and video confirming for the first time that *Saw - The Ride* would be the name of their 2009 attraction. The announcement was perfectly timed for both parties, allowing Lionsgate to generate some publicity around *Saw V* which was being released later that month. The release also made several major claims saying *Saw – The Ride* would be[412]:

"...the world's first ever horror movie-themed rollercoaster"

"...the scariest ride in the world"

"Shocking and intense; both physically and psychologically"

And feature:

"the steepest freefall drop in the world"

The announcement had the desired effect, garnering a lot of attention for the project amongst the media and the public. To help capitalise on the attention a mini-site was created online for people to find out more, and follow the rest of the construction process. Much like *Stealth* it also offered a competition to win the chance to ride before anybody else.

The Saw – The Ride entrance sign. Credit: Alex Rowe

With the cat out of the bag, work continued apace to get everything completed in time for opening in March 2009. Huge effort went into dressing the main warehouse style building, with large shipping containers installed to be converted into an official *Saw – The Ride* shop. Giant blades/saws were added to the main drop, giving riders the appearance of a near miss with them. An American style police interceptor car, previously used for a *Blues Brothers* show, was parked outside the main building. To help get the operations team up to speed they visited Southend to experience how a Gerstlauer *Euro-Fighter* worked, watching *Rage* in action.

To create an authentic *Saw*-like experience the extensive outdoor queue section had fake razor wire fences added, with the final section of the queue inside featuring horror items, with a couple of jump scares including a gunshot that fires occasionally. There were also several references and genuine torture props from the films. Videos featuring the puppet Billy were also created and played during this section, to help prepare guests before boarding. Despite the original announcement that the ride would be situated in *Canada Creek*, the relationship with Lionsgate meant this was changed to a separate newly created zone called *Saw Island*.

Samurai in action with Saw – The Ride beside it. Credit: Alex Rowe

The final ride experience was an impressive mix. It starts with passengers boarding the train, with a countdown clock indicating how long it is until you begin your journey. Two trains of eight riders each head off at once passing a physical Billy puppet on a tricycle, and then the trains split with one holding back to allow the other to continue ahead. You continue through the dark inside section, going down a very steep hidden drop, followed by a number of special effects such as compressed air that imply you are being attacked from either side. Still in the dark you complete a heartline roll which takes you over a fake dead body squirting fake blood, and head out of the warehouse.

After this entertaining indoor section, you stop to watch another quick Jigsaw video, with the traditional ride element still to begin. After an intimidating vertical climb up 100 feet, you experience the 100 degree drop under the spinning blades. Following this there is a number of tight turns, dive loop and the airtime hill that was added at the last minute of design. It's a thrilling ride, which leaves you pretty disorientated and packs a decent punch. As it should be, it's an awful lot of fun rather than outright terrifying. With the queue line acting as the most intimidating part of the whole experience.

The usual camera captures your face gurning at an intense moment of the ride, but in a new twist technology was introduced to each vehicle that allowed visitors to be filmed during the experience. You could then choose to pay extra and take this home on a DVD if you wished, another first for Thorpe Park.

The official opening of the ride was set for Saturday 14th March, with a media night shortly before. An advertising campaign asked the public to "face your fears" with the slogan also being emblazoned on each of the eight ride vehicles. Frustration hit the media launch though, as with guests such as Jonathan Ross and Chantelle from *Big Brother* already in attendance, the ride broke down due to a software malfunction[413]. When engineers got it working, another extended stop led a journalist to report having a panic attack. Arguably though, that just fuelled the publicity.

When *Saw – The Ride* opened to the public it was met with strong reviews. *Coaster Critic* gave it a positive review of 8.5 out of 10 saying[414]:

"...a ride that'll scare the living daylights out of the general public. Thorpe Park have it in the bag with this one"

Teething problems were to strike again, meaning not enough of the public were getting their chance to experience the new attraction. For the first days and weeks there were continuous issues with getting the coaster working smoothly, with the team having to resort to severely reducing the number of cars on the track[415]. Signs were placed near the entrance stating that visitors should expect longer queues due to "reduced seating capacity". Gerstlauer worked quickly to make some small modifications, and these helped increase the hourly throughput of the ride close to the original projections.

Regardless of any small initial issues, the new headline ride was working wonders in pulling in new visitors to the park. Attendance was up massively in 2009, with close to two million people visiting during a season for the very first time[416]. The project was a substantial success; entertaining the public and rewarding the park's £13.5 million investment.

Saw's record for steepest drop would not last for long however, as just a few months later *Mumbo Jumbo* opened at Flamingo Land, boasting a 112 degree drop[417]. It was arguably irrelevant by this point, as Thorpe Park had already cashed in on the publicity.

Following the success of *Saw – The Ride* Merlin Entertainments would return to Gerstlauer, purchasing an updated version of the *Euro-Fighter* to create *The Smiler* at Alton Towers in 2013. *The Smiler* was very popular with thrill seekers, and looked remarkable, thanks to the lengthy track cramped into a relatively small space. Everything was good until it suffered an infamous accident in 2015, injuring a number of riders when two of the trains collided[418]. As a precaution *Saw – The Ride* was closed but re-opened shortly afterwards[419].

After the accident at Alton Towers hit the headlines, any small incident, however common, tended to be picked up by the media. Therefore, when *Saw – The Ride* went through a standard safety stop procedure in late 2006 the *Metro* led with[420]:

"Saw ride leaves thrill-seekers terrified as they're stuck for 90 minutes"

Meanwhile the local papers must have been having a slow news day, as articles appeared on their websites with the headline[421]:

"Group of teens screamed 'help' when *Saw* ride plunged them into darkness"

The beyond vertical drop. Credit: Alex Rowe

Meanwhile in 2018, just a short nine years after opening, *The Sun* newspaper ran an article blazoned with "EXCLUSIVE" alongside the headline[422]:

"Both *Saw* at Thorpe Park and *The Rage* at Adventure Island in Southend were built by the same manufacturer"

The same year a less delayed story was covered by *Surrey Live*. It explained that a young lad called Tom Stokes was "obsessed" with watching *Saw – The Ride* in action, despite not being tall enough to go on it. Tom has autism and Thorpe Park invited him on a behind-the-scenes tour of the ride much to his delight. His dad told the paper[423]:

> "Some days we go there and stand and watch the ride, among others, for hours. If my wife comes sometimes I have to go on it for him while he watches, close to chundering many times"

Away from *Saw – The Ride*, the Thorpe Park marketing team were trying other wacky PR stunts to try and get the attention of the British media, and journalists were lapping it up. In August 2009 a press release claimed that Thorpe Park were banning guests from putting their arms in the air on rides, after complaints about body odour. Staff were apparently issued with cans of deodorant to help, and a huge number of media outlets ran with the story, including the *BBC* who included quotes from director Mike Vallis[424]:

> "The human body reacts to being scared and being thrilled by sweating a bit more. We are asking people to keep their arms down in the present hot spell. In some extreme cases we may even ask people to move to the back of the train so the whole ride doesn't have to go through a cloud of someone else's BO. People may say it's all a publicity stunt but we take our customer feedback seriously"

The *Saw* films continued to be released annually until 2010, when the seventh instalment called *Saw 3D*, was advertised as the last chapter. After a seven year break the franchise returned in 2017 with *Jigsaw*, and another called *Spiral* will be released in 2021 written by comedian Chris Rock[425].

Gerstlauer's rollercoasters remain popular around the world, including modified versions of the *Euro-Fighter* still being installed. The ride manufacturers themselves being cleared of any wrongdoing in *The Smiler* incident[426].

Saw – The Ride has continued to be an incredibly popular attraction, constantly drawing some of the biggest crowds of all the rides over a decade since it was introduced. There have been some valid criticisms that as the ride matured it became a little rough, but it doesn't seem to distract from the experience of most. At some point the agreement with Lionsgate might not be renewed, meaning the attraction will require a new name, but until then it stays very much synonymous with the *Saw* films. Considering the ride system itself was already available elsewhere in the UK, it's a credit to the power of the *Saw* brand, and the effort that went into the project to create something distinctive, that it continues to perform so well.

In fact after being introduced it was performing so well that Thorpe Park would return to create another *Saw* attraction the following year....

2010

Since arriving in the 1980s, the *Thorpe Belle* steamboat had served many purposes during its time at Thorpe Park, acting at various points as a restaurant, boat, and an education centre. For 2010 it was decided that it would once again get a new lease of life. Following the success of *Saw – The Ride* the previous year, an extension of the branded area was agreed upon. The steamboat was floated towards the new piece of land that the rollercoaster sat on, with its entrance placed onto a brand-new path alongside *Colossus*. The decoration of the boat was given a complete overhaul, bringing it in line with the rundown, creepy feel of the main *Saw* attraction.

The concept was a live action horror maze, of the type that had become very popular at the annual *Fright Nights* event. This maze, however, would be open all year round for guests to enjoy. It was appropriately titled *Saw Alive*. Six traps themed to the various Saw movies were portrayed in different rooms, featuring everything from a toilet to a freezer. As each group of ten people made their way around they would witness some horrific scenes, with one of the highlights a corridor featuring an electric fence, although the voltage was set very low. Actors were placed around the dimly lit attraction to create some genuine scares, and mixed in with costumed mannequins being tortured by Jigsaw throughout.

To promote the opening of the attraction the usual quirky PR stories were released to drum up attention. The most outrageous of these was offering £500 for the person with the most pungent urine[427]. The "winner" would have their distinctive wee smell used in the attraction to help scare visitors. After over 30 years of hard work from generations of park staff to create a professional image and high-quality experience all round, it was disheartening to see the park resort to such measures for some easy media coverage. It was a sign of an external agency working on the project, looking for some headlines to hit their targets, and having no connection and care for the wider reputation.

There was also some small controversy around the age limit of the ride, which was set at those twelve and over. *The Mirror* ran a story claiming[428]:

"Gruesome scenes will be open to young children in a maze based on the 18-rated Saw films"

The new attraction opened in 2010 to mixed reviews from visitors. As with many of these mazes, the experience differs greatly depending on the number and skill of the actors inside at the time. However the consensus seemed to be that the actors were of a high quality, and the *Saw* theming lived up to the high standard set the previous year. *Saw Alive* operated throughout the 2010 and 2011 seasons, but was reduced to a *Fright Nights* only attraction the following year. It remained part of the annual celebration until 2018 when it was finally retired.

A ticket to Thorpe Park had now reached a new high of £38 per person (equivalent of £46.50 in 2020). A price that whilst hefty was possibly justified by the huge range of attractions now contained on the island. What was more contentious was the increasing prominence and reliance on guests purchasing upgrades to skip the queues. Since the early 2000s the *Fasttrack* queue jump option had been steadily introduced to the most popular rides - with a separate entrance for those who possessed one. From five pounds to bypass a single attraction, to £60 for all of them, the initiative was certainly a money spinner[429]. However, the two-tiered system was leaving a bitter taste in the mouth of those spending hours waiting their turn only to have others ushered past them. If the British know anything it's how to queue properly, and giving jumps to those who can afford it seemed offensive to many. For the park it was a necessary evil to boost revenue, but perhaps systematic of the change in attitude from the 80s and 90s where experience and quality were put first.

From distasteful marketing tactics to frustrations about money grabbing, the public perception of Thorpe Park was starting to change. Management were not ignorant of the issues they faced, but reputations take a lifetime to build, and only a moment to lose. Record revenues were perhaps justification of the tactics in the short term, but they might come to regret them when bigger prizes were desired in years to come.

2011

In 2010 Merlin Entertainments acquired the Cypress Gardens theme park in Florida, which had been closed the year before, and planned to convert it into a Legoland branded park due to open in 2011[430]. This meant a complete overhaul of the Cypress Gardens site to fit with the prestigious Lego brand, including moving the *Jungle Coaster* from Windsor across the Atlantic.

A number of Cypress Gardens rides were identified as no longer required, one of which was a 60-foot-tall spinning rapids ride called *Storm Surge* manufactured by Canadian based WhiteWater West. This water ride saw guests sit in a round boat similar to *Thunder River/Rumba Rapids*, and immediately head up a conveyor belt the full height. The boat then makes it way down a twisting water slide style track with a dash of water and gravity propelling riders forward at moderate speeds. After a final small drop into a larger pool the ride is over, and riders return slowly to the station.

With the attraction up for grabs, and nothing else confirmed for the 2011 season, Thorpe Park took ownership of the ride. As frantic work began on the new Legoland, *Storm Surge* was packed into containers and shipped across the Atlantic. The space in front of the X pyramid was chosen to host the water ride, but would sadly necessitate removing the *Octopus Garden* area that had hosted a variety of small rides for young children since the earliest days of the park[431].

As usual the Thorpe Park PR hype machine for the new ride was fired up, and issued a statement to the press. This time the claim was that *Storm Surge* was planned to be placed on or near Monk's Walk, a public footpath that roughly runs in line with the old *Canada Creek Railway* line to *Thorpe Farm*. It appears, so to speak, that when preparation work began, workers had been spooked by sightings of ghostly figures such as a headless monk. It just so happened that this location could be the site of an ancient burial ground. The claim regarding the original location was a complete fabrication, but some of the press picked up on it, with the *Daily Mail* running the story[432]:

"A paranormal detection agency was then called in to the park in Chertsey, Surrey, to carry out tests and found that a burial ground or settlement could have been disturbed. Managers at the park decided to relocate the ride to another area of the park and also called in a forensic team to carry out further investigations"

Unfortunately, the person in charge of naming the ride was not feeling as creative, and decided to stick with the original *Storm Surge* name. The ride would form part of an ever-expanding *Amity* area, but fail to live up to the high standards of original theming. As installation progressed it became obvious that very little would be added to decorate the gaudy ride, which had each part of the track coloured differently alternating between red, yellow and blue. Admittedly the name and concept did generally sit well alongside *Tidal Wave*, however it stuck out like a sore thumb in terms of quality compared to other newer additions, and seemed slightly counterproductive to the atmosphere the park was trying to achieve. A nice entrance area was added to the beginning of the queue, but the budget appeared not to stretch any further for this modest addition.

Ahead of opening on Thursday 17th March 2011, the project team had found that the boats would not spin very much, so added rough material to the sides of the tube to help create some friction and spin more. This helped to an extent, but there was a larger issue that was impossible to fix. Compared to other similar attractions at the park, *Storm Surge* had an extremely low capacity. This resulted in queues moving slowly and visitors being frustrated. Even more annoying was the addition of a *Fasttrack* option to ride, with the normal queue remaining static for long periods at a time.

Visitors to the park met the ride with mediocre reviews. Surprisingly for a water ride you didn't really get splashed by the ride naturally, so water sprays were added to try and add some excitement. Additionally, the boats featured hardly any drainage, giving guests soggy feet on the occasions enough water got inside. Other issues included long waits to exit the boats, which sat queued behind others waiting for dispatching, blocking return to the station. Considering the decent height, it surprisingly lacked excitement and intensity, taking the turns at a pretty mundane speed. Nick Sim's review for *Theme Park Tourist* summed up saying[433]:

> "In the end, *Storm Surge* just about serves its purpose as a stop-gap attraction...It can't live up to the standard of the park's best rides, but it does offer a fun experience that can't be found elsewhere in the UK"

Storm Surge with Colossus in the background. Credit: Alex Rowe

A TV advert to promote the new ride did however, do a great job of editing together footage of the ride to make it look quite thrilling - featuring teenagers having the absolute time of their lives, ending with the tagline "thrill out"[434]. In truth this was a solid family ride, but it was very unlikely that Thorpe Park would ever have chosen *Storm Surge* if purchasing a new installation. The park already had a glut of similar rides such as *Depth Charge*, *Rumba Rapids* and *Tidal Wave* that did a much better job of putting smiles on faces and chewing through the crowds. It also accentuated the issue of limited guest choice on rainy days due to the unpredictable British weather.

Storm Surge. Credit: Alex Rowe

In another attempt to steal some media attention during the summer holidays, a press release in August 2011 claimed that extra-large seats had been added to *Nemesis Inferno* to accommodate an increasing number of larger riders. The truth was that these seats were standard on most B&M coasters, including *Nemesis Inferno* since 2003, but the truth wouldn't get in the way of a good headline. Again, Mike Vallis was wheeled out for quotes, this time apparently telling the *Mail Online*[435]:

"We listen to the concerns of our customers and continually monitor trends, so that we can modify our offering to ensure we're giving them the very best possible experience. The reality is that we are super-sizing - and that's a fact we're embracing. Why shouldn't people be comfortable when they are enjoying a day out with their friends or family?"

The 2011 season would be the final one for another classic, with the *Canada Creek Railway* finally succumbing to a Beeching-like fate. The railway had entertained families for 22 years, but lacked purpose since *Thorpe Farm's* closure. Some nice efforts had been made to keep it engaging for youngsters, with a bear hunt angle added to the reduced route, but with the focus now squarely on thrills it was time to say a very fond farewell.

Thorpe Park's long-term love/hate relationship with firework events also continued, with a display returning after a three-year absence. A poll was held in advance asking followers of their Facebook page who they would like to see an effigy of burnt, Guy Fawkes style. The winner was celebrity brothers, and former *X Factor* contestants, John and Edward Grimes, known collectively as *Jedward*. Videos online from the event showing the giant *Jedward* papier-mâché recreation burning sent the internet ablaze against Thorpe Park. A statement was quickly issued, covered by *Surrey Live*[436]:

"This was not meant in a malicious way and was to be a celebration of their explosive rise to fame. As fans of the singers, we would very much welcome John and Edward to the park should they wish to visit us"

Storm Surge continues to mildly entertain visitors to this day. Thankfully though, something much more extravagant was coming together for the following season...

2012

Under the stewardship of Merlin Entertainments hopes for the future of Thorpe Park remained high. Having had time to fully consider their options, a development plan was created by the latest set of management, outlining how expansion could be successfully achieved. The park was hitting capacity on a semi-regular basis, especially during the key summer holiday and Halloween periods. With space on the "island" at a premium, a further two moderate sized manmade islands were planned that would allow new attractions to be built and raise the total capacity. It was a notion that Tim Hartwright had foreseen as far back as 1982, when he wrote[437]:

> "If anything, Thorpe Park is blessed with too much water, leaving insufficient areas available for the siting of leisure facilities. To some extent this limitation can be overcome by the judicious filling-in of certain lake areas and no doubt this will be necessary in the future"

The expansion would require parts of Manor Lake to be filled in, and would create a direct route, for the first time, between the main entrance and the former *Treasure Island* site. It was an expensive exercise, but placing attractions on this land would open up a new world of opportunities and could eventually result in huge financial gains. Work on the first new island began as early as 2008, before *Saw – The Ride* had even been completed. Filling in part of a lake means the displaced water has to go somewhere, potentially resulting in flooding. Therefore, to get the go ahead to start the ambitious new plans, parts of the former *Thorpe Farm* site were sunk, keeping the water levels consistent[438].

Merlin Magic Making, responsible for creating and delivering the large majority of the company's new attractions, were preparing ideas for the next big investment. Despite being priced at a premium, they admired the work of Bolliger & Mabillard (B&M), and were keen to work with them again. The company still had an outstanding reputation in the industry but had struggled to diversify their product range after the huge success of their early models. After a series of successes Wardley had a strong personal friendship with the founders, and was collaborating on a proposal for a new model that would have riders sit either side of the track, rather than above or below it. The belief was that this *Wing* coaster would offer an unrivalled feeling of freedom, with passengers having their legs dangling below like their popular Inverted product. Explaining the thought process Wardley said[439]:

> "Walter Bolliger and I came up with an idea partly inspired by classic film scenes, where a vehicle would make dramatic last-minute turns to fit through a small space. Like an X-Wing attacking the Death Star in *Star Wars*, or Roger Moore flying through aircraft hangar doors moments before they shut in *Octopussy*"

The new configuration would allow riders to replicate this experience whilst sat two either side per row, ducking and diving close to the landscape, giving the impression of coming close to impact before a "near-miss".

When the Swiss manufacturer was approached to suggest ideas for the first of the new development islands, they were strongly against using the new *Wing* model. The flat piece of land really didn't play to the strengths of the concept, and Wardley also felt a different B&M option should be utilised instead. His preference was a *Hyper Coaster*, a tall ride that offers high speeds and massive airtime. Having good knowledge of planning restrictions, he was confident that permission could be agreed and it would be the perfect complement to the four major rollercoasters already in operation at Thorpe Park[440]. However when the suggestion was put forward the message from the very top of Merlin was a familiar one. They were adamant that any major new attraction would need to have some kind of unique selling point in order to attract the public and getting their hands on a *Wing Coaster* would give them an exclusive.

Confident that the B&M *Wing Coaster* would be a sure-fire hit, one was immediately ordered for Gardaland, opening as *Raptor* in 2011[441]. The area *Raptor* resides in is a more natural fit for the model, offering a varied environment to swoop through, and plenty of opportunities for near-misses. Before it was even open Merlin placed an order for a second, confirming Thorpe Park's 2012 headline attraction. The timing coincided with the predetermined three-year cycle for major investments, but also with the all-pervading London Olympics. There was a strong belief that opening the same year as the global event would capitalise on the expected boom in tourism to the capital.

Reluctantly accepting the decision to go with the *Wing Coaster* concept he himself had helped develop, Wardley began work on possible configurations alongside creative director Candy Holland. Starting with a traditional chain lift to the height of 127 feet, an element was developed that would roll riders upside down at the very top before diving to the ground, in what was called a "dive loop" element. Wardley had used a special advanced version of the *No Limits* computer design software to play around with the idea, and engineers in Switzerland confirmed it was indeed possible[442]:

> "I thought it was a pretty dastardly thing to do on a rollercoaster, and everyone agreed it was a marvellous idea"

Following the dive loop the trains would complete a number of traditional twists, turns and helixes over its 2,540 feet of track, including inverting riders five times.

Happy with the proposals, detailed plans were submitted to the local council at the beginning of 2011. These plans revealed the extensive amount of theming that would be applied across the new island, creating the sense of an apocalyptic attack. To take advantage of the *Wing Coaster's* strengths without having an interesting landscape to work with, Holland devised clever set-piece near misses for the ride to interact with. Structures were carefully planned throughout that would be placed as close as safely possible to the track, including a number of narrow gaps that would initially appear too tight to fit through. Features would include a station depicting a ruined church, alongside wrecked vehicles such as planes, helicopters and fire engines. The project was titled *LC12* (short for Long Count 12), relating to the Mayan long count calendar, which predicted the end of the world in 2012. The attention to detail and scope of the area design was incredible, but it wasn't to everyone's liking.

On the 7th March, before final planning permission had been granted, the *BBC* ran a story stating the British Airline and Pilot Association (Balpa) were unhappy with the theme of the planned new rollercoaster. Balpa were quoted as saying[443]:

"We think this ride is staged in a tasteless way. The park is fairly close to both Gatwick and Heathrow and the last thing families want to be reminded of is a tragic crash, which fortunately are rare, but nevertheless devastating. We urge Thorpe Park to think again."

Thorpe Park rejected the claims, stating that the ride itself was nothing to do with a plane crash. It seemed that Runnymede Borough Council agreed, granting permission for the project to go ahead at the end of March.

It was still a year until the first members of the public would get to ride, but Thorpe Park were keen to start the hype early for their fifth major rollercoaster. By April clues had started to appear around the park to tease visitors, including stickers planted around the park proclaiming "the end is coming". Actors were hired to dress as conspiracy theorists and walk around the main island wearing sandwich boards stating the same slogan, with the now customary teaser website also promoted. The website featured a countdown clock, that indicated an announcement would be made sometime in August.

With the green light to go ahead, construction started to accelerate, with foundations and footers being placed. The new island would be accessed from a pathway behind the *Depth Charge* ride and could be accessed by passing the *Flying Fish*.

Because *LC12* would be away from the core island a whole new full set of facilities would be required to cater for guests. One benefit of using the new land being that it would allow construction to progress away from the day-to-day operation of the park, meaning deliveries and machinery could continue without disruption. The construction team put together was led by veteran engineer Keith Workman, and included 15 specialists from Germany.

Using the prime summer holiday period as a backdrop, the ride details were announced publicly, along with the name confirmed to be *The Swarm*. Alongside the name reveal was a new "War is Coming" tagline, which was subsequently plastered around the park, most noticeably on a large replica tank. In another smart move some promotional military style gates complete with warning lights were placed near *Stealth*.

By October *The Swarm* was starting to rise into the Chertsey sky, becoming a great advert for itself[444]. The crack team assembled the 1,000 tonnes of quality B&M metal track without any major issues, in fact completing the twisting circuit two weeks ahead of schedule. The ambition of the project meant that months of theming work were still to be undertaken to turn the site into an apocalyptic urban landscape, that appeared to have just been attacked by an alien threat. The basics of this included a reported 100,000 paving blocks being placed on the site, but it was the unusual set-pieces that would prove a little more difficult[445].

The most ambitious part of this was perhaps the controversial crashed plane. For this effect Merlin decided that, rather than create a replica from scratch, they would instead buy a real 737 plane that was no longer in operation. The wing of the plane would form one of the many near misses for riders, with this particular one seeing guests duck underneath at 59 miles per hour. The plane's fuselage, engine and wing were adapted to fit perfectly into the specifics required to make the illusion work safely. Other striking theming features included a helicopter wreckage, sitting crash landed into a small lake by the final turnaround, and a giant fake billboard. Riders would fly through the middle of the latter, which was adorned with a rather relevant advertising slogan either side.

A decommissioned fire engine was also added, with gas cylinders providing a blast of fire from the rear of the vehicle. Around the site charred trees were also placed as if burnt by the devastation. Even the two trains received a neat makeover to represent the predatory swarm creature that was responsible for the attack, complete with eyes that light up. As continuing layers of more spectacular theming were added, it was clear that it was the most well realised creation since *Tidal Wave*, maybe even surpassing it. Merlin had backed their creative team with a significant budget for this one, and their faith was being repaid.

The first drop under the plane wing. Credit: Alex Rowe

With the team happy with progress the first test runs were held in January 2012, and *The Swarm* performed admirably, easily making it round the track. To aide with the promotion the park followed the progress through the final stages with a developer's diary online, that also allowed followers to ask questions of the construction team. It was an open and welcome approach to sharing news about the new attraction, and helped spread the word amongst rollercoaster enthusiasts across the globe.

For some promotion a little closer to home the PR machine went into action with their latest stunt. In early February many media outlets were reporting on a story released by Thorpe Park around *The Swarm's* testing, where apparently a number of test dummies had lost limbs[446]. Accompanying pictures showed the devastation caused with headlines such as:

"Test dummies have limbs ripped off on new £20m rollercoaster ride"

Most acknowledged the fact this was probably a publicity stunt, but the stories did the job of spreading the word[447]. It's worthwhile noting that this was before the horrible incident on *The Smiler*, and it's unlikely that Merlin would ever consider such an approach now.

With the decapitating parts of the ride now "fixed" four pilots from the famous Red Arrows were recruited to test out the new ride. It was another chance to interest the media, with the *Metro* newspaper declaring[448]:

"New *Swarm* ride at Thorpe Park even scares former Red Arrows pilot"

The following month just ahead of park opening it was announced that local rock band *You Me at Six* would be recording a theme song for the ride, publicised as the world's first rollercoaster single[449]. Titled appropriately *The Swarm* it was released digitally and reached number 23 on the UK charts[450].

With construction complete, and the ride performing well during tests, season pass holders were invited to the latest *Premiere Screaming* event to try out the new attraction. Early reviews were positive praising the ride experience and the incredible effort that had gone into creating the new area. The full public opening followed with *The Swarm* ready for the first day of the new season on Saturday 10th March 2012. To help keep those waiting entertained televisions had been added to the queue line showing a fake rolling news channel covering the attack, and helping to explain the backstory. However, with the media following the first day a perfectly normal delay hit the news, including the BBC who reported[451]:

"A new rollercoaster came to a halt at Thorpe Park theme park, leaving visitors stuck halfway up a steep ascent for several minutes"

At a reported cost of £18 million this was a massive investment, which had been delivered professionally and on time. Many praised the attraction for its smooth ride, and comfy restraints that resembled those used on B&M *Flying* rollercoasters. Others reported being slightly disappointed with the ride saying that it was not as fast or intense as they expected. The website *Theme Park Tourist* summarised[452]:

"It may have fallen just short of our sky-high expectations, but it's still a ride that every theme park fan in the UK should make a pilgrimage to experience"

Former employee David McCubbin is a big fan[453]:

"My favourite rollercoaster at Thorpe Park is definitely *The Swarm*. I think it's absolutely amazing, everything about it, even the way the train looks"

Theming connoisseur Justin Rees felt it set a new high bar for quality[454]:

"It's a thrilling ride with the right amount of speed, inversions and turns that mean you come off it with a smile on your face and not like you've been in washing machine like some big coasters do. Plus I really like the theming around it. While queuing for a ride I like to see and hear a story around the ride to help get excited for it. This is what they do so well in the US theme parks and for me it's one of the few rides in Thorpe Park that does this well"

Despite the positivity and media attention surrounding the ride, *The Swarm* was struggling to attract visitors to the park in the desired numbers. In fact, attendance at the park dropped by nearly 200,000 people for the year[455]. Arguably launching in the same year as the London Olympics could have actually been counterproductive, with many choosing to either avoid the capital for fear of crowds, or follow Team GB in action. It was a year jam packed of major events, with the Euro 2012 football tournament and the Queen's Diamond Jubilee.

The Swarm goes through an advertising hoarding, with Stealth behind. Credit: Alex Rowe

Attempts continued throughout the year to promote the ride with an announcement in September now claiming that Thorpe Park would be breathalysing students before they rode *The Swarm*. *The Express* newspaper ran the story writing[456]:

"Thorpe Park has seen a 250 per cent increase in the amount of people being sick due to alcohol as they go to the park still suffering from the night before"

Since Merlin introduced the B&M *Wing Coaster* to the world at their parks, many more have appeared around the world. They seem to be especially popular in China where seven of the first 15 in existence were built[457]. Merlin soon built one more, at Heide Park in Germany for 2014. They were later to express disappointment commercially with how *The Swarm* had performed for Thorpe Park, and in an interview with enthusiasts claim they were unlikely to ever build a B&M *Wing Coaster* in their parks again. That was to change almost a decade later when the technology was surprisingly re-utilised for several of their family parks such as Legoland Germany. A launched, shuttle version was also installed at Chessington World of Adventures as part of their *World of Jumanji* for 2023.

The Swarm itself still stands proud at Thorpe Park and continues to rate well with guests. Its installation might not have given the park the instant financial boost it desired, but as a long-term investment it continues to prove its worth. The quality manufacturing means the ride operates smoothly, with very little downtime, especially compared to some of the more troublesome attractions nearby.

As the 2012 season ended management felt there was more to be made of their new headline attraction, and with little budget available for something new the following season, they came up with an alternative plan to turn things around....

2013

After a what was perceived to be a lacklustre revenue year in 2012, options were explored about how a new spin could be found for *The Swarm* to keep marketing fresh. After consultation with ride manufacturers and park engineers, it was found possible to turn sets of seats on *The Swarm* so they faced backwards[458]. It was decided to switch the rear two rows of seats on each train round, giving visitors the option to ride either way. This new experience was promoted as *Swarm – Brave it Backwards*.

Little was different with the experience when riding, and in fact in many ways it was detrimental to the large amount of work that had gone into creating the near miss elements. Riding backwards meant you had no idea what was coming, however close that might be. On the positive side it gave you an unobstructed view which was usually only available in the front row. To help promote the new feature on *The Swarm* a promotional deal was agreed with popular London based radio station *KISS FM*, who held competitions and ran adverts on the *Rickie, Melvin and Charlie Breakfast Show[459]*.

Brave it Backwards seating would remain in place for three seasons, before all rows were returned to their original forwards formation. John Wardley would later describe the act of turning seats round on a rollercoaster as "desperate"[460].

Elsewhere the opposite was happening. For its 18th season in operation *X:\ No Way Out* had a minor overhaul to become just *X*. The park had finally had enough of guests becoming nauseous and ill, so Vekoma refurbished the cars so they would now be facing forwards, a decision that had been considered for over a decade. Gone was the original computer mayhem concept and in its place was some kind of loose nightclub theme. Loud dance music, disco style lights and lasers were added to the ride section, ruining the illusion created by riding in the darkness. Effort went into creating a new soundtrack, and the overall results were interesting. One of *X:\ No Way Out's* original operators

David McCubbin went back to try out the update[461]:

"I never liked it as X with the club music and flashing lights, it was really bad. I remember going in it and not being very impressed. I walked out and thought, this is really bad, what have they done to it"

Many found the new X all a little too random, some amusingly so. In Thorpe Park's defence the ride wasn't advertised anywhere as a new addition, and they had put effort into revitalising an aging ride when it would have been easier to leave it. Small changes would be made for the next few seasons, before a larger overhaul in 2018.

The biggest change, senior management at Merlin Entertainments were keeping an eye on for 2013, was the first ever overnight accommodation at Thorpe Park. Seen as testing the waters before potentially installing something more ambitious, the *Crash Pad* was a basic hotel run by external company Snoozebox situated on the entrance side of the *Dome*. This was described delightfully by the *Mail Online* as[462]:

"…a temporary structure on the edge of the park, made of two storeys of shipping containers, held up and surrounded by scaffolding"

Crash Pad's small rooms could fit up to four people, providing you didn't mind bunk beds. Whilst basic, it was far more affordably priced than the accommodation options at Merlin's other UK parks, with the hope that it might appeal to younger groups. Free WiFi was also added across what was now being termed as the "resort"[463].

Ahead of officially opening the gates for the 2013 season the media covered a couple of stories released by the park. The first was an impressive selection of pictures of maintenance team members inspecting the rides, including hanging off the top of *Stealth's* 205 feet high top hat[464]. With so many gimmicky attempts at getting news coverage, this was a refreshing change, highlighting the efforts that go into safety around the park every off-season. For Valentine's Day they went for a more conventional effort, teaming up with online dating platform *eHarmony* to reveal that Thorpe Park is one of the best places for couples to date[465].

Interestingly, there has been a constant stream of relationships, marriages and new babies from not just the guests, but staff working at Thorpe Park over the years. It has been the catalyst for many long-term relationships to flourish, with love blossoming for its workers since the earliest days of opening. Pirates have married ferry drivers, rides hosts have fallen in love with entertainers, and farm vets have got hitched to each other[466][467]. Working at a theme park seems an incredibly prolific place to meet your future partner, or at least your next one, as David McCubbin explains[468]:

"I still have a really strong friendship group from the people I worked with, I met some of my best friends and my partner there. There are so many Thorpe Park relationships, babies, it was some of the best years of our life. It really was a great time, and a great place to work. Because so many of us have ended up with husbands, wives and partners that legacy lives on"

Proposals at Thorpe Park are a common occurrence, with many examples over the years. One of the more creative ways to do this was in 2012, when Lawrence Key got his friends to hold up various signs reading "Will you marry me?" as they plunged down *Loggers Leap*. It wasn't until the ride photo booth that partner Sophie saw the message, and instantly accepted[469]. A Thorpe Park wedding featured in an infamous episode of the BBC Three television programme *Don't Tell The Bride* in 2011, when a groom's plan to surprise his bride with a ride on *Stealth* didn't go down too well[470]. A more successful ceremony had taken place in 2009, when Karl Anderson and Gaynor Cooper were the first people to get married on a rollercoaster in the UK, choosing *Saw – The Ride* as their venue[471].

Back in 2013, it was unfortunately also a year for some more controversial stories in the media, not instigated by the PR team themselves. BBC One television show *Your Money, Their Tricks* conducted an undercover operation, working on some of the park's many games stalls. These are the carnival style games that allow you to try and win prizes by taking part in a challenge for a small fee. *The Independent* followed up on the TV show claiming unfair tricks were used by staff[472]:

"...distracting people as they threw balls at a target; using wax on a game's surface to increase friction, making it harder to knock blocks off; and altering the position of baskets into which balls should fall. The programme also found stallholders demonstrating a game with one type of ball but giving the customer another"

The games themselves were staffed by a third-party company called HB Leisure, and they largely denied the claims alongside Thorpe Park themselves, pointing out that 100,000 toys are won every single year. HB Leisure did commit to re-training staff to ensure there were no unethical incidents in the future.

Later in the year there was a bigger storm to come. *The Asylum* scare maze had been a regular part of the *Fright Nights* line-up since 2005 being a favourite with visitors. When a petition to ban it by a student called Katie Sutton started gaining momentum, Thorpe Park were again under the microscope. Many media outlines including the *Mail Online*[473], *Guardian*[474] and *Metro*[475] started carrying the story saying that *The Asylum* stigmatises mental illnesses. As word started to spread campaigners waited outside the gates holding placards to protest. A BBC article stated[476]:

"Thorpe Park said the attraction was not offensive or a realistic portrayal of a mental health institution"

This was a topic that was a lot larger than just Thorpe Park, with supermarkets pressured to remove mental asylum Halloween outfits from their shelves. *The Asylum* continued as planned for the 2013 *Fright Nights* event, but it was to be a final swansong for the maze, with a replacement coming in the following year.

On a more upbeat note *The Telegraph* reported the bizarre story of a young child managing to make their way inside one of the grabber machines where people can attempt to win plush toys[477]. Keen to secure one of the characters, the young girl crawled in through the prize chute, as horrified parents watched on. Thankfully she was quite happy playing amongst the furry creatures until a member of staff could free her.

Undoubtably the biggest development for parent company Merlin was the decision to sell shares to the public and float on the stock market[478]. Since alluding to this during the Tussauds takeover, they had considered the move in 2010 but changed their minds due to volatile market conditions. Taking the plunge now would allow them to clear almost a quarter of a billion pounds of debt and invest in their most famous brands. The plan was still to create cookie cutter copies of Madame Tussauds, Dungeons and Legoland parks for undeveloped territories around the world.

It wasn't immediately obvious what the new structure would mean for Thorpe Park, but the changes would have repercussions in the years to come, with a greater need for short term profit to appease shareholders. After an incredible 12 years the Chertsey skyline had been forever changed by an influx of huge investments, as Thorpe Park was seen as a priority to the wider business. However, that was all about to change. Although nobody realised it at the time, *The Swarm* was to be the last major thrill ride for over a decade.

PART FIVE

AUSTERITY, INTELLECTUAL PROPERTY AND DELAYED TRAINS

2014

Saw – The Ride's huge success and the comparative disappointment of *The Swarm*, meant Merlin had witnessed the pulling power that having a brand's intellectual property (IP) had added. Using an IP was nothing new in the theme park business and was a core part of the success of Disney, Six Flags, Universal and many more attractions for countless years. Adding a well-known story or set of characters can convert a perfectly standard new addition, into a must-do for hard core fans. In fact, two IPs had transformed the fortunes of parks on opposite sides of the Atlantic in recent years.

The *Wizarding World of Harry Potter* opening at Universal Studios Islands of Adventure in Florida magically changed the performance of the park, that had been struggling to hit attendance targets for over a decade[479]. Closer to home Paultons Park in Hampshire had, in 2011, introduced a land based on pre-school character *Peppa Pig* which had been seriously bringing home the bacon, doubling their attendance to one million guests a year[480]. Whilst both areas that were introduced offered decent to tremendous rides in their own right, it's hard to imagine that they would have been anywhere near as commercially successful without using brands that came pre-disposed with millions of faithful fans. From this point onwards the new additions at Thorpe Park, and many of Merlin's other attractions, would almost exclusively come with an IP attached.

First introduced in 2009, the mobile phone game *Angry Birds* had become a phenomenal success, being downloaded tens of millions of times in the first year alone. The touchscreen gameplay revolves around different coloured cartoon birds being propelled by slingshot towards a group of enemy green pigs, who are arranged in increasingly convoluted manner amongst various structures. Its simple but addictive gameplay, alongside its cheeky style, had helped it become a hit with critics and players alike around the world.

Angry Birds had been developed by a Finnish company called Rovio, who had capitalised on the early success of the game by creating a number of sequels. The new versions had attracted partnerships with the likes of *Star Wars*, with *Facebook* also securing an exclusive version for their platform worldwide. Sensing the opportunity to exploit the brand further in the following years all sorts of licensing agreements were hastily progressed. Angry Birds would become toys, TV series, movies, cookbooks and sweets amongst many other things.

One of these new branches for expansion was in the theme park world, with Rovio agreeing to open the very first *Angry Birds Land* in their homeland Finland at a park called Särkänniemi in 2012[481]. The colourful section contained play areas, small rides and shops featuring the distinctive cartoon birds and their piggy foes. The same year the *Angry Birds* hit the UK attraction market for the first time at the Sundown Adventureland in Nottinghamshire[482]. Aimed at the under 10s, it consisted of a large outdoor play area with many traditional playground rides, given a bird-shaped makeover. Another followed at Lightwater Valley in Yorkshire[483].

The next destination on the *Angry Birds* expansion train would be Thorpe Park. Merlin management were confident that the brand had a sufficiently large and hardcore following, especially with a younger family market - they had not invested in significantly for a while - but were now keen to attract alongside the many teens and young adults. Planners identified an area in the middle of the park that would be suitable to re-brand and worked alongside the Rovio team to create a number of ride concepts that would work for both parties.

Announced to the media in January 2014, Rovio were excited by this latest expansion into the theme park world. Their director Dan Mitchell stated[484]:

"It's great to be teaming up with Thorpe Park Resort, and we hope this will be just the first of many projects together. Having the game jump out of the screen and come to life around you is going to be incredible and we're confident that this partnership will bring that amazing experience to life"

The centrepiece of the new area would be utilising the 4D cinema that had sat unused since *Time Voyagers* was stopped at the end of 2011. A brand new *Angry Birds 4D* cartoon film lasting just under 15-minutes was written by Robert Henny and directed by Howard E Baker. Ride technology specialists Simworx refurbished the theatre[485], working alongside 7thSense Design[486] to add new water sprays, air blasts, leg ticklers, plus smoke, lighting and bubble effects that would function in accordance with the action happening in the movie. The seating was also updated to add vibrations and a leaning effect that would simulate the catapult movement which the mobile game was famous.

The movie itself was aimed at children, but palatable for everybody else. Its simple story contains no speaking, and follows a clash between the birds and pigs, ending up in space. As per the previous films shown in the same theatre, guests would be required to wear 3D glasses. Whilst rather novel back in the *Pirates 4D* days, the 3D glasses were now a regular option for many blockbuster films at your local multiplex, thus losing some of the mystique.

Sitting just a catapult throw away from the entrance to the 4D theatre was *Detonator*, the Fabbri Drop Tower. Its proximity meant it was also to get a minor *Angry Birds* makeover, although mainly in name, becoming *Detonator: Bombs Away*. No changes were made to the ride experience itself, with just a few small parts of theming added. The name is a reference to the black coloured character from the game named "Bomb", who explodes shortly after landing. A large model of him was added next to the entrance, along with a few *Angry Birds* style boxes.

The final ride in the new land would be a completely new addition, albeit a rather classic concept that had been at the park in a different form previously. *Dodgem* or "bumper car" rides have been a staple at fairgrounds and theme parks since the 1920s allowing visitors of all ages to take the wheel of a small electric powered car and have the freedom to drive it round a designated space. Being so iconic you can only imagine most people have seen or participated in the dodgems at one point.

Placed on a space opposite the 4D theatre next to *Tidal Wave* which had been used sporadically before for upcharge attractions. Thorpe Park acquired a version from experienced Italian manufacturers Bertazzon, which had each of the cars customised to represent either "Red" (the red bird) or the villainous green pigs. The ride was named after the greediest of all the bad pigs, officially becoming *King Pig's Wild Hog Dodgems*.

The entrance to Angry Birds Land. Credit: Alex Rowe

Colourful *Angry Birds* characters were painted on the walls in the new area between the three rides, plus entrance archways were added either side of the pathway in the style of the structures from the game. Branded games stalls were also dotted around, with merchandise being available from the old sweet shop. A spot to have your picture taken with the mascot version of the lead character Red, and a total of seven high quality character models were placed around the area too.

Celebrities signed up to speak to the media and pose for photographs to promote *Angry Birds Land* when the usual launch event was held in mid-May. These included radio presenter Sara Cox, *X Factor* star Stacey Solomon; and long-term theme park advocate Jonathan Ross[487]. The marketing team also invested in an external agency called Space to create a number of experiences to help spread the word. The first of these was an Easter egg hunt, where children could claim a chocolate egg for completing a number of riddles and finding hidden items[488]. A likely unintentional nod to the same activation that Thorpe Park had used at Easter 20 years previously.

Warm, if slightly underwhelming reviews, followed the opening. The main praise coming for the new film, which offered the type of good quality rain proof family attraction the park had been lacking for a number of years. The area still exists with the original line-up of attractions, although one common criticism is that the choice of IP was a little too late, already on the wane by the time the section of the park opened, and even less prevalent years later. 2014 was however one of the largest ever years for attendance, comfortably attracting over two million visitors.

Rovio's expansion into the attraction world has continued somewhat, with *Angry Birds* branded areas popping up in various places. You can try out their *Space Encounter* interactive section at the Kennedy Space Centre, and also at the Space Centre in Houston[489]. The *Angry Birds 4D* movie was adapted into a new type of ride system for a theme park in Istanbul, where visitors would sit in large cars which would react to the action played on a screen rather than individual chairs in a large cinema[490]. Two full length *Angry Birds* movies have also been released theatrically, together grossing over £500 million at the worldwide box office[491].

Alongside the work to gain coverage for the new land, the PR team were also up to their usual tricks to get Thorpe Park's name in the media. The latest approach was to jump on the April Fool's Day bandwagon and announce a fake new annual event for owners and their dogs, appropriately named *Thorpe Bark*. A press release stated[492]:

> "After constant requests from owners, we have decided to finally open the park to dogs so they too can enjoy the thrilling rides. We've tested

each ride extensively with our volunteers and apart from a few nervous
barks on *Stealth*, our guests rated it five woofs out of five"

Crash Pad also underwent some changes, with Thorpe Park now taking
full control and re-branding the basic accommodation as the *Thorpe Shark
Hotel*. Whilst remaining as modest as before, it had some intricate
decoration added in parts, including an impressive large metal shark at
the entrance. This was sculpted using recognisable signs and metalwork
from around the park, with visitors having to walk through the mouth to
reach reception. This development was always supposed to be for the
short to medium term, with Merlin keen to progress plans for permanent
solution.

The entrance to the Thorpe Shark Hotel. Credit: Alex Rowe

In May 2014, Thorpe Park submitted detailed plans to Runnymede
Borough Council, asking for final permission to construct a new
permanent hotel that would eventually boast 250 rooms, along with
restaurants, health club, spa and conference facilities[493]. The
development would not be placed on the main island, instead on the
other side of the lake closer to the A320. Its position next to the water
would be a big selling point, with the architecture planned to be in a
classic style, with terraces where guests could sit and watch over the
lake. A ferry service was intended to take hotel guests across to the

theme park directly. The plans were quite stunning, and noticeably classier and more mature in tone than more recent projects, reminiscent of the classic Thorpe Park style of the 1980s.

A permanent hotel had been in the planning stages for almost a decade already, with public consultation initially happening way back in 2006, and early versions of planning permission being submitted and provisionally approved in 2011. These latest plans changed to request the project being completed in two stages, now starting with 150 rooms, and upscaling at a later date.

The hotel was part of Merlin's vision to turn Thorpe Park into a proper resort, encouraging multi-day visits and maximising profits from visitors who could afford to spend a little more on a short break. It had already proved a successful plan at other Merlin attractions in the UK including Alton Towers, Chessington World of Adventures and Legoland Windsor, which they also wanted to expand further. The plans stated that vertical construction would begin in 2016, with the *Thorpe Park Hotel* opening to the public in 2018.

To date the elegant *Thorpe Park Hotel* has never materialised. Apart from some extremely early preparation work undertaken in 2016, the project remains stagnant despite accommodation projects continuing at other Merlin parks. The most likely reason for this is a lack of confidence in the demand for premium lodging based on the teenage and young adult audience that currently visit. *Thorpe Shark* remains, but has not delivered enough to allay fears that the larger waterside accommodation would be a sensible investment. There's also the challenge with the park's operating season, which means they would face a serious task to fill rooms over the winter.

Whilst no construction work is imminent, ambitions still remain to one day add a permanent hotel and truly earn that resort name. Whether that is the version of the lakeside accommodation they have permission for, or something completely different, is yet to be seen. Elsewhere in the Merlin group Alton Towers now has three hotels, over 100 lodges in an

Enchanted Village area, and 100 "Stargazing Pods". Both Legoland Windsor and Chessington World of Adventures have two hotels, and are also moving into lodge style accommodation. The seemingly standard process of adding hotels to parks is now common practice both inside Merlin and in the wider theme park industry, which has left Thorpe Park somewhat isolated.

2015

With a big headline attraction underway and ready to open in 2016, the 2015 season would have to be a little less ambitious. With the preference to now work alongside existing IPs to help bring in the crowds, they were about to work with the biggest show on British television.

In 2002 *ITV* were searching for a reality show to rival the success of *Channel 4's* imported reality TV concept *Big Brother*, which was a runaway commercial and ratings hit since it had launched in 2000. In response ITV had licensed the rights to the big US reality show *Survivor*, where members of the public are stranded on an island and are forced to fend for themselves whilst taking part in challenges. Frustrated that the UK version of the programme was failing to captivate viewers, a replacement was sought. Producers came up with a twist on the concept that would instead strand people in the Australian jungle rather than on a desert island and replace boring old members of the public with familiar showbiz faces. High adrenaline or disgusting endurance challenges were devised for them to undertake, and the appallingly titled *I'm a Celebrity...Get Me Out of Here!* was born.

Despite the title, the programme became a ratings juggernaut for *ITV*, pulling in viewers every night of the week for a fortnight each year. Presented by the nation's sweethearts Anthony McPartlin and Declan Donnelly (Ant & Dec), it unsurprisingly returned annually (twice in 2004). What's more whilst the initial wave of reality formats that had filled television schedules early in the new millennium were starting to lose popularity, *I'm a Celebrity* was bucking the trend, with record viewing figures reported for the 2013 season (won by Kian from *Westlife* if you're interested). Not even a (unsuccessful) lawsuit from *Survivor* creators *CBS* could slow it down[494].

A deal was agreed between Merlin Entertainments and *ITV* to bring an *I'm A Celebrity* experience to Thorpe Park, but as the show's concept didn't particularly suit a traditional ride system, this attraction would be a little different. Using space where *Fright Night* mazes *Studio 13* and *The*

Asylum sat near the old *Ranger County*, this would instead be a walkthrough, giving visitors the chance to try a number of the so-called "Bushtucker Trials" from the programme. Guests would take on five different challenges, finishing with the notorious *Celebrity Cyclone* which is featured towards the end of each series of the show[495]. Ant & Dec recorded a special video to be shown to each group before they started, and the attraction would rely heavily on performers acting as guides who would be responsible for entertaining each group and moving them on in good time. Whilst completely different in tone, it was somewhat similar setup to the *Saw Alive* maze.

Unlike the television version, no real creepy creatures would be used or eaten, with special effects tools such as leg ticklers being used to recreate the feelings. One of the highlights would be "Screamer Showers" themed to the *Chamber of Horrors* challenge, with each group member inside an individual booth, and given the impression that creatures such as snakes were falling onto them[496]. The experience would be completely enclosed and hidden from the public, with visitors exiting through a tunnel slide into the gift shop. The shop would be shared with *Nemesis Inferno* and given an updated jungle theme, along with the option to get your own personalised t-shirt, just like the show.

To help create the immersive feeling of a camp from the Australian jungle, the team from Scruffy Dog Creative came on board to assist[497]. Scruffy Dog had delivered an excellent job on the *Thorpe Shark Hotel* and were to become regular collaborators with Merlin moving forward. The attraction came together quickly, taking just a few months to install from start to finish. A couple of set-pieces were added outside including a classic Mini Cooper that was given a makeover to appear overgrown[498].

In February of 2015 Thorpe Park announced the new attraction with a press release to the media. Resort divisional director Mike Vallis was quoted saying[499]:

"After thirteen years of watching *I'm A Celebrity…Get Me Out Of Here!* on the small screen, we're delighted to offer our guests the chance to brave

Bush Tucker Trials inspired by the hit TV show"

Referencing the show's reputation to get celebrities to eat animal testicles he added[500]:

"the good news is that we don't expect any of our guests to chew on a kangaroo's less palatable parts"

The new attraction opened on Friday 27th March, preceded by a VIP event the evening before attended by celebrities such as Tamzin Outhwaite, Katie Price, David Haye and Angela Griffin[501]. Opening went generally smoothly with some warm reviews from early riders, especially for the actors who were responsible for engaging with each group. Enthusiast website *Theme Park Insider* attended the launch night and summarised[502]:

"I came out somewhat bemused by the experience, and with reservations as regards its execution, yet impressed by the audacity of the attempt"

Following the introduction of *Angry Birds Land*, this was another step towards the family market, with the aim to recover some of the goodwill lost from the years concentrating solely on thrill seekers. They also saw it as an opportunity to get into the corporate market, positioning the attraction as a team building challenge for work groups.

During its first season operating it seemed to be a pull for visitors, often forming a queue in excess of an hour. The long queues may also have partly been a consequence of the relatively low throughput of the ride, meaning it could churn through far less guests every hour than many of the traditional rides. Being heavy on guest interaction, it also quickly started to pick up a number of faults, with effects and buttons not working at times. Changes were made to sections to try and improve the experience for each guest, and get people moving through as fast as possible. However, by the summer both the *Celebrity Cyclone*, and final slide sections were removed.

The experience lasted a total of four seasons at the park before being remodelled into an unbranded escape attraction. During its final couple of years, *I'm a Celebrity Get Me Out of Here* was only opened on peak days, presumably as it needed decent performers for it to operate, making it rather expensive. Increasingly visitors reported maintenance issues, and reviews declined. Some of the initial enthusiasm from those leading the groups was lost, although this obviously varied depending on the individual. Whilst the attraction might have lost popularity, the show continues to remain a huge hit for *ITV*.

A new music festival style event was also introduced this year for the key summer holiday period. *Island Beats* was a collaboration between Thorpe Park and Universal Music, bringing some big-name music acts to play gigs on Friday and Saturday evenings[503]. These included *Rizzle Kicks*, *Conor Maynard*, *Ella Eyre*, *The Vamps* and *Professor Green* playing sets on a stage in the *Lost City*. Rides remained open until 10pm and lesser known acts were given the chance to perform during the day on a stage in *Amity*. It was a neat idea but was to remain a one-off.

Unfortunately, much of the season was overshadowed by *The Smiler* incident at Alton Towers, which caused a decline in attendance across the board for Merlin's UK attractions. The intense media coverage of the crash would mean some lost faith in attending rollercoaster heavy theme parks, and there was no quick fix. Thorpe Park had however already signed off a massive addition for the following season, that would be a rather large gamble.

2016

Whilst both *I'm a Celebrity* and *Angry Birds Land* had been welcome family additions, they had been moderate investments compared to the five multi-million-pound rollercoasters introduced during the previous decade. Merlin management had now identified a strategy of making one major outlay on a headline attraction every four years, and 2016 would be the next opportunity to loosen the purse strings and add something they hoped would offer game changing appeal.

Derren Brown is described as a mentalist and illusionist, and had first come to prominence in 2000 with his *Channel 4* television programme *Mind Control*. After the success of the series he worked on a number of television and theatre shows to display skills he describes as "magic, suggestion, psychology, misdirection and showmanship". A very basic, possibly unjust, description would put him as the British version of David Blaine.

Brown's fame had risen thanks in a large part to a number of high profile controversial stunts he had performed. The most famous of these included playing a game of *Russian Roulette* with a loaded gun on live television and claiming to predict the results of the *National Lottery*. Other shows had focused on him using his mind control techniques to convince members of the public to perform actions which ranged from landing a plane, to committing a robbery or pushing somebody off the edge of a building. He was undoubtably an incredible showman, who had earned a loyal following, allowing him to conduct lengthy successful theatre tours along with West End residencies.

Not convinced that another rollercoaster was the right move as they were attempting to evolve into a fully-fledged resort, Thorpe Park approached Derren Brown and his team about working on a new attraction that they wanted to be something a little different. Merlin Magic Making contained a number of fans of his work, and Brown's theatrical skills, plus knack of grabbing headlines was attractive to management. By this time previous ride consultant John Wardley had retired, and Candy Holland was now focusing on the Legoland franchise, opening the door for new creatives at the company to express themselves. Merlin put their faith in Paul Moreton and Bradley Wynne to drive the project forward[504].

An ambitious plan was hatched to create a new kind of dark ride, given the project name *Whitechapel*, leaning heavily on technology and actors to perform Brown's mind-bending illusions on an industrial scale. There was no precedent set for how this would work, it was a brand-new concept that couldn't be purchased off the shelf from a manufacturer. Developing new systems always comes with extra challenges, but if it could be pulled off would give Thorpe Park a ride truly unlike any other in the world.

After over a year in development considering various options and speaking to potential suppliers, a decision had to be made on the concept, so they had time to complete the project for the 2016 season. They settled on a plan to take riders on an incredibly unusual train journey taking place inside a mysterious abandoned station/warehouse. Whilst some initially assumed the second development island created years earlier would house the next big headline attraction, instead a space was located right in the middle of the main island. A huge building would need to be constructed adjacent to the X pyramid, and creating the space would require the removal of some existing infrastructure. This meant the end of both the *Ranger County Arena*, utilised for various uses but probably most fondly remembered for the high diving shows, and the nostalgia laden *Chief Ranger's Carousel*.

With the new attraction housed entirely indoors local residents didn't have much to object to, and Runnymede Borough Council approved planning permission for the mysterious ride in January 2015[505]. An overview of the plans was visible to the public as always, but gave very little away about what was to be expected from the attraction - which was being kept completely secret - including the involvement of Brown. His passion for Victoriana was apparent from the building designs though, and that theme would continue throughout the experience.

What was this secret revolutionary experience going to be? Well it was certainly different to anything ever created before. After an outdoor queue and going through a preshow room, riders would enter the warehouse where a full-size Victorian train carriage would be hanging by chains from the ceiling. In groups riders would enter the train via a metal bridge, only to find that the interior was actually that of a typical modern-day London Underground carriage. Each of the seats would be equipped with a VR headset that is compulsory to wear, and a video would play accompanied by effects in the carriage matching the film. Eventually riders would be instructed to remove headsets and leave the train, only to find that they are no longer inside the same Victorian warehouse and instead in a tube station where a theatrical walkthrough style set piece happens. Guests are instructed to return to a train via another platform, and once again go through a VR experience complete with effects. At the end of this riders find themselves leaving the original Victorian train carriage and the experience is over.

The whole experience from entering to leaving the building would take between 12-15 minutes, far longer than any average ride you'd usually find in a theme park. It is impossible to overemphasise just how different and brave a move this was from Thorpe Park. The temptation to play it reasonably safe and install another rollercoaster or water ride must have been strong. A huge amount of credit must be given to them for allowing the team at Merlin Magic Making to try something quite so ambitious, and back it with a huge eight figure budget. Moreton and Wynne were quoted as saying[506]:

"At Merlin Magic Making we are constantly striving to push the boundaries of innovation; we don't just want to be specialists in creating entertainment, but also inventors. This concept is an entirely new invention. You can't simply call it a ride, an attraction or an experience – this is an original concept and we can't wait to see people's reactions to it"

If it worked though it had a number of positives going for it. Since the destruction of *Wicked Witches Haunt* there had been no true dark ride attraction, something other leading theme parks were offering. Additionally, it was another indoor ride, and what's more it was a headline attraction that could potentially open all-year round. Unlike the rollercoasters that struggle in the cold weather, this could be part of a future winter resort opening and be another part of the jigsaw to get the permanent hotel project off the ground. It was also hoped this might be another step towards changing the reputation of the park that had suffered from an overabundance of teenagers, by offering something on a par with the premium parks such as Disney and Universal. Basically, a lot was being gambled on this being a success.

Behind the scenes a British company called Simworx had been commissioned to provide three high tech vehicles that would form the transport part of the ride. Inside each of these vehicles sit 58 HTC Vive VR headsets, each powered by an individual hard drive[507]. Played on each of these headsets would be the specially commissioned films, created by Guildford based digital media production company Figment[508]. Each of these elements, along with dozens of other pieces of equipment, would need to work seamlessly together to create the desired effect.

Work to remove the existing structures, and build the warehouse required to house the attraction, took place during the 2015 season. Large banners teasing *Project Whitechapel* were added to the construction walls, and pointed towards a mysterious website called *Minds Wanted* where those curious could register for updates and try to solve clues to find out more. Unlike a rollercoaster, keeping the concept of the ride was going to be a lot easier.

By the end of October 2015 Thorpe Park were willing to show their hand a little to start the publicity going for the following year. Derren Brown was officially revealed as the mastermind behind what was being billed as[509]:

"The world's first psychological theme-park ride"

A press release also featured Brown with his mouth sewn up, with references to a secret he was keeping, and that it would "derail people's minds". In the same release Mike Vallis teased[510]:

"This truly is the world's first 'smart' theme park attraction, paving the future for the leisure industry"

No name or details of the ride were given at this point, although hints towards the train theme continued, with images of five people with outreached arms standing next to each other widely used. If you squinted a little these could be seen as a trainline.

Following the end of the 2015 season, work continued apace to try and hit the advertised March opening date the following year. This included installing 110 metres of track, and the 65-foot replica Victorian train carriage, which would actually be a shell that the Simworx underground styled vehicle would fit into. To make it appear like it was hanging loose in a completely empty warehouse an old magicians' trick was applied, literally using smoke and mirrors to create a simple but highly impressive illusion and hide the secrets from unsuspecting passengers.

Another classic from the magician's repertoire, *Pepper's Ghost*, was to be used for the pre-show. The illusion which has been around since the 19th Century, and used on many dark rides, would allow a version of Derren Brown to speak with each group of passengers, and apparently interact with several physical objects such as a whiteboard and toy train.

Filming of the VR sections continued in January, with the ride's loose story following how controversial drilling technique fracking had caused some disturbances underground. Six versions of the first section were filmed using different characters, meaning that passengers who sat next to each other could be experiencing separate journeys. To those wearing the VR headsets it would appear as if the relevant character had entered the train carriage, and was speaking directly to them. In addition, two versions of the second VR section were created, meaning in total there were twelve possible variants of ride experience.

To reinforce the psychological suggestions made during the VR sections, a number of physical effects would be in action too. These included vibration and leg ticklers, with the carriage impressively also being lifted off the track by a 35-tonne motion platform. Whilst the technology was immense, maybe the most effective trick was a simple one. The ride hosts tapping each guest on the leg with a stick, which they would be signalled to do at relevant points in the VR by lights inside the vehicle.

At the start of 2016 Thorpe Park were ready to reveal a little more about what guests should expect, including the final name for the attraction, which would officially be known as *Derren Brown's Ghost Train*[511]. To accompany the name reveal was some outline details of the ride, along with some more of Brown's thoughts including[512]:

"The team has been galvanised by the positive reaction to the first announcement we made last year and we are even more determined to deliver a revolutionary experience; as such we are constantly tweaking things to ensure they're the best they can be... I firmly believe that this kind of multi-sensory, mind blowing attraction represents a glimpse of what the future holds for theme parks the world over"

The tweaks alluded to were proving to be something a little more significant. The immense amount of technology that needed to work together was having some serious difficulties. In addition, the teams working on the ride had concerns about the middle section where riders would leave the train. This section relied heavily on the performance of the actors within the ride for it to work, and position people ready for an illusion where a tube train would appear to crash into the room. Whilst it originally worked on paper, in practice it would need some amendments.

One of the most serious problems was the VR headsets working consistently inside each carriage. Reportedly they were being particularly sensitive to light reflections inside the shiny tube interior, and that was not something that could be easily amended. One solution was to remove the poles you find on a standard underground train, but these amendments were putting the project well behind schedule[513].

Publicly the park was portraying positivity about the opening, and organised an offer to let 1,871 people pre-purchase tickets for just 12p each (the equivalent of a Victorian shilling) on Good Friday[514]. The number of tickets available was based on the year the ride is set, which apparently was chosen as it is one hundred years before Derren Brown was born. The promotion proved to be a little too popular, leading to all the tickets being sold before the advertised time they went on sale. News outlets were full of angry people complaining that it was fixed, with Thorpe Park eventually agreeing to run the offer again with another 1,871 12p tickets available[515].

In other attempts to spread the word about the new arrival the restrictions board that sat outside the attraction's entrance was claimed to be the longest in the world[516]. Most importantly it confirmed that visitors would need to be over 13 years old if they wished to experience it. Agency Taylor Herring were appointed to help drum up further interest, and arranged to film Derren Brown "testing" aspects of the new addition, which in this instance involved scaring park staff in their offices with a demon creature[517].

Intrigue and interest were high, with fans of the illusionist and theme parks around the world keen to find out the full extent of what had been created. In further media interviews Brown was slowly revealing more about his involvement. In an interview with *Digital Spy* where he also claimed he came up with the idea in his front room, he said[518]:

> "I was given basically carte blanche to do anything which was a phenomenal situation to be in and making a ghost train felt right immediately"

The mysterious building that houses the attraction. Credit: Alex Rowe

The various promotions and media releases were timed to lead up to the big opening that had been announced for Friday 6th May[519]. If what was being promised was true, Thorpe Park was to be home to one of the most advanced and innovative theme park rides in the entire world. However, with technical issues continuing to plague the testing, a delay was confirmed just three days beforehand. With no obvious fix possible, no new date was given for the opening with the media told[520]:

> "...the reason for the delay is purely creative, there are still elements of the show yet to be completed"

The delay was a disaster for the marketing team who had been planning the campaign for over a year. In addition to the lost momentum from the extensive media coverage, an expensive television advertising campaign had been booked and was too late to cancel. Adverts were amended to say that the attraction would open in May but with no specific date. Even that would eventually turn out to be overly optimistic, with the delays dragging from weeks into two months as problems persisted.

Whilst inside the mysterious building teams from various suppliers were working to try and get everything working, the outside was finished and looking magnificent. It had been transformed from a modern corrugated warehouse into a Victorian station called *Thorpe Junction*. The level of detail was impressive, although the bespoke metal entrance gates remained firmly shut for now. Much of the queue line had been covered to protect guests during either wet weather, or bright sunshine. Added throughout were bespoke posters hinting at the fracking theme, which had been deliberately aged and graffitied on.

The queue also included two rooms, that worked as photo opportunities. There was no on-ride photo because it would be difficult to capture and spoil some of the secrets. So, these spots in the queue were a chance to get a memento, with those waiting posing in specially designed holes, and the resulting pictures being turned into unique souvenirs. It also had the positive side-effect of breaking up the wait a little and giving those outside something to do before entering the building.

Opened before the ride itself was the gift shop, which is undoubtably the best themed and most creative merchandise outlet they had ever achieved. In line with the ride and the queue, the level of detailed theming was exceptional with several bespoke items added. This included a Derren Brown fortune teller machine (think Zoltar from the movie *Big*), a fake portrait that moved, and various other tricks. The items available to buy included backwards clocks and floating train carriages amongst the usual logo emblazoned t-shirts, teddies and stationery. You could also purchase items relating to the fictional companies created for the ride, such as Sub Core Energy. It was impressive stuff, that also helped whet appetites for the real thing. A second fortune teller machine was added in the *Dome*, inside a promotional destroyed train.

Eventually *Derren Brown's Ghost Train* opened exclusively to *Thorpe Shark* guests in small numbers to try it out, before soft opening to visitors from 1st July. It finally officially opened to all on Friday 8th July, just in time for the summer holidays[521]. To begin with only one of the two options for the second VR section would be used, which involved an explosion causing the train to suffer a catastrophic accident. Brown seemed to see the funny side of the delays tweeting[522]:

> "My Ghost Train at Thorpe Park is finally open. After all the delays you'd expect from an actual train. Enjoy x"

Confident everything was good to go; the usual VIP launch night was arranged. The random celebrity generator this time turned out *Masterchef*'s Gregg Wallace, *Harry Potter's* Rupert Grint, and former Arsenal and England goalkeeper David Seaman[523].

Reviews of the ride started to flood in, and they seemed to vary greatly, veering from completely blown away to massively underwhelmed. Some of the disappointment might have been from setting expectations a little bit too high, with even representatives from Disney and Universal Studios travelling to try it out[524]. Despite mixed reviews there was a consensus that the physical decoration was fantastic, with praise for the actors who played an instrumental role in creating a suitably intense atmosphere.

Whilst praising the first half of the ride *Digital Spy* tech editor Luke Johnson was critical of the second VR section, stating[525]:

"The second VR experience, however, feels awkward and disjointed. It's more farcical than fantastical and even with the willing suspension of disbelief, never feels real. And that's largely down to the grainy graphics. Seriously, this looks like a 2007 video game, not a 2016 sign of the future"

Many, including Jamie Feltham at Upload, felt the scariness was overplayed[526]:

"Obviously, you can't make this ride too scary, but I couldn't help but feel disappointed that the Ghost Train hadn't even troubled me, a man that often has to hold his breath, cover his ears and close his eyes when re-watching Aliens. After spending such a long time building up the experience I was left wishing it had made me laugh less and got my heart racing ever so slightly"

A common criticism seemed to be that whilst the attraction was interesting and enjoyable, it lacked cohesion between the different sections, leading to a confusing experience. Nick Summers review for *Engadget* summed it up stating[527]:

"There's no grand reveal at the end. Nothing that explains what you were feeling, or acts upon those feelings to do something new. It's a flashy but ultimately hollow experience"

Not everybody was as critical though, with the *Thorpe Park Mania* fan website exuding praise[528]:

"In one word I think I would describe it as 'amazing'. It's like nothing I have been on before and it's totally unique"

Understandably visitors were keen to make up their own minds, with huge lines forming beyond the usual queue area, with some waiting several hours. Not helping was a continuation of operating issues, with a number of "technical delays" causing queues to move slowly, and many riders unable to receive the proper experience. Many would sit for several minutes with just green fog filling the VR headset screen, presumably because there was a delay in reaching the next part of the ride. Throughput was also not helped by the need to clean each headset between groups, with staff rushing through with antiviral wipes as quickly as possible.

Unsurprisingly the *Mail Online* had found something to sensationalise about the new attraction, running a story that claimed[529]:

> "Derren Brown's latest trick may be his most controversial yet – brainwashing thousands of teenage theme park visitors against fracking by making them believe it could have apocalyptic consequences"

With over 1,000 people involved in the creation, and at a reported cost of over £13 million, it had taken an incredible amount of time and money to make *Project Whitechapel* a reality[530]. The mixture of technology and illusions deployed was a truly ground-breaking endeavour that was always going to be a risk. The end result whilst not a total catastrophe, was a frustrating experience, with the nagging feeling that it could have been so much better. There's so much potential to create a memorable journey for every guest, which has not been realised. Whilst some effects don't quite work as well as expected, it's maybe understandable given the ride's ambitious nature. What is completely inexcusable is the lack of a cohesive story, that should surely be one of the critical success factors for any attraction of this nature.

John Wardley was even asked by several senior staff to return to see what improvements he could suggest, but with so much already in place at a great cost, it was too late[531]. Ironically it was a project his pedigree was perfect for, having come from a career of working in special effects, magic and ride consultancy. It appeared this time many talented people had come together from different backgrounds, but the project lacked an individual who had copious theme park operations experience in their heart, leading to it losing focus on its core purpose. Reliably entertaining as many people as possible.

The heavy reliance on VR also has its issues. It is a shame that the train passengers spend the majority of such an incredibly themed dark ride; inside a headset blocking everything out. It also takes you out of the moment whilst inside the tube carriage, somewhat dampening the reveal when you leave the first time to see the Victorian carriage has gone. There's also a worrying whiff of short-termism about such technology, knowing the rate such things progress, it could quickly become dated. The same year Merlin also added VR headsets to the *Air* rollercoaster at Alton Towers, giving riders the impression they were travelling through space[532]. The re-branded *Galactica* was an initial draw, but quickly riders tired of the experience and as the novelty wore off, headsets were reduced and eventually removed just a couple of years later. With so many classic dark rides enduring decades, there was a danger that Thorpe Park's investment would not be futureproof.

It seemed that Merlin agreed to some extent, and plans were quickly revisited to see what changes could be made for the following season to try and rescue their new star attraction.

In 2016, away from the new attraction, Thorpe Park received some welcome publicity from superstar rapper *Stormzy*, who claimed he had hired out the park for his birthday and invited his millions of social media followers to enter a competition to join him[533]. For his birthday at the end of July he did indeed visit with a couple of hundred friends and winners that included musician *Wretch 32* and *Crystal Palace* footballer Wilfred Zaha. Nando's provided packed lunches, and Adidas a cake and goodie bags[534]. Stormzy himself performed a short set after riding the likes of *Nemesis Inferno* and *Rush*.

During the season website *Trusted Reviews* used wearable technology to indicate what the park's scariest rides were. The article suggested that *Nemesis Inferno* was the most heart racing stating[535]:

"All of this combined to make my heart rate leap to 64% of its maximum
– equivalent to 124bpm"

Stealth and *Saw* were close behind. *Derren Brown's Ghost Train* failed to make much of an impact, with the reviewer Richard Easton suggesting the queue times might be more terrifying than the experience.

The final PR move of the summer was to try and attract an older audience to the park, by releasing a specially commissioned survey, and offering pensioners half price entry for the rest of the season. The *Evening Standard*[536] reported that more Over-65s than ever had visited in 2015, and the "Old Aged Coaster Pass" (OACP) was to encourage more to try out the rides. Considering most theme parks struggle to attract large numbers on weekdays outside of school holidays, there is some logic in the idea.

2017

Inside Merlin there was great frustration that *Derren Brown's Ghost Train* was not the trailblazing attraction envisioned, and with so many hopes for the future of Thorpe Park riding on its success, it was decided that action would be required, and quickly. Any budget that was going to be set aside for a small addition or improvements in 2017, would now instead be used to upgrade the experience on the underperforming dark ride.

For the upgrade, Merlin Magic Making would be going back to some of their original ideas that were not incorporated. By October 2016, just three months after the official opening of the ride, a new planning application was submitted to the council to extend the attraction's building by a small amount[537]. Posters were then spotted at *Fright Nights* promising "a new terrifying destination" for the following season. The plans were quickly approved by the council, and a trademark application for *Rise of the Demon* followed.

The Drum reported that television adverts for the attraction planned to be shown during the Christmas holidays were banned, being too scary for a pre-watershed audience[538]. The 20 second planned ads featured white bunnies playing amongst a snowy train line, before a loud demonic creature fills the screen for a split second, designed to make the audience jump. By March 2017 Thorpe Park were ready to confirm that *Derren Brown's Ghost Train: Rise of the Demon* would be their latest attempt to excite and terrify guests, with some minor details revealed about the changes[539].

Over the winter work had been completed to construct the extension of the building, adding a new surprise ending. Once riders had exited the chained carriage and had likely relaxed, they would now enter a fake shop building carefully designed to look like the real thing, complete with merchandise and photo spot. Once stopped by a member of staff due to a fake unspecified issue, the group would be subjected to some spooky activities including the room shaking, pipes splitting apart and lights flickering. The pièce de résistance was the magical appearance of a life size demon in the room, which would then disappear again within a flicker of light. It was impressively realised, and genuinely works as a surprise.

The second VR section of the ride was also changed to incorporate the demon theme. This was in fact one of the original two films that were promised for 2016, but only one ever used. The official line was that this video was not used previously because the content was too intense. The more likely reason was to remove headaches encountered during testing and get the ride open. The new film was more realistic, featuring what appeared to be fellow riders sitting around you on the carriage who are attacked, followed by the train being torn apart by a demon. The teaser pictures and videos of Derren Brown and a demon from a year earlier now made sense, giving away that this was a plan for the original concept.

The middle section where riders leave the train a first time was also changed to feature a more defined route for each group making their way through, defined by metal fencing. There were a few added effects too such as a demonic shadow lurking. The section was now more of a Halloween walkthrough than the previous theatrical piece.

Once again Derren Brown was promising big things to the media, telling the *Evening Standard*[540]:

"We are making this bigger, better and scarier than last year. The changes and improvements that have taken place will scare the shit out of guests"

Despite this, early reviewers concurred that the attraction was no scarier than before. *WIRED*'s Rowland Manthorpe summarised[541]:

"Was it the scariest ride ever? Perhaps not. But then again it's hard to say for sure. When the going got tough, I took Derren's advice and closed my eyes"

In general, many agreed that the attraction was a mild improvement, but was no silver bullet to fix the overall feeling of disappointment. As more of the public tried out the updated experience many familiar moans returned around technology not working correctly, or being left confused by the (lack of) storyline.

Since the re-launch struggles have continued in living up to the high expectations of visitors, perhaps fuelled by Thorpe Park's marketing. The operation of the ride itself has also failed to deliver, with slow moving queues often frustrating those waiting. Additionally, many headsets sit broken or unusable in each carriage, further limiting the hourly capacity. Damningly for what should be a headline attraction, it no longer opens with the rest of the park, instead waiting until noon every day to make it cost effectives. As a major investment, costing more than a new major rollercoaster, it was a huge disappointment. *The Swarm* might have initially failed to boost attendance, but at least it continues to offer a high-quality experience that churns through the crowds. *Derren Brown's Ghost Train* has achieved neither, and is perhaps the most high-profile failure in the history of Thorpe Park. It certainly has parallels with the other big budget experimental ride installed 20 years earlier - when *X:\ No Way Out* also struggled to re-define the audience of the park.

The repercussions of the performance probably go well beyond its day to day appeal though. A permanent Thorpe Park hotel was not justifiable, further delaying its journey from concept to possible reality. It is also a blow to dark rides in the UK, and potentially further afield, with it being unlikely that Merlin will take another big gamble on such a ground-breaking concept anytime soon. The business argument for backing this type of creativity just doesn't make sense, which is in many ways heart-breaking. That is not to say there are not some great ideas in the finished product, they just didn't quite work as everyone had hoped.

You could also make some loose connections between *Derren Brown's Ghost Train* and Disney's *Star Wars Rise of the Resistance* mega attraction, which opened in 2019. The core idea of taking visitors through several different parts of a journey rather than one basic transport system is the same. Most agree Disney's ride delivers on so many levels, possibly making it the most complete attraction in the world, no doubt helped by an outrageous nine figure budget.

The future of Thorpe Park's most distinct and interesting ride is uncertain. It is far too big of an investment to discard, but at the same time suffers from high operating and maintenance costs. Whilst the big five rollercoasters are proudly promoted at the top of the bill on the website, and all other promotional material, the *Ghost Train* plays a reduced role. Would they dare slash its operating time further to just peak days? Or worse will it be reduced to only the packed *Fright Night* events? It's unlikely we've seen the final ever version of the ride, but that is not to say any future changes will be for the better. It is probably more likely these changes would be made to reduce costs rather than spend further to try and rescue the concept. One popular theory is that the attraction could undergo a branding makeover to a more popular IP, as whilst Brown's style fits the mystique of such a ride, he's possibly just not enough of a draw. Even something such as a Sherlock Holmes mystery storyline might work better (and is an out-of-copyright IP). As David McCubbin comments[542]:

"Maybe the biggest gamble in many ways was tying it to Derren Brown"

The 2017 season also saw a couple of small surprise additions to the former *Canada Creek* area of the park, now designated as *Old Town*. Merlin Entertainments had been having a clear out of the Weymouth Sealife Centre and found a couple of childrens' rides that were no longer required. These were *Rockin' Tug* and *Jumpin' Star* models, both manufactured by Italy's Zamperla[543]. The former was named *Timber Tug Boat* and consisted of a small vessel sliding from side to side, and spinning in a gentle manner. The other was a very small drop ride named *Lumber Jump*. It is likely Thorpe Park inherited these as both Alton Towers and Chessington World of Adventures already boasted similar rides. They stuck out at Thorpe Park, with no effort made to theme either to their new surroundings. However, they did offer something for the smallest members of a family, which had been lacking since the removal of *Octopus Garden*. Both would move location again in 2022, *Lumber Jump* joining the ride line-up in Amity and being re-branded as *High Striker*, whilst (despite being almost identical to another ride there) *Timber Tug Boat* made its way to Chessington World of Adventures, becoming *Trawler Trouble*.

The television singing competition *X Factor* also made a debut at the park in 2017. Strangely relevant given the song competitions that had been a regular event at the park over 25 years previously. This was an episode of the auditions stage of the programme where hopefuls try and impress the judges. It also worked as a wonderful primetime advert for the park, with judges (at the time) Simon Cowell, Louis Walsh, Sharon Osbourne and Nicole Scherzinger being shown riding various attractions, including the updated *Ghost Train* which Cowell described as "terrifying"[544].

Another General Election in the UK on 8th June was dominating the media narrative, so keen as ever to be part of the story, the PR team unleashed a couple of initiatives. First was the opportunity for young people to get entry for just £20 if they registered to vote[545]. The second was a rename of *Derren Brown's Ghost Train* to *POLL-TERGEIST* for election day, complete with actors dressed as the party leaders Theresa May, Jeremy Corbyn and Tim Farron inside the ride[546].

It was also a newsworthy year for *Stealth*, initially featured in many articles surrounding the 200th anniversary of the rollercoaster. To celebrate, engineers enjoyed a birthday cake at the highest point of the 205-foot ride, with the posed photograph circulated to the media[547]. Then in less welcome coverage a small group illegally entered the park at night and climbed to the top without safety equipment. The whole thing was captured on camera, with the resulting video going viral online. The culprit was unsurprisingly banned from all parks for life[548].

In another shocking story it was revealed, in the *Mail Online,* that one couple had left their one-year old baby unattended in a pram by the attraction entrance, as they took an hour queueing for and riding *Colossus*[549]. Security were called, who reported the incident to social services.

Ahead of the 2017 *Fright Nights* event, it was announced that *AMC's The Walking Dead* would be featuring in two mazes. To help promote the popular IPs appearance, a truck toured round London as a "live billboard" complete with zombie actors and props. Marketing publication *The Drum* summarised[550]:

"It is unlikely the gory ad format will be widely adopted by the industry but it inarguably provides a not-so-subtle alternative to online adblocking"

Whilst *Fright Nights* offered welcome escapism for many visitors, the real world was unfortunately becoming scarier. Terrorist attacks in London, including one on London Bridge killing eleven people, were impacting on the tourism industry[551]. Thorpe Park was one of the lesser affected attractions, but Merlin Entertainment's central London sites such as Madame Tussauds and the *London Eye* were harder hit. The subsequent poorer than expected financial results for the company was putting their stock price under pressure, and by November they were relegated from the FTSE 100 index[552].

2018

Following the introduction of *The Walking Dead* at the 2017 *Fright Nights*, the brand would make a more significant appearance the following season with a permanent attraction proposed.

Since premiering in 2010 on American network *AMC*, *The Walking Dead* had been a runaway ratings success, and been shown around the world. It focuses on the survivors of a zombie apocalypse with an ensemble cast led by actor Andrew Lincoln. It has a reputation for shock twists and gory fights, leading to it being massively popular with the much sought after 18-49 age demographic. It celebrated its 100th episode in late 2017 and spawned a spin-off series called *Fear the Walking Dead*, which shows how the fictitious pandemic apocalypse started. Whilst not quite as ubiquitous in the UK, it seemed a good fit for Thorpe Park's existing audience, and Merlin Magic Making's love of installing disaster style decoration.

Thorpe Park's indoor Vekoma coaster, known originally as *X:\ No Way Out* before a small makeover to *X* in 2013, had been operating for 22 years. Once the biggest investment in the history of Thorpe Park, it now largely failed to inspire visitors, and was underwhelming in comparison to the five major rollercoasters elsewhere in the park. It was now to receive a *Walking Dead* makeover, and creatives went about working out how to best realise this with a small budget. It would be unfeasible to change any of the actual rollercoaster system, so instead focus was put into integrating the TV series in other ways.

How visitors entered the distinctive pyramid building was the only main structural change, with permission sought from the council to build a replica watchtower from the series in December 2017[553]. Inside this a new pre-show was developed that briefed riders on a zombie outbreak happening at Thorpe Park, complete with synchronised lights and video screens replicating an attack. The outside queue line was extended to resemble a compound complete with chain line fences and cattle pen style queuing system. Giant letters added to the side of the building declared it as "THE SAFE ZONE".

Once through the pre-show many of the meandering corridors remained, with spinning warning lights the only clue to guide your way through the darkness. Towards the end of the queue, more graffiti and artwork was added including many Easter eggs for fans of the series. The ride itself continued to run in its updated forwards positioning, but a new on-board soundtrack was added, along with effects such as smoke and sparks at the stopping sections. No *Walking Dead* ride would be complete without some zombies, so these are visible during key sections of the ride, including quite effectively towards the final brake run.

John Burton was the creative lead on the project from Merlin Magic Making, and he turned to frequent collaborators Scruffy Dog to realise many of the more ambitious moments[554]. Highlights of these included giant entrance gates made from corrugated iron, and a delivery truck that surprises riders as they disembark with a loud horn. The number plate of which is a nod to the ride's predecessor reading "XNWO". Expert media creation company Holovis developed the new audio and video required, including what they describe as "immersive media scenes"[555]. This would sit inside an area of the park designated the *Dock Yard*, encompassing *The Walking Dead* and *Derren Brown's Ghost Train*. The attention to detail, and standard of decoration throughout the experience is top notch, although riders believing it's a brand-new attraction might be disappointed when they reach the end of the queue.

Overhauling rides with new theming to create a "brand new" attraction is of course nothing new in itself, and has been present nearly as long as theme parks themselves. Thorpe Park had previous examples with *Space Station Zero/Flying Fish* as well as *Phantom Fantasia/Wicked Witches Haunt*, but it was common practice throughout the industry. Even theme park titans Disney are happy to update existing systems with IPs to create a new attraction. Recently this has led to the iconic *Tower of Terror* in California becoming *Guardians of the Galaxy*, and in Florida the *Maelstrom* ride at EPCOT had a makeover to be known as *Frozen Ever After*. Neither ride system has changed, but both have incorporated a new IP storyline to a level that is believed enough to justify it as a new attraction.

Thorpe Park proudly announced their latest addition in February 2018 declaring it to be[556]:

"The UK's first and only multi-sensory and multi-part rollercoaster as guests are invited to flee *The Walking Dead* in a terrifying and relentless ride for survival"

To add extra panic, actors dressed up as zombies would be deployed throughout the dark corridors before and after the ride section. Although like many attractions of this nature, you're only likely to see them at peak times.

Before the planned opening for the Easter holidays, the usual marketing blitz started to take place. The most bizarre attempt this time was to claim that the rollercoaster would be literally powered by the screams of riders. *The Mirror* picked up on the story and said the "Scream-O-Meter" developed by Queen Mary University London would be in operation for a trial period[557]. Reading beyond the headline, it seemed the device would more likely pick up power from the coaster's vibrations and G-forces, and only enough to power a phone charger, by that probably does not make such a good PR piece.

Soon after the media were getting their chance to try it out, alongside some influencers. *Theme Park Incorporated* summed up their review with[558]:

"Overall this is probably the most effective use of the original *X:\ No Way Out* building and coaster. If it wasn't for the unbelievable amount of theming and creative planning that has gone into the attraction then this would still be the same old, now boring, coaster"

However, *The Sun* newspaper, who probably represented more of the casual theme park visitor clientele, were more enthusiastic stating[559]:

"The worst part of the ride is that you don't know what's going to happen around each corner – it's also the best part"

David McCubbin, who had passionately worked on the original *X:\ No Way Out* for many years, returned to try out the new version, and felt it compared favourably[560]:

"It finally feels it has achieved what it set out to do in the beginning. It's a completely immersive themed experience from the moment you walk in, to the moment you walk out"

The attraction would form the centrepiece of what Thorpe Park were calling their *"Year of The Walking Dead"*, which also included a couple of new seasonal events[561]. These were in the form of the Halloween live action maze being opened up for May Half Term, and an interactive *Zombie Hunt* during the summer break. After a successful debut the previous year, *The Walking Dead* mazes would also be the core to the 2018 Fright Night celebrations.

Another TV brand was also signed up to help bring in the crowds, with Thorpe Park partnering with *ITV2's Love Island* for their late night summer openings[562]. The show had been somewhat of a surprise hit for the digital channel when it was revived in 2015, and its popularity was surging with teenagers and young adults keen to find out what shenanigans the latest bunch of horny youngsters on a paradise island would get up to. By 2018 nearly four million people were watching every night. *Love Island Lates* would transform Thorpe Park's beach (now part of the constantly expanding *Amity*) into a scene from the series, complete with photo opportunities, fire pit and dunk tank. The park remained open until 10pm at weekends, featuring the likes of live music, cocktails and games[563]. Scantily clad contestants from the series were signed up to launch the concept, although they wouldn't be in attendance most of the time. *Love Island Lates* was a creative, low risk way of trying out something new, but did not return the following year despite the TV series continuing to set new records for *ITV2*.

2019

2019 marked the 40th anniversary of Thorpe Park, and regardless of the significance of the year, there was a reluctance to celebrate. There were no new attractions announced or constructed, and whilst that was rare, it wasn't unheard of during difficult times[564]. What was fishier was the lack of development on the horizon for future years. Having previously hinted to enthusiasts that 2020 would be the year of a major new investment, with a major new rollercoaster once in the pipeline, it soon became clear that something was holding back their future plans. By June that year the cause of this became a little clearer, when Merlin Entertainments announced a deal had been struck to be acquired for £5.9 billion[565]. The new joint owners were Kirkbi, Blackstone and the Canadian Pension Plan Investment Bond, taking the company off the stock exchange, and into private hands once again.

With the deal in the pipeline for a while, it's likely the decision was taken to hold back on any major plans until the new owners could do a proper assessment of where funds should be spent. Kirkbi is the investment vehicle of Lego's founding family, and already had a 30% stake in Merlin. Their interest in the Legoland franchise is obvious, but where Thorpe Park fits into a business with an overwhelmingly family friendly portfolio isn't immediately obvious.

With no new rides to entice visitors, faith was instead put in several low budget small events taking place across the year. The hope being they could capture some of the crowd pulling magic performed by the annual *Fright Nights*. The first of these was called *GameFX*, a celebration of computer games, from retro classics to the latest technology[566]. Taking place in a hospitality marquee between *Depth Charge* and *The Swarm*, it allowed guests to get hands on and try out many different games at no extra cost. Partnered with *HYPD* and Coke Zero it seemed an attempt to cash in on the popularity at the time of online gaming, led by the extraordinary success of the computer game *Fortnite*. Most of these could of course be simply played at home, which might have made justifying an expensive theme park ticket difficult for families, but the opportunity of trying out the latest VR technology added some additional value.

To promote the *GameFX* event Thorpe Park captured and released a number of pictures of iconic computer games characters around the park. However, the costumes used were obviously from a local fancy dress shop, looking similar in quality to the pre-*Thorpe Park Rangers* Mr Rabbit outfit, and certainly not official mascots. Adam Starkey in *The Metro* picked up on the unintentionally funny photoshoot, writing under the headline "Thorpe Park is hosting an esports event with a very low barrier for cosplay"[567]:

> "The event promises a 'fully-immersive audience experience' – with immersion only possibly broken by a Mario and Luigi combo fresh from Del Boy's van"

If *GameFX* was a bit of a leftfield choice, the second special event of the year was something straight out of early Thorpe Park. BounceZilla was a 90-metre-long inflatable obstacle course set up in the *Lost City* area of the park[568]. Visitors were asked to remove their shoes and make their way round the ultimate childrens' party bouncy castle, in what many found surprisingly exhausting fashion. Whilst it seemed slightly tacky of the park to be promoting this rather than a new cutting-edge ride, it did add something different and most importantly fun, allowing guests to have a laugh rather than promising to terrify them for once. *BounceZilla* remained in action until the end of the summer holidays, leaving those visiting after this time feeling a little deflated.

Another new option for visitors was *Jungle Escape*, which was the re-working of the *I'm a Celebrity Get Me Out of Here* attraction. Escape rooms had become increasingly popular during the previous decade, and the nature of these means they offer very low capacity per hour, ruling them out of a theme park environment. However, creatives came up with a way to churn through as many people as possible and charge them an additional £6 for the privilege. Reviews suggested that *Jungle Escape* offered a fun, albeit short experience. Others were disappointed to see something that was in effect previously included in the entrance fee, now being something for which they had to pay extra.

Entry into Thorpe Park hit an all-time high of £55 per person, a far cry from the £1 original entry price in 1979. Whilst that figure is substantial, the truth is that hardly anybody visiting pays that amount. Due to the plethora of deals available from third-party partnerships (such as soft drinks companies, newspapers and many others), most visitors pay a heavily reduced fee. Many of these are "buy one, get one free" deals, but the promotions vary. The Thorpe Park website also offers a cheaper price, saving around £20 per person, when booking several days in advance. An annual pass can also be obtained for the same £55 fee (no vouchers valid), offering further evidence that it's a rather small percentage of visitors who pay that amount in the first place. Another very popular option is a Merlin annual pass, which covers all their attractions, which works out as especially good value if you live close to the triumvirate of Chessington World of Adventures, Legoland Windsor, and Thorpe Park.

Whilst billion-pound deals were dictating the future of the park behind the scenes, the public were given the chance to see some business amateurs in action during filming of BBC One's *The Apprentice* at the park[569]. Candidates were briefed by Lord Alan Sugar to design a potential new Thorpe Park rollercoaster, and also got to try out the existing ones. Whilst it's unlikely Merlin Entertainments will be reaching for the phone to offer them a job, the show did an excellent job of showcasing the park, much like the *X Factor* the previous year.

With it being the 40th anniversary some small celebrations were held to commemorate the past four decades. Whilst these were subdued there were some nice touches in place, including the use of the classic logo and original rabbit mascot on the anniversary weekend. A new range of merchandise was also launched featuring classic rides and attractions. Locals were also offered cupcakes when visiting on the actual anniversary weekend so they could join in the fun[570].

Everyday life was soon to change for everyone, with 2019 being the last time for a while that you could visit a theme park anywhere under normal circumstances.

2020-2022

Just a couple of months ahead of opening for the 2020 season, Thorpe Park made a surprise announcement. They had teamed up with another television show, this time *Netflix*'s *Black Mirror*, to create a new walkthrough attraction[571]. *Black Mirror Labyrinth* was promoted to visitors saying[572]:

> "Get lost as you enter a hypnotic maze using cutting-edge visual technology and sensory-defying environments"

Black Mirror was a British show written by comedian and journalist Charlie Brooker. It started life on *Channel 4*, where it proved to be a sleeper hit for three series, before being picked up by *Netflix* for international distribution. When it performed particularly well for them, *Netflix* offered to fund future series, with upcoming episodes becoming available exclusively through their platform. The show itself is a kind of take on the old fifties and sixties television series *The Twilight Zone*. Each episode being self-contained with its own storyline and cast. The series explores unintended consequences of technology, with most episodes set in the near future. It has also dabbled with technology itself, becoming one of the first shows on the streaming platform to offer an interactive episode, where viewers can dictate the story by choosing from various options throughout.

The Thorpe Park attraction is located indoors, at the back of *The Walking Dead* pyramid which previously housed the *Living Nightmare* scare maze during *Fright Nights*. With so many different creative directions that could be taken from the *Black Mirror* back catalogue, rumours started to fly about what this experience would actually be about[573]. Some were alarmed though, when mastermind Charlie Brooker admitted he knew nothing about the attraction, telling *NME* in an interview[574]:

> "Well, I'm not really involved in any of that, so I'll be as interested as anyone will be to find out what it is"

With much of the installation possible during the closed season without having to battle the elements, a launch date of Friday 27th March was confidently set.

2020 was the year the COVID-19 pandemic changed everyday life around the world. Although Merlin Entertainments were one of the final members of the leisure industry to do so, they did reluctantly announce the closure of all their parks just days before the start of the season. The real tragedy was of course the tens of thousands of lives that were lost in the UK, and around the world, but for businesses it was also disastrous across the travel and tourism industry. Thorpe Park took advantage of the government furlough scheme, with team members released of their duties until lockdown started to ease.

After several months of strict restrictions in place, Thorpe Park was allowed to start planning to open again in July providing social distancing measures were in place. Due to the way restrictions were being eased the park became the centre of social media discussion, with many users pointing out how ridiculous they felt it was that children could ride *Nemesis Inferno* but not go to school. With so much uncertainty around what would be possible during the 2020 season, the decision was taken to delay the opening of *Black Mirror Labyrinth* until 2021[575]. This was a choice not unique to Thorpe Park, with Alton Towers and Paulton's Park amongst others in the UK delaying new investments to attempt to launch them fresh when things had returned to more usual operating conditions.

When opening was finally allowed by the government, significant changes were put in place to ensure social distancing was possible. Measures introduced included limiting the daily capacity, requiring visitors to pre-book, and markers added throughout the park to avoid people standing too close to each other. Rides needed to leave gaps to ensure riders from different groups were well separated, significantly reducing their capacity. Guests were asked to wear face masks whilst indoors and on rides. Completely enclosed rides, including the two newest additions *Derren Brown's Ghost Train* and *The Walking Dead*, were left closed. The collective result was huge queues during the summer holidays despite the reduced capacity[576]. The big five rollercoasters would regularly hit around a two hour wait, with *The Swarm* the only real exception. *The Swarm* was allowed to operate at near full capacity as the seats are more spaced out, ensuring the coaster had the fastest moving queue in the park.

On Saturday 18th July 2020, just as staff and guests were getting used to the new arrangements, reports of a horrific incident started to break. Towards the end of a busy but perfectly normal day of operations a fight broke out between two groups on the bridge between the *Dome* and admissions area. This resulted in one person being stabbed, receiving a slash to their stomach[577]. With the individual injured and requiring significant medical attention, the remaining guests in the park were blocked from exiting and, in the age of social media, the news spread fast of the shocking incident. Officials from Merlin released a statement that included[578]:

> "An incident took place at the Thorpe Park Resort today, where a guest was seriously injured by another. The health, safety and security of our guests is our number one priority and we have never had any incidents of this type in over 40 years of operating"

As suggested, nobody had been stabbed before at Thorpe Park since opening at 1979. Nothing excuses such a horrible act of evil, but it was a sign of Thorpe Park's changing atmosphere, culture, and clientele, that this possibly wasn't as much of a surprise as it should be. After spending over a decade celebrating and glorifying torture, along with largely abandoning the family atmosphere that it had worked so hard to earn for the first half of its existence, reports of anti-social behaviour, both anecdotally and in the media, had been on the rise for a while. Security checks at the entrance had been put in place years earlier, but the few young team members who were responsible for conducting these had no chance of performing their jobs to the required standards when thousands of guests needed to pass them every hour. Four individuals were identified and arrested by the police, with Thorpe Park investing in additional security team members to beef up their efforts at the entrance from the following day.

With the British public having to postpone any plans for a foreign summer holiday, UK based resorts were having a mini boom. Beaches across the country were rammed during heatwaves, and Thorpe Park and its peers were a welcome domestic trip to entertain the family after being locked in their homes for so long. The UK government also stepped in to try and support the industry, offering Thorpe Park and its peers a 5% VAT rate, compared to the usual 20%[579]. This enabled them to keep a larger chunk of each ticket price. Looking to make up for lost time (and revenue) it was confirmed that *Fright Nights* would return from October, preceded by a new *Oktoberfest* event featuring traditional German lager and food[580].

The *Oktoberfest* event was simple, but a lot of fun. It was reassuring to see another attempt to bring a fun and joyous event to life around the park, especially at a tough time for many. The area in the centre of the park outside the closed *Ghost Train* was turned into a mini German village, complete with live music and market stalls. Small touches were also made around the park, with some classic rides receiving a slight German makeover, including the former *Thunder River* becoming the *Oompah Rapids*. Many areas also received a twist on their distinctive music, the originals having been fittingly created by German company IMAscore.

Black Mirror Labyrinth finally opened in 2021. The experience challenges visitors to make their way through a high-tech maze in small groups. Using data and pictures taken before you begin, it utilises facial recognition technology to give you a personalised experience lasting 5-10 minutes. With only a small group able to enter every minute or two, the hourly capacity is low. To mitigate this, reservations were required during the opening year, with visitors needing to secure a timeslot during the day to come back and join the queue.

Reviews for *Black Mirror Labyrinth* were largely positive, with most agreeing it was a worthwhile small addition, if not particular re-rideable. The need for a timed ticket was dropped in 2022 as restrictions eased and demand for the experience appeared to settle.

With so much uncertainty around there was understandably little else in the way of new hardware added for 2022. Instead, events were scheduled to take place throughout the season featuring live entertainment. *Oktoberfest* and *Fright Nights* returned, along with *Mardi Gras* during May/June, and *Carnival* in July/August. The more recent additions were reasonably similar but added a refreshing energy around the park. Regular music performances and roaming entertainers helped add a welcome spark during peak times.

The self-styled "Island Like No Other" was finding ways to successfully survive during a period like no other. But with so much changing in society, and behind the scenes, what will the next part of the Thorpe Park journey look like?

PROJECT EXODUS (2024/25)

By late-2021 Merlin were finally ready to show part of their vision for what the future holds. A public consultation in December revealed a planned development of the former Loggers Leap site that would also encompass Old Town (née Canada Creek). Documents revealed that a new major rollercoaster was finally on the horizon, due to open in 2024. It would be very clearly visible for all on that horizon in fact, as if approved it will take the UK height record by standing at 236 feet tall. That's around 30 feet taller than *Stealth*, and roughly 20 feet higher (depending how you measure it) than the current record holder *The Big One* in Blackpool.

Paperwork submitted suggests the station will be located roughly where the disused Canada Creek Railway platform was, then rising high into the Staines sky over Abbey Lake using a traditional lift hill rather than a launch. At the top riders will be subjected to a breath-taking twisted drop of over 200 feet, before soaring and plummeting through several huge elements. Despite the size it is contained within a reasonably small footprint compared to other 'hyper' coasters, which may help keep construction and material costs down by reusing supports and footers. It's proposed that part of the ride's finale will be a 'splashdown' section which could soak riders and surrounding crowds in a similar style to Tidal Wave.

No manufacturer for the new rollercoaster was confirmed at the time of publication, but it's highly likely to be another collaboration with Mack Rides. As the company was responsible for some of the earliest classic attractions in Thorpe Park's history, it seems fitting that they would be part of the next historic ride. The new rollercoaster is likely to invert riders several times, and take the UK speed record, although details around this will be released during later promotional phases.

In preparation for the massive development, Old Town was closed at the end of the 2021 season, retiring the longstanding *Rocky Express*, plus the more recent toddler additions of *Timber Tug Boat* and *Lumber Jump*.

Delays in securing planning approval led to the area remaining largely untouched during 2022, however on Wednesday 2nd November that year Runnymede Council gave the green light for *Project Exodus* to move ahead. The late start could put the original opening date of 2024 in jeopardy, with 2025 realistically looking like the first chance visitors will have to ride this latest multi-million pound investment.

THE FUTURE

From Tim Hartwright's original vision for an adventure in leisure, to the modern thrill capital, it has already been over four decades of change for the former RMC extraction site. Despite differing attitudes from owners and management of what the park should encapsulate; one thing has never changed, and that's the constant need to evolve. It's impossible to tell what the next forty plus years will look like, or if it will even survive that long.

David McCubbin summed up the situation in 2020[581]:

"I don't think Thorpe Park is sure what it's is trying to be at the minute. I don't know what direction it's heading in now. I hear people say a lot what's next, and currently it seems like a lot of filler, everybody is waiting for that next big thing"

Plenty of hard work is going into rediscovering the level of guest experience that was once held in such high regard, but scores for Thorpe Park of 1.8 out of five on Trustpilot[582], and 3.5 on Trip Advisor[583], suggest there is still plenty that can be done. Even acknowledging that this type of review site tends to attract more critical visitors, it still falls short of the high scores achieved by Alton Towers and Paultons Park.

One way or another, the new ownership is going to define the next era of development. Thorpe Park had gained a reputation at Merlin Entertainments for being the "problem child" of the portfolio, struggling to fit into the group's overall aims and strategy. Since the withdrawal from the stock market, there is no longer an immediate share price to worry about, meaning funds could be available, if deemed appropriate, to back huge long-term investments across the park. However, like any well-run business there needs to be proof that the money invested will eventually be recuperated somehow. Especially as a major new competitor is potentially on the horizon.

The London Resort is an ambitious new plan for a major new theme park resort close to the M25 in Swanscombe, Kent[584]. Millions of pounds have already been spent on development of the project, with detailed plans at a 2020 public consultation showing that the area could eventually boast two theme parks, a waterpark, an esports arena, plus hotels and amenities. The focus would be on attractions based on popular films and television shows, with deals struck with *Paramount Pictures*, the *BBC* and *ITV*. Tactically located close to a Eurostar terminal, alongside road and rail links, it certainly would tick all the boxes identified by RMC fifty years ago. The project to this point has seen many parallels with the original Thorpe Park concept, with push backs around planning consent leading to costly delays. Some, including Merlin's former CEO Nick Varney, don't believe it will ever come to fruition[585]. However, if it does it will be an almighty challenger to Thorpe Park and the rest of the UK leisure industry.

It's unlikely that dreams of a full-scale hotel have been completely crushed. Expect to hear more about that in due course. In terms of what specific rides and attractions visitors can expect in the future beyond *Project Exodus*, that is very much up in the air. Inevitably this will happen, but with plans liable to change quickly, and none currently publicly shared by the park, it would be pure speculation to suggest particulars. Enthusiasts will be hopeful that the success of *Wickerman* at Alton Towers, a much longed for wooden coaster, might open the door for one at Thorpe Park. However, with technology advancing and updating endlessly, there's no knowing what the latest trend will be when it comes time to invest.

The 1981 guide book promised[586]:

"The first thing to understand about Thorpe Park is that you have never been anywhere like it before. Because there isn't anywhere like it."

That statement remains true to this day, and many millions are likely to be entertained and amazed by the huge collection of attractions from far and wide for years to come. Thousands of people have worked tirelessly to bring together a collection of special experiences, spending millions of pounds to bring safe and revolutionary technology to sleepy Surrey in order to achieve one thing, entertaining you on a day out. Looking back at the last fifty years has showed that you never know what's going to happen next, but we know that more adventures in leisure are still to come.

ACKNOWLEDGEMENTS

This book would not be possible without the help of lots of lovely people to whom I am incredibly grateful.

Much of the content has come from people who generously gave up their time to speak to me at length about their achievements and experiences. These include Tony Audenshaw, Graham Clatworthy, David McCubbin, Ian Minshull, John Wardley, and Stephen Wyatt-Gold. All of whom have gone above and beyond over the years to create experiences that make millions of people happy, which is a wonderful thing. In particular, ride consultant John Wardley is an icon to me, and it was a relief that such a talented and successful legend is a true gentleman in real life.

Many of the pictures inside are taken by my good friend, and annoyingly talented colleague, Alex Rowe. Alongside being a promising young digital marketer, podcaster and vlogger, he is also a fine photographer. David McCubbin kindly supplied a number of pictures from his Thorpe Park Nostalgia Instagram account. If you find any of this book interesting, I strongly recommend you check it out.

The front cover is designed by another hugely gifted person, Tom Wells. I became aware of his work when following the excellent ParkWorks account on Instagram, and it immediately became my first and only choice to be used as the cover art. Despite my embarrassing budget, Tom graciously agreed to help, and I would encourage you to check out his other quality graphic design work.

Many historic items about Thorpe Park have been kept impeccably by the dedicated team at the Surrey History Centre, located near Woking. It's a wonderful resource that not enough people know about and appreciate. The team were very helpful in finding items during the coronavirus pandemic under difficult circumstances.

It's unlikely I would have had the motivation to continue writing without the support of several of my friends, who didn't laugh me out of the room when I revealed the project. Sam Keir is possibly the most accomplished writer I know, so his words of advice and encouragement were invaluable. Phil West and Steve Day kept my spirits high when I felt I had taken on too much.

I must say a special thank you to the two most important people. My father Michael Atkinson has worked tirelessly to check every single word I have written. Simply, this book would never have been finished without him. Funnily enough, it probably wouldn't have been started either, as it was a trip with him in 1992 that sparked my fascination. Thank you Dad. Sorry I didn't include some of your suggested "jokes".

Finally, and most crucially, my phenomenal partner Naomi has been the most incredible person throughout. Whether it be a pep talk when I've had enough, a cup of tea late at night, or arranging interviews with the media, she has never once waivered in her support. She's suffered the most, as many evenings and weekends have been spent researching and writing this book, when I should have been devoting them to her. I love you and promise to make it up to you over the rest of our lives.

ABOUT THE AUTHOR

Chris Atkinson is a senior marketing professional from Surrey, specialising in sports and events. He leads the marketing strategy for some of the UK's leading running events such as the Manchester Marathon and London Winter Run 10k.

Growing up a stone's throw from Surrey's most popular theme parks, Chris has been an avid fan from a young age. He spends too much time sleeping, but when he's not, he'll be working on his podcasts, walking his two favourite dogs Winnie and Penny, or catching the latest film in his local cinema.

Twitter: @ChrisA_Tweets
Instagram: @achrisogram

NOTES

1 The Ready Mixers, Michael Cassell, Pencorp Books

2 The Ready Mixers, Michael Cassell, Pencorp Books

3 The Telegraph, 28 September, 2004

4 Evening Post, 29 June, 1970

5 The Ready Mixers, Michael Cassell, Pencorp Books

6 The Ready Mixers, Michael Cassell, Pencorp Books

7 Hartwright, Planning for Leisure in the Countryside, Joint Planning Law Conference, 17-19 September, 1982

8 Ravenscroft, Recreation Planning and Development, 1992

9 Hartwright, Planning for Leisure in the Countryside, Joint Planning Law Conference, 17-19 September, 1982

10 Chertsey Museum www.chertseymuseum.org

11 The Ready Mixers, Michael Cassell, Pencorp Books

12 Hartwright, Planning for Leisure in the Countryside, Joint Planning Law Conference, 17-19 September, 1982

13 Evening Post, 27 November 1970

14 Herald and News, 29 August 1996

15 Ravenscroft, Recreation Planning and Development, 1992

16 Hartwright, Planning for Leisure in the Countryside, Joint Planning Law Conference, 17-19 September, 1982

17 The Birmingham Post, 14 August, 1975

18 Country Life, 1 November, 1973

19 Hartwright, Planning for Leisure in the Countryside, Joint Planning Law Conference, 17-19 September, 1982

20 International Waterski and Wakeboard Association www.iwsf.com

21 Ravenscroft, Recreation Planning and Development, 1992

22 Hartwright, Planning for Leisure in the Countryside, Joint Planning Law Conference, 17-19 September, 1982

23 Thorpe Park, The Book of the Park, 1981

24 1979 Thorpe Park Map

25 Thorpe Park, The Book of the Park, 1981

26 London Archaeologist, 1980

27 Daily Mirror, 9 June, 1979

28 Thorpe Park, The Book of the Park, 1981

29 1979 Thorpe Park Map

30 Thorpe Park, The Book of the Park, 1981

31 1979 Thorpe Park Map

32 Thorpe Park, The Book of the Park, 1981

33 The Ready Mixers, Michael Cassell, Pencorp Books

34 1979 Thorpe Park Map

35 Gazette and Post, 24 May, 1979

36 Evening Post, 6 July, 1979

37 Evening Post, 29 June, 1981

38 Hartwright, Planning for Leisure in the Countryside, Joint Planning Law Conference, 17-19 September, 1982

39 Hartwright, Planning for Leisure in the Countryside, Joint Planning Law Conference, 17-19 September, 1982

40 The Ready Mixers, Michael Cassell, Pencorp Books

41 Hartwright, Planning for Leisure in the Countryside, Joint Planning Law Conference, 17-19 September, 1982

42 Thorpe Park, The Book of the Park,

1981

[43] Thorpe Park, The Book of the Park, 1981

[44] London Archaeologist, 1980

[45] Thorpe Park, The Book of the Park, 1981

[46] The Ready Mixers, Michael Cassell, Pencorp Books

[47] Hartwright, Planning for Leisure in the Countryside, Joint Planning Law Conference, 17-19 September, 1982

[48] Hartwright, Planning for Leisure in the Countryside, Joint Planning Law Conference, 17-19 September, 1982

[49] Thorpe Park, The Book of the Park, 1981

[50] Evening Post, 29 May, 1981

[51] Evening Post, 6 July, 1981

[52] Evening Post, 19 June, 1981

[53] Thorpe Park, The Book of the Park, 1981

[54] Hartwright, Planning for Leisure in the Countryside, Joint Planning Law Conference, 17-19 September, 1982

[55] Evening Post, 29 May, 1981

[56] Evening Post, 24 April, 1981

[57] The Ready Mixers, Michael Cassell, Pencorp Books

[58] Evening Post, 28 August, 1981

[59] International Waterski and Wakeboard Association www.iwsf.com

[60] Hartwright, Planning for Leisure in the Countryside, Joint Planning Law Conference, 17-19 September, 1982

[61] Chertsey Museum www.chertseymuseum.org

[62] Hartwright, Planning for Leisure in the Countryside, Joint Planning Law Conference, 17-19 September, 1982

[63] Interview with Ian Minshull, 4 September, 2020

[64] Liverpool Echo, 29 December, 1982

[65] Midweek, 30 March, 1982

[66] Evening Post, 17 April, 1982

[67] Interview with Ian Minshull, 4 September, 2020

[68] 1982 Thorpe Park Map

[69] Hartwright, Planning for Leisure in the Countryside, Joint Planning Law Conference, 17-19 September, 1982

[70] 1982 Thorpe Park Map

[71] Freaky Trigger, 23 April, 2000

[72] Space and Place Website , www.space-place.com

[73] Stephen Wyatt-Gold, Bowie and Me: Unparallel Careers, 2019

[74] Interview with Tony Audenshaw, 21 August, 2020

[75] Stephen Wyatt-Gold, Bowie and Me: Unparallel Careers, 2019

[76] Miniature Railway World www.miniaturerailwayworld.co.uk

[77] Hartwright, Planning for Leisure in the Countryside, Joint Planning Law Conference, 17-19 September, 1982

[78] John Wardley, Creating my own Nemesis, 2013

[79] Phantom Fantasia ONRIDE, Neilfever, YouTube

[80] Evening Post, 24 April, 1984

[81] Mack Rides official website

[82] The Stage and Television Today, 25 June, 1987

[83] 1986 Thorpe Park Map

[84] Evening Chronicle, 3 July, 1984

[85] 1984 Thorpe Park Leaflet

[86] The Press and Journal, 30 July, 1984

[87] John Wardley, Creating my own Nemesis, 2013

[88] Mack Rides official website

[89] J-D Games Wiki

[90] Western Foodservice, March, 1979

[91] Showbiz Pizza, www.showbizpizza.com

[92] Memories of Thorpe Park www.memoriesofthorpepark.co.uk

[93] Captain Andy's River Band at Watermouth Castle, RetroPlayPlanet, YouTube

[94] Gizmodo, 17 August, 2017

[95] Today Online, 21 August, 2017

[96] Herald and News, 7th September, 1989

[97] The Mercury, 1 November, 1985

[98] Interview with Ian Minshull, 4 September, 2020

[99] The Stage and Television Today, 11 December, 1986

[100] The Kingston Informer, 14 March, 1986

[101] Interview with John Wardley, 20 July, 2020

[102] Evening Chronicle, 3 July, 1984

[103] The Stage and Television Today, 25 June, 1987

[104] Advertiser and Gazette, 28 August, 1986

[105] The Mercury, 31 October, 1986

[106] Herald and News, 22 October, 1987

[107] Herald and News, 19 March, 1987

[108] Thunder River debuts at Astroworld, ABC13 newscast, YouTube

[109] Herald and News, 5 March, 1987

[110] Herald and News, 17 April, 1986

[111] Herald and News, 17 April, 1986

[112] Herald and News, 18 June, 1987

[113] Herald and News, 5 March, 1987

[114] 1986 Thorpe Park Map

[115] Herald and News, 24 December, 1986

[116] Herald and News, 24 December, 1986

[117] Herald and News, 19 March, 1987

[118] The Courier and Advertiser, 16 April, 1987

[119] Herald and News, 23 April, 1987

[120] Herald and News, 23 April, 1987

[121] Evening Post, 13 August, 1987

[122] Evening Post, 30 July, 1987

[123] Evening Sentinel, 30 July, 1987

[124] The Journal, 30 July, 1987

[125] Kingston Informer, 10th July, 1987

[126] Evening Post, 12 August, 1987

[127] Evening News, 8 September, 1987

[128] Evening Post, 27 August, 1987

[129] Evening Post, 30 July, 1987

[130] Interview with Graham Clatworthy, 28 August, 2020

[131] The Stage and Television Today, 25 June, 1987

[132] International Waterski and Wakeboard Association www.iwsf.com

[133] BBC News, 21 July, 2020

[134] Mirror Online, 10 May, 2017

[135] The Sun Online, 10 May, 2017

[136] Herald and News, 10 December, 1987

[137] The Stage, 23 December, 1987

[138] The Stage, 18 August, 1988

[139] The Stage, 18 August, 1988

[140] The Stage, 18 August, 1988

[141] Herald and News, 10 December, 1987

[142] The Stage, 23 December, 1987

[143] Adrian Kaye website, www.adriankayeclown.com

[144] Herald and News, 10th November, 1989

[145] Stephen Wyatt-Gold, Bowie and Me: Unparallel Careers, 2019

[146] Interview with Stephen Wyatt-Gold, 24 August, 2020

[147] The Stage, 15 August, 1991

[148] Interview with Stephen Wyatt-Gold, 24 August, 2020

[149] Stephen Wyatt-Gold, Bowie and Me: Unparallel Careers, 2019

[150] The Stage, 1 June, 1995

151 Stephen Wyatt-Gold, Bowie and Me: Unparallel Careers, 2019

152 Interview with Stephen Wyatt-Gold, 24 August, 2020

153 The Stage, 1 June, 1995

154 Herald and News, 9 November, 1989

155 Herald and News, 23 April, 1987

156 Herald and News, 30 March, 1989

157 Herald and News, 22 March, 1989

158 Interview with John Wardley, 20 July, 2020

159 The Kingston Informer, 14 March, 1986

160 Interview with Ian Minshull, 4 September, 2020

161 Herald and News, 30 December, 1987

162 Herald and News, 16 March, 1989

163 Herald and News, 30 March, 1989

164 Herald and News, 30 March, 1989

165 Herald and News, 30 March, 1989

166 Herald and News, 22 March, 1989

167 Herald and News, 9 March, 1989

168 Evening Post, 27 March, 1989

169 Herald and News, 27 July, 1989

170 Herald and News, 7th September, 1989

171 Interview with Tony Audenshaw, 21 August, 2020

172 Interview with Steve Day, 27 September, 2020

173 Herald and News, 9 November, 1989

174 Interview with Ian Minshull, 4 September, 2020

175 Interview with Stephen Wyatt-Gold, 24 August, 2020

176 1989 Thorpe Park Map

177 Evening Mail, 9 September, 1989

178 Herald and News, 9 November, 1989

179 Reading Post, 4 August, 1989

180 Herald and News, 30 March, 1989

181 The Stage, 4 June, 1998

182 Herald and News, 4 May, 1989

183 Herald and News, 1st June, 1989

184 1989 Thorpe Park Map

185 Herald and News, 9 November, 1989

186 Surrey Live, 20 February, 2019

187 Case study on official Garmendale website

188 Mail Online, 12 April, 2019

189 Manchester Evening News, 12 April, 2019

190 Evening Sentinel, 26 February, 1990

191 Business Mail, 30 March, 1990

192 Evening Mail, 5 March, 1990

193 Evening Mail, 30 March, 1990

194 Evening Sentinel, 9 October, 1991

195 Evening Sentinel, 9 October, 1991

196 Park World interview with John Wardley, 1990

197 Gazette, 4 April, 1990

198 John Wardley, Creating my own Nemesis, 2013

199 Herald and News, 1 February, 1990

200 Herald and News, 1 February, 1990

201 Herald and News, 1 February, 1990

202 Stephen Wyatt-Gold, Bowie and Me: Unparallel Careers, 2019

203 Interview with Tony Audenshaw, 21 August, 2020

204 Interview with Stephen Wyatt-Gold, 24 August, 2020

205 Interview with Tony Audenshaw, 21 August, 2020

206 Herald and News, 12th July, 1990

207 Interview with Tony Audenshaw, 21 August, 2020

208 Stephen Wyatt-Gold, Bowie and Me: Unparallel Careers, 2019

209 Interview with Stephen Wyatt-Gold,

24 August, 2020

[210] www.reride.net , August, 2007

[211] Herald and News, 1 February, 1990

[212] Gazette, 4 April, 1990

[213] Herald and News, 1 February, 1990

[214] Herald and News, 25 October, 1990

[215] Herald and News, 4 April, 1991

[216] Herald and News, 17 January, 1991

[217] Herald and News, 27 March, 1991

[218] The Kingston Informer, 17 May, 1991

[219] Herald and News, 6 June, 1991

[220] Evening Post, 5 July, 1991

[221] Evening Post, 5 July, 1991

[222] Herald and News, 6 June, 1991

[223] The Stage, 15 August, 1991

[224] Press and Journal, 1 April, 1991

[225] Herald and News, 4 April, 1991

[226] Sunday Mirror, 31 March, 1991

[227] Interview with Tony Audenshaw, 21 August, 2020

[228] Sunday Mirror, 19 April, 1992

[229] Herald and News, 31 January, 1991

[230] Evening Mail, 13 August, 1991

[231] 1991 Thorpe Park Guide Book

[232] Herald and News, 19 March, 1992

[233] Herald and News, 19 March, 1992

[234] Herald and News, 16 April, 1992

[235] Herald and News, 11 June, 1992

[236] Stephen Wyatt-Gold, Bowie and Me: Unparallel Careers, 2019

[237] Herald and News, 8 October, 1992

[238] 1992 Thorpe Park Map

[239] Herald and News, 30 January, 1992

[240] The Stage, 27 August, 1992

[241] Interview with Stephen Wyatt-Gold, 24 August, 2020

[242] Interview with Tony Audenshaw, 21 August, 2020

[243] Stephen Wyatt-Gold, Bowie and Me: Unparallel Careers, 2019

[244] Evening Post, 28 October, 1992

[245] Evening Post, 28 October, 1992

[246] Liverpool Echo, 2 December, 1992

[247] Evening Post, 13 May, 1993

[248] Evening Post, 12 March, 1993

[249] Evening Sentinel, 21 May, 1994

[250] Herald and News, 8 July, 1993

[251] Evening Sentinel, 21 May, 1994

[252] The Journal, 18 March, 1994

[253] The Mercury, 28th July, 1994

[254] Herald News, 24 March, 1994

[255] www.metallbau-emmeln.de

[256] The Mercury, 28th July, 1994

[257] Stephen Wyatt-Gold, Bowie and Me: Unparallel Careers, 2019

[258] Interview with Stephen Wyatt-Gold, 24 August, 2020

[259] Herald News, 12 May, 1994

[260] Stephen Wyatt-Gold, Bowie and Me: Unparallel Careers, 2019

[261] Herald News, 14 July, 1994

[262] The Mercury, 28th July, 1994

[263] Interview with Phil West, 27 September, 2020

[264] Herald News, 24 March, 1994

[265] Gazette, Easter 1994

[266] Herald News, 21 April, 1994

[267] The Stage Summer Preview, 1994

[268] Herald News, 28 April, 1994

[269] Herald News, 28 July, 1994

[270] Uxbridge & West Drayton Gazette, 25 January, 1995

[271] Evening Sentinel, 18 January, 1995

[272] Interview with Tony Audenshaw, 21 August, 2020

[273] Stephen Wyatt-Gold, Bowie and Me: Unparallel Careers, 2019

[274] Herald and News, 10 July, 1997

[275] The Stage, 11 February, 1999

[276] Herald and News, 13 April, 1995

[277] Herald and News, 30 July, 1998

[278] Herald and News, 6 July, 1995

[279] Herald and News, 13 April, 1995

280 Interview with Stephen Wyatt-Gold, 24 August, 2020

281 Herald and News, 19 October, 1995

282 Independent, 31 March, 1996

283 John Wardley, Creating my own Nemesis, 2013

284 Press and Journal, 1 July, 1996

285 ParkVault, 20 December, 2014

286 X:\ No Way Out Promotional Video, 1996

287 Herald and News, 10 November, 1994

288 1995 Thorpe Park Map

289 Expo:\2018

290 X:\ No Way Out Promotional Video, 1996

291 Independent, 11 August, 1996

292 Campaign, 28 June, 1996

293 Herald and News, 11 January, 1996

294 Herald and News, 11 April, 1996

295 Independent, 31 March, 1996

296 Gazette, 21 February, 1996

297 Interview with Stephen Wyatt-Gold, 24 August, 2020

298 Herald and News, 15 August, 1996

299 Crawley News, 31 July, 1996

300 Campaign, 28 June, 1996

301 X:\ No Way Out Promotional Video, 1996

302 Herald and News, 4 February, 1999

303 Interview with Graham Clatworthy, 28 August, 2020

304 Interview with David McCubbin, 4 September, 2020

305 Herald and News, 8 May, 1997

306 Interview with Tony Audenshaw, 21 August, 2020

307 Herald and News, 8 May, 1997

308 Campaign, 20 June, 1997

309 Herald and News, 31 July, 1997

310 Herald and News, 17 July, 1997

311 Herald and News, 4 September, 1997

312 Herald and News, 23 October, 1997

313 Herald and News, 19 February 1996

314 Sunday Mirror, 30 July, 1989

315 Herald and News, 26 February, 1996

316 1998 Thorpe Park Map

317 Sunday Mirror, 24 Mirror, 1998

318 Liverpool Echo, 21 May, 1998

319 Herald and News, 3 September, 1998

320 John Wardley, Creating my own Nemesis, 2013

321 Interview with John Wardley, 20 July, 2020

322 Staines and Ashford News, 18 June, 1998

323 RMC Press Release, 12 June, 1998

324 Staines and Ashford News, 18 June, 1998

325 Herald and News, 5 November, 1998

326 Staines and Ashford News, 25 June, 1998

327 Press and Journal, 20 October, 1998

328 Kingston informer, 5th June, 1987

329 www.simex-iwerks.com

330 Herald and News, 1 October, 1998

331 Thorpe Park Press Release, February, 1999

332 Herald and News, 4 February, 1999

333 Herald and News, 8 April, 1999

334 Interview with Graham Clatworthy, 28 August, 2020

335 Reading Evening Post, 13 September, 1999

336 Herald and News, 17 September, 1998

337 SouthParks www.southparks.co.uk

338 ARTEM case studies, www.artem.com

339 Thorpe Park Blog, 1 August, 2017

340 Interview with David McCubbin, 4

September, 2020

341 Thorpe Park Press Release, February, 2000

342 Interview with Graham Clatworthy, 28 August, 2020

343 BBC News, 21 July, 2000

344 Interview with John Wardley, 20 July, 2020

345 2001 Thorpe Park Map

346 Thorpe Park 2001 Television Advert

347 Watchdog, BBC One, 27 April, 2001

348 BBC News, 29 March, 2004

349 The Argus, 30 March, 2004

350 Surrey Live, 1 August, 2017

351 The Sun Online, 16 September, 2018

352 Thorpe Park 'Park Rangers' Underwater Diving Experience, ThemeParkCollective, YouTube

353 Interview with Graham Clatworthy, 28 August, 2020

354 Interview with John Wardley, 20 July, 2020

355 Interview with John Wardley, 20 July, 2020

356 Interview with David McCubbin, 4 September, 2020

357 Interview with Graham Clatworthy, 28 August, 2020

358 Thorpe Park official website, July, 2020

359 Interview with David McCubbin, 4 September, 2020

360 South Parks construction archive www.southparks.co.uk

361 Thorpe Park 2002 Television Advert

362 2001 Thorpe Park Map

363 Interview with David McCubbin, 4 September, 2020

364 Tomorrow's World, BBC One, March, 2002

365 Interview with David McCubbin, 4 September, 2020

366 Airtime Issue 29, May/June, 2001

367 Interview with John Wardley, 20 July, 2020

368 Interview with John Wardley, 20 July, 2020

369 South Parks construction archive www.southparks.co.uk

370 2002 Thorpe Park Map

371 Thorpe Park Press Release "Get ready for Nemesis Inferno", 2003

372 Interview with David McCubbin, 4 September, 2020

373 Surrey Live, 23 June, 2018

374 The Inbetweeners "Thorpe Park" (Series 1, Episode 3), 8 May, 2008

375 Screamscape, 8 October, 2002

376 South Parks www.southparks.co.uk

377 Theme Park Insider

378 Coaster Kingdom, 29 March, 2005

379 S&S press release, Ride Entertainment, www.rideentertainment.com

380 South Parks www.southparks.co.uk

381 The Sun, June, 2008

382 2005 Thorpe Park Map

383 Games Industry International, 15 August, 2005

384 South Parks, 4 April, 2017

385 Interview with John Wardley, 20 July, 2020

386 Runnymede Borough Council website

387 South Parks construction archive www.southparks.co.uk

388 The Engineer, 17 October, 2006

389 Interview with John Wardley, 20 July, 2020

390 Thorpe Park official website, 2006

391 Holiday Extras, 15 March, 2006

392 Theme Park Insider

393 The Guardian, 17 April, 2006

394 Thorpe Park official website, 2007

[395] Thorpe Park official website, 2007

[396] The Guardian, 23 March, 2005

[397] New York Times, 5 March, 2007

[398] Reuters, 5 March, 2007

[399] Financial Times, 2007

[400] South Parks, 10 February, 2008

[401] Gardaland Time Voyagers, YouTube

[402] www.themeparkjames.co.uk

[403] Surrey Live, 2 July, 2013

[404] John Wardley Q&A, Oakwood, 2013

[405] Great Coasters International

[406] Season Pass Podcast Episode 103

[407] South Parks construction archive
www.southparks.co.uk

[408] Thorpe Park Press Release, 27
November, 2007

[409] Thorpe Park Press Release, 31
January, 2008

[410] South Parks, 20 May, 2008

[411] Season Pass Podcast Episode 103

[412] Thorpe Park Press Release, 13
October, 2008

[413] The Telegraph, 13 March, 2009

[414] www.coastercritic.com

[415] South Parks, 31 March, 2009

[416] www.statista.com

[417] Flamingo Land official website

[418] BBC News, 2 June, 2015

[419] Get Surrey, 5 June, 2015

[420] Metro Online, 9 October, 2016

[421] Surrey Live, 10 October, 2016

[422] The Sun, 7 August, 2018

[423] Get Surrey, 30 August, 2018

[424] BBC News, 29 August, 2009

[425] Den of Geek, 5 February, 2020

[426] The Guardian, 24 November, 2015

[427] Mail Online, 25 February, 2010

[428] Mirror.co.uk, 11 March, 2010

[429] The Telegraph, 12 June, 2010

[430] Attractions Magazine, 15 January,
2010

[431] Thorpe Park Twitter, 28 February,
2019

[432] Mail Online, 8 February, 2011

[433] Theme Park Tourist, 26 March, 2011

[434] Thorpe Park television advert, 2011

[435] Mail Online, 30 September, 2011

[436] Surrey Live, 8 November, 2011

[437] Hartwright, Planning for Leisure in
the Countryside, Joint Planning Law
Conference, 17-19 September, 1982

[438] South Parks construction archive
www.southparks.co.uk

[439] Interview with John Wardley, 20
July, 2020

[440] Interview with John Wardley, 20
July, 2020

[441] Inpark magazine, 5 May, 2011

[442] Interview with John Wardley, 20
July, 2020

[443] BBC News, 7 March, 2011

[444] South Parks construction archive
www.southparks.co.uk

[445] Thorpe Park Developers Diary,
Facebook

[446] The Telegraph, 24 January, 2012

[447] Mirror Online, 25 January, 2012

[448] The Metro, 23 February, 2012

[449] Thorpe Park official website, 31
March, 2012

[450] Official Charts Company

[451] BBC News, 15 March, 2012

[452] Theme Park Tourist, 18 March, 2012

[453] Interview with David McCubbin, 4
September, 2020

[454] Interview with Justin Rees, 27
September, 2020

[455] www.statista.com

[456] The Express, 25 September, 2012

[457] www.coasterpedia.net

[458] Mirror, 17 April, 2013

[459] The Drum, 20 March, 2013

[460] An Evening with John Wardley, 6
May, 2017

461 Interview with David McCubbin, 4 September, 2020

462 Mail Online, 14 April, 2013

463 Think Broadband, 8 May, 2013

464 Mail Online, 28 February, 2013

465 Surrey Live, 27 February, 2014

466 Herald and News, 26 June, 1997

467 Interview with Ian Minshull, 4 September, 2020

468 Interview with David McCubbin, 4 September, 2020

469 Daily Mail, 13 September 2012

470 Don't Tell the Bride, Series 5 "Steven & Kaleigh", BBC Three

471 BBC News, 13 February, 2009

472 Independent, 3 July, 2013

473 Mail Online, 22 October, 2013

474 The Guardian, 22 October, 2013

475 The Metro, 9 November, 2013

476 BBC News, 22 October, 2013

477 The Telegraph, 12 August, 2013

478 The Guardian, 21 October, 2013

479 USA Today, 12 September, 2014

480 Blooloop, 28 February, 2018

481 Los Angeles Times, 27 April, 2012

482 The Telegraph, 29 August, 2012

483 Mail Online, 23 May, 2013

484 Digital Spy, 9th January, 2014

485 Blooloop, 23 July, 2014

486 www.7thsensedesign.com

487 Get Surrey, 30 May, 2014

488 The Drum, 30 May, 2014

489 USA Today, 11 March, 2013

490 www.themeparkjames.co.uk

491 Box Office Mojo

492 Surrey Live, 1 April, 2014

493 South Parks, 16 May, 2014

494 The Guardian, 14 January, 2003

495 Surrey Live, 23 March, 2015

496 Thorpe Park Press Release, 14 April, 2015

497 Blooloop, 2015

498 Theme Park Guide, 17 March, 2015

499 The Guardian, 12 February, 2015

500 Metro, 12 February, 2015

501 Digital Spy, 27 March, 2015

502 Theme Park Insider, 4 April, 2015

503 Campaign, 20 April, 2015

504 Blooloop, 19 January, 2016

505 South Parks, 7 April, 2015

506 Thorpe Park Press Release, 18 January, 2016

507 Attractions Management Promotional Feature

508 Figment Productions Website

509 The Independent, 26 October, 2015

510 Thorpe Park Press Release, 25 October, 2015

511 Huffington Post, 18 January, 2016

512 Digital Spy, 18 January, 2016

513 Season Pass Podcast, ERT #33

514 BBC News, 25 March, 2016

515 Metro, 12 April, 2016

516 Digital Spy, 10 May, 2016

517 The Drum, 19 April, 2016

518 Digital Spy, 10 May, 2016

519 The Independent, 9 May, 2016

520 Surrey Live, 3 May, 2016

521 Express, 8 July, 2016

522 The Sun, 8 July, 2016

523 The Sun, 25 July, 2016

524 Season Pass Podcast, ERT #33

525 Digital Spy, 22 July, 2016

526 Upload VR, 22 July, 2016

527 Engadget, 15 July, 2016

528 Surrey Live, 12 July, 2016

529 Mail Online, 13 August, 2016

530 Modern Mann Podcast, Season 2, Episode 4

531 Interview with John Wardley, 20 July, 2020

532 The Guardian, 12 January, 2016

533 BBC News, 21 July, 2016

534 Evening Standard, 28 July, 2016

535 Trusted Reviews, 28 July, 2016

536 Evening Standard, 25 August, 2016

537 South Parks, 19 October, 2016

538 The Drum, 22 December, 2016

539 South Parks, 9 March, 2017

540 Evening Standard, 16 March, 2017

541 WIRED, 31 March, 2017

542 Interview with David McCubbin, 4 September, 2020

543 Theme Park Central, 15 March, 2017

544 Huffington Post, 4 July, 2017

545 The Sun, 17 May, 2017

546 Surrey Live, 1 June, 2017

547 Surrey Live, 22 March, 2017

548 Evening Standard, 21 April, 2017

549 Mail Online, 2 June, 2017

550 The Drum, 5 September, 2017

551 Financial Times, 21 June, 2017

552 Sky News, 29 November, 2017

553 Document 246839, Runnymede Council Website

554 Blooloop, 4 April, 2018

555 Holovis official website, 12 June, 2018

556 The Independent, 20 February, 2018

557 The Mirror, 26 March, 2018

558 Theme Park Incorporated, 1 April, 2018

559 The Sun, 30 March, 2018

560 Interview with David McCubbin, 4 September, 2020

561 2018 Thorpe Park Map

562 Thorpe Park Official Blog, 17 July, 2018

563 Surrey Live, 27 July, 2018

564 Proactive Investors, 28 February, 2019

565 Express Online, 28 June, 2019

566 Thorpe Park Official Blog, 9 April, 2019

567 Metro, 27 February, 2019

568 Surrey Live, 19 May, 2019

569 Mail Online, 7 November, 2019

570 Thorpe Park official website, 21 May, 2019

571 Digital Spy, 25 February, 2020

572 Lad Bible, 16 March, 2020

573 Blooloop, 25 February, 2020

574 NME, 14 May, 2020

575 Screamscape, 8 June, 2020

576 MyLondon, 27 July, 2020

577 Surrey Live, 18 July, 2020

578 BBC News, 18 July, 2020

579 Express, 8 July, 2020

580 Thorpe Park official website, 24 August, 2020

581 Interview with David McCubbin, 4 September, 2020

582 www.trustpilot.com

583 www.tripadvisor.co.uk

584 Blooloop, 3 June, 2020

585 Ride Rater, 18 March, 2017

586 Thorpe Park, The Book of the Park, 1981

Printed in Great Britain
by Amazon

13668002R00188